UNITED ROUMANIA

BY

CHARLES UPSON CLARK, Ph.D.

MEMBER OF THE ROUMANIAN ACADEMY

WITH ILLUSTRATIONS
AND MAPS

DODD, MEAD AND COMPANY

NEW YORK   1932

PRINTED IN THE UNITED STATES OF AMERICA
BY THE VAIL-BALLOU PRESS, INC., BINGHAMTON, N. Y.

PREFACE TO "UNITED ROUMANIA"

The warm reception accorded "Greater Roumania" (1922) soon carried it out of print, and the publishers desired a new edition; but my observation of the country's progress convinced me that the book must be rewritten, not merely revised. In 1923, 1925 and 1927 I visited Roumania on lecture trips, the last covering the entire country from Temeshvar to Kishineff; each time I made a thorough investigation of the charges of minority oppression, and I gathered quantities of material, some of it utilized in my "Bessarabia" (Dodd, Mead and Co., 1927). In 1930, I had the good fortune to be in Roumania upon King Carol's accession, and felt that the time was ripe for a new book upon the country. I call it "United Roumania" because in 1922, Bessarabia and the Banat, the Bucovina and the Dobrudja, were still strangers to each other; now, after ten years of business, political and intellectual association, there is genuine union.

In rewriting the book, I have omitted much that I hate to leave out, like the story of our American Red Cross, Food Commission, and Y. M. C. A. contributions to Roumanian upbuilding; interviews with King Ferdinand and Queen Marie, and sketches of Bratiano, Take Jonesco, Marghiloman and other distinguished Roumanians. I have condensed or rewritten much of the remainder. Having had unusual opportunities for learning the truth in highly controversial matters, I have preserved most of the material on Roumania's part in the War (still so widely misrepresented), and especially the Buda-Pesth episode and the treatment of

Roumania at the Peace Conference. I have taken great pains to bring statistical material up to date. I have added a chapter on the Minorities, for which at any rate I have had one advantage; so far as I know—it sounds incredible —no other foreign investigator of this subject was able to speak the language! The new chapter on Roumanian Politics since the War is based on a wide and sympathetic acquaintance with the men prominent in public life; the one on recent literature has a like basis. Thousands of miles of travel in the country, and countless conversations with business men, bankers, etc., underlie the new chapter on Reconstruction, and the revision of every part of the work. The Bibliography represents far more work than is obvious; I am especially grateful here to Prof. A. Marcu of Bucharest and to the Yale University Library. There are many new illustrations.

I contemplated additional chapters on the people, their home and city life, their customs and ways; but as these would make the book unwieldy, I have decided to issue them in separate form, as "Town and Village in Roumania."

Again I thank my scores of Roumanian friends, and especially Messrs. Gr. Antipa, I. Bianu, Antoine Bibesco, George Cantacuzino, N. Ciotori, E. Filotti, N. H. E. Lahovari, A. Marcu, Ion Pillat, Alex. Rosetti, Vasile Stoïca, and N. Titulesco, for constant help and encouragement.

CHARLES UPSON CLARK

Seville, July 23, 1931.

PREFACE TO "GREATER ROUMANIA"

In my study of anti-Italian propaganda during and after the war, I became interested in the similar campaign of misrepresentation directed against Roumania. The two Latin sisters had much in common in their relation to the Austro-Hungarian monarchy; but Roumania was far less known in the West than Italy. Accordingly I welcomed an invitation of 1919 from the Roumanian Government to come out and observe the post-war situation on the spot. This book is based on those personal observations.

Our ignorance of Roumania is so great that I have thought it desirable to sketch the geography and history of the country, as an introduction; her part in the war has been so maligned that I have inserted a brief account, based on official sources, of her heroic defence and of the great victory she won over Mackensen at Mărăsheshti; her campaign against Béla Kun's attack has been so distorted that I have devoted a chapter (also embodying an official report) to the story of her clever and successful parrying of the blow. Having had the unusual good fortune to be in Buda-Pesth under the Roumanian occupation, as well as in Paris during part of the Conference, and to have access to several documents hitherto unpublished, I am enabled to give a fuller and more accurate story, I hope, of her relations with the Peace Conference, than has yet been attempted. Through the courtesy of the American Relief Administration, the American Red Cross and the Y. M. C. A., I include résumés of their activities, which have made the American name beloved throughout Roumania. Since she offers remarkable

opportunities to the farsighted American capitalist and manufacturer, I have tried to make the book a trustworthy work
of reference for the business man, as well as for the traveler
and the student of history and literature.

It is a grateful task to acknowledge unbounded courtesies
and hospitality from those mentioned in these pages, and
many others. My chapters on the history, language and literature have had the advantage of kind criticism and cor-
rection by my friends Mr. Nicholas H. E. Lahovari,
Dr. I. Lugosiano and Capt. Basil Stoïca; but these gentlemen are not to be understood as sharing my views, nor are
they to be held responsible for any of my statements and
opinions.

In Roumanian proper names, I have in general followed
their convention, by which, on visiting cards printed for
Western Europe, Carol Brătianu becomes Charles Bratiano,
and Tache Ionescu, Take Jonesco. I would urge every
reader first to study the pronunciation of the language, explained on p. 278; it is almost as melodious as the Italian it
so closely resembles. An agreeable surprise of my lecture
tour devoted to Roumania was the delight shown over the
Roumanian poems which I quoted; and this has emboldened
me to print several of them in this book, with only a literal
translation.

In fine, my attempt has been to provide the reader with
the necessary elements for a sympathetic understanding of
Roumania, her policy, her ambitions and her future. I have
tried to embody my deep impression of a national education, through centuries of storm and oppression, to the present marvelous development of this attractive and gifted
people—how misunderstood and misrepresented, I hope to
have made clear. May the reader end sharing my conviction
that Roumania has the future of Southeastern Europe in her

hands, and that any Western nation will honor itself, as well as profit, by helpful association in Roumanian development.

CHARLES UPSON CLARK

Paris, October 24, 1921

CONTENTS

xi

ILLUSTRATIONS

UNITED ROUMANIA

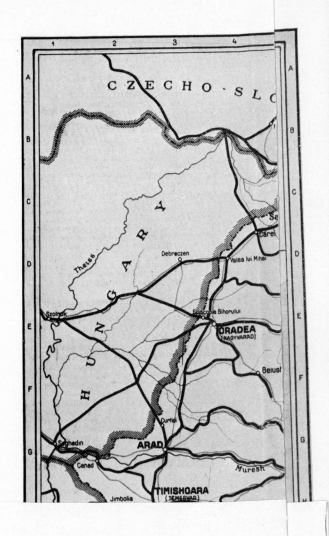

CHAPTER I

THE LAND

ROUMANIA's life-blood is sustained by four elements—the Danube, whose main stream and affluents are her arteries; the Carpathians and their smiling vine-clad hills, rich in minerals and oil; the plains, sweeping down from Hungary on the west to the narrow thread of the Iron Gates, and then expanding eastward into the steppes of the Ukraine; and the Black Sea, her route to the Dardanelles and the Orient. Roumania lies across the Danube, a bar to German-Austro-Magyar penetration eastward; she fronts upon the Euxine, and thus blocks Russia's path toward Constantinople. This strategic position forms her strength and her weakness, and explains her neighbors' covetousness.

In general, the new Roumania has well-marked boundaries: the Dniester against the Ukraine (though the Roumanian peasantry prevails beyond the river, to within a few miles of Odessa itself); the Theiss against the Magyars (but the Peace Conference drew the line some miles east of the river); the Danube against the Serbs and Bulgarians (with some overlapping here also); and the Black Sea to the east. It forms a compact mass of some 300,000 square kilometers (say 115,000 sq. m., greater in area than Italy or England, or than New York, New Jersey and Pennsylvania combined). Its southernmost point (43° 15′) lies even with Nice, Detroit and Vladivostok; the extreme north of the Maramuresh (48° 45′) is on the same meridian with Paris, the Saguenay River, Vancouver and northern Manchuria. East and west,

1

it runs between 17° 40′ and 28° 5′ E.—about the distance between Vienna and Geneva, or Pittsburgh and St. Louis. This northern trend, together with the lofty mountains and the illimitable plains running up into Russia, makes the climate highly variable. In the July harvesting in southern Wallachia, the peasant faces a truly African heat, sometimes 108° in the shade; in the long winter, he fights a cold which occasionally drops to —30°, with a freezing wind off the steppes. These extremes toughen his constitution, and perhaps explain why malaria is less of a scourge than in Albania and Italy, although the anopheles seems quite as abundant.

In a typical Roumanian season, cold nights and snow-squalls last into April; spring comes on with a rush, and by the end of May summer heat shimmers over the plains. Autumn arrives with the same brusqueness, and yields to winter sometimes as early as October; but the heavy frosts generally hold off until the turn of the year. In November of 1919 I ran into zero weather in the Bucovina, and have rarely felt the cold as I did in the fetid unheated train from Czernowitz to Bucharest the night of the 19th; yet the peasant soldiers who crowded the roofs of the coaches faced the biting wind all night long without complaint. There is of course a great difference between south and north, and plain and mountain; lilacs bloom along the Danube and the Theiss five weeks earlier than in the upper Maramuresh and Bucovina. Late spring frosts are a scourge and the Transylvanian peasants consecrate May 8–12 to "the ice saints." Late summer weather is generally fine and clear, and Roumanians whom business calls to western Europe sigh constantly for the soft blue skies and the endless green fields and hillsides of their home. In the Banat and Wallachia, just about half the year is cloudless altogether; fair days wholly overcast hardly come except in winter, and then especially in the mountains. While there is really no rainy season, more rain generally falls about the summer solstice than at any other period. May, June and July are apt to be wet; August and September, and January and February, are usually dry. The rain fall is not heavy; only in the Carpathians does it approach the average of the Atlantic sea-board, though there are mountain valleys where it reaches 50 or 55 inches. Over most of Roumania no more rain falls than in Kansas or Nebraska; the steppes of Wallachia, the Dobrudja and southern Bessarabia (the Budjac) get only about 15 inches a year. The summer rains are often accompanied by frightful thunder and hail-storms; the record downfall is of 8 inches in 20 minutes at Argesh, and at Cara-Omer in the Dobrudja 13 inches once fell in 4 hours! Two years out of five are generally dry; in a century of observation, there were three years of extreme drought; 58 of partial drought (¾ of the normal rainfall, which for Roumania as a whole is about 24 in.); 24 wet years, with precipitation decidedly over the average, and 15 when it ran ¼ beyond the normal. In an agricultural country relatively undeveloped, like Roumania, these relations are vital; a dry year means hunger and distress even yet, and in 1899 (a very dry year) and 1904 the Kingdom found itself forced to import corn in order to avert famine. The droughts of 1925–1928 contributed powerfully to the recent agricultural distress.

Like our own plains, Roumania is a land of ever-blowing breezes. The strong East wind (E.-N.-E., called the Crivătz) off the Russian steppes brings their baking heat in the summer, and in January will freeze the Danube almost over night. The Southwest wind, the Austru, blows just as often; it is really a continuation of the African sirocco, which reaches Hungary and the Banat, and so is usually a warm wind. Still warmer is the Southeast wind, the Băltăretz, which brings in the moisture of the Black Sea and the Danube delta. During the summer heat, whirlwinds and even cyclones arise occasionally, and do much damage. But in general one thinks of the Roumanian breezes as rippling the infinite grain-fields, bearing off the floating plum petals, or breathing the cool resinous fragrance of the Carpathian spruce forests.

CHAPTER II

MISTRESS of the mouth of the Danube, Roumania has a closer interest in the great river than any other nation. The Danube is to Roumania not merely a great trade channel, connecting the Baltic and the North Sea with the Euxine; but since the river forms a delta comparable with that of the Nile or the Mississippi, overflowing an area of more than two million acres, it brings up unusual agricultural and fishery problems. The difficulty is increased by the variation of the river's volume. At low water, the Danube discharges only 2000 cubic meters per second; at high water, up to 36,000! It is to be hoped that the International Danube Commission will carry through its plans for systematic regulation of the river, with a series of reservoirs. Meanwhile, Roumania's distinguished scientist, Dr. Gregory Antipa, succeeded for a time, at least, in harmonizing the opposing claims of agriculture and the fisheries. The farmers would like to have the river dyked in by levees for its lower course, and reclaim, at least for pasturage, all the overflowed area; but much of this region is light sandy soil, quite worthless without the annual deposit of river mud; and much is made up of permanent lakes and canals. Furthermore, the fisheries are a State monopoly and bring in an income of about a million dollars a year. To show how dependent the fisheries are on the Danube overflow, I reproduce Dr. Antipa's figures for the fisheries on the island of Braila alone, taking an average period:

5

Year (Apr. 1 Mar. 31)	Extreme High Water at Braila (in meters)	Duration of Flood, in days over the bank (4 meters)	in canals	Fish Catch (in tons)
1903–04	4.45	20	28	2650
1904–05	3.57	...	...	1000
1905–06	4.57	74	142	3630
1906–07	4.73	71	129	5830
1907–08	5.40	128	154	7050

The total catch in recent years has varied from 17,162 tons in 1922, to 26,328 in 1927. The fish are the same as in such muddy deltas elsewhere—carp, catfish, sturgeon (which, like the mullet and herring, run up from the Black Sea to spawn) and pike-perch; the sturgeon caviar is second only to that of the Volga. There is also a fascinating bird-life in these lagoons and swamps—wild-fowl in numbers unbelievable, even yet; egrets, cranes, cormorants, pelicans and an occasional flamingo.

The Danube is a stately stream, the largest in Europe west of the Volga—some 1800 miles long, or about the length of the Arkansas or the Rio Grande. After receiving the Save at Belgrade and the Morava at Semendria, it meets the barrier formed by the southern foothills of the Carpathians, and the northernmost extensions of the Balkans; at Cazane it dashes between cliffs less than 400 feet apart; on the north side are still to be seen the remains of the roadway hewn in the rock by the Romans under Trajan. Widening enough for the town of Orshova, the river soon narrows again, with dangerous rocks; here are the famous "Portzi de fer" (Iron Gates), which used to block navigation for over a mile and a half. This defile is some 80 miles long, and the Serbian side is hilly throughout; but from Turn Severin on, the Roumanian bank flattens out, and lagoons and marshes fill the northern landscape. The hills rise again as the river approaches the sea, and it makes a great bend to the north to avoid them; once past the Dobrudja uplands, it loses itself in the delta, renowned even in antiquity for its seven channels. 675,000 acres are covered with high reeds; the famous "floating islands" take up nearly a quarter of this area. Much use is made of the so-called "Bulgarian wheels"—mill-wheels set into the river's bank, which dip up the water into irrigating canals for early vegetables. Dr. Antipa, who had discovered that the plants and micro-organisms which small fry eat, survive exposure to sun and frost for at least one year, developed an ingenious system of alternating cultivation and fishing on the same land in successive years; and it is to be hoped that it will be given a thorough trial on a large scale.

The Danube carries down so much fine sand and clay that it pushes its delta seaward 15 or 20 feet a year; the turbid yellow flood overlies the clear green of the Euxine for many miles. This sea receives such a volume of fresh water that it is much less salt than the Mediterranean; at the surface there is only 1.9% salt, but at the greatest depth, of 6500 ft., the percentage rises to 2.2. The temperature varies curiously; at the surface the water runs from 55° to 75°, according to the season; at 50 fathoms, there is a constant temperature of about 45°; but in the lower strata the temperature rises again, to nearly 50°. Life ceases in this sea below 50 fathoms, chiefly in consequence of the large percentage of sulphuretted hydrogen in the deep water.

The Dniester, which rises in the Carpathians in central Galicia, bounds Roumania to the northeast as the Danube does to the south. A mountain torrent till it issues from its rocky gates at Soroca, it then becomes a sluggish and very winding river, navigable for barges; it empties into the Black Sea near the city of Cetatea Alba (Akkerman), the key to Bessarabia; its mouth is a long and narrow gulf, which it has silted up. The chief rivers of Moldavia are the Pruth and the Sereth, two much embattled streams—the Sereth being witness of the heroic victory of the Roumanians over Mackensen at Mărăsheshti in August, 1917; both rivers empty into the Danube beside Braila and Galatz. The Pruth has become fixed in Roumanian literary tradition as a melancholy river of defeat and death, the channel of the invader, to whom the peasant sang:

> Prutule, râu blestemat,
> Face-te-ai adânc shi lat
> Ca potopul tulburat!
> Mal cu mal nu se zărească
> Glas cu glas nu se lovească
> Ochi cu ochi nu se ajungă
> Pe a ta pânză cât de lungă!
> Lăcustele când or trece
> La ist mal să se înece!
> Holerele când or trece
> Pe la mijloc să se 'nece!
> Dushmanii tzării de-or trece
> La cel mal să se înece!
> Iar tu 'n valurile tale
> Să-i tot duci, să-i duci la vale
> Pân' la Dunărea cea mare
> Pân' în Dunărea shi 'n mare!

O Pruth, accursed stream
You must make yourself deep and wide
Like a muddy flood!
Let one bank not be seen from the other
Let one voice not carry to the other
Let eyes not reach one another
Over thy waters so broad.

THE DANUBE "IRON GATES"

ON THE LOWER DANUBE; HILLS OF THE DOBRUDJA IN THE BACKGROUND

Whenever the locusts pass
At the further bank may they drown!
Whenever the plagues pass
In the middle may they drown!
Enemies of our country if they pass
At this bank may they drown.
While you in your waves
May you carry them all down-stream
Down to the Danube, that great river,
Down into the Danube and the sea!
(*Popular ballad collected by Alecsandri.*)

The streams of the Wallachian plain are not much more than mountain torrents; they are fine trout-brooks in their upper courses, and have great power possibilities; but they carry little water in the dry months, and are practically useless for navigation. Best known are the Ialomitza and the Dâmbovitza, the muddy creek which flows through Bucharest. A grandiose project is under way to utilize the latter in a canal system which will make a seaport out of Bucharest. But the two westernmost rivers of Wallachia, the Olt (Aluta or Alt) and the Jiu, are respectable streams. Both of them rise in Transylvania, and pierce the Carpathians by romantic gorges; the Olt has its wealth of ballads also, having been a favorite course of the bandits who fought the Turks and the Magyars.

The largest river in the western Roumanian area is the Theiss (Roum. Tisa, Hung. Tisza), which would naturally form the boundary on the west; but the Paris Conference drew an artificial line to the eastward, leaving the upper course mostly in Hungary and the lower in Jugo-Slavia. It rises in the mountains of the Maramuresh; after it reaches the plains, its descent is so gentle—about one foot in ten miles—that it meanders in every direction; its actual length, some 750 miles, is double what it would be in a straight line; and like the Missouri and the Danube, its bed changes constantly, working westward over 100 feet a year along much of its course. There is a heavy river traffic on the Theiss, and the affluents from Transylvania and the Banat are also important; the Bega, which passes through Temeshvar, floats down thousands of fir logs from the Banat hills. The Bega canal, between Temeshvar and the Theiss, is an active waterway. Largest of all these tributaries of the Theiss is the Muresh (Hungarian, Maros)—a river sacred to the Roumanian aspirations for unity. After issuing from its picturesque mountain defiles, it passes Alba-Julia (Karlsburg, Karolyfejérvar), where Michael the Brave made his triumphal entry in November, 1599, after his great victory over the Magyars; where, in the early winter of 1918, was held the assembly which voted the annexation of Transylvania with the Kingdom of Roumania; and where, in October, 1922, Ferdinand and Marie were crowned sovereigns of Greater Roumania. A few miles east lies Blaj (Balizsfelva), scene of the "Field of Liberty" of 1848, where the Transylvanian Roumanians drew up a charter of liberties, which had to wait two generations for realization.

Roumania is also rich in lakes; but only those along the Danube and the sea-coast are of any size; Lake Razilm, where the Dobrudja touches the Danube delta, is the largest, and is rich in fish. Lake St. Anne, in the upper Olt valley, fills an extinct crater; Lake Tekirghiol, near Constantza, and Salt Lake near Braila are famous for the medicinal mud which forms their beds. The Bessarabian coast is one series of lakes formed by bays of the sea which have silted up; and further north, not far from the Dniester, is a country which boasts of hundreds of small ponds. The problem of reclamation of swamp lands calls for solution all over Roumania; and millions of capital will find profitable employment in power projects, irrigation schemes and other uses of this wealth of water courses.

CHAPTER III

THE MOUNTAINS

THE Carpathians form the back-bone of Roumania, and are in addition the cradle of the race, beloved by every patriot. Rising along the Danube near Vienna, they sweep in a great crescent about the Hungarian plain till their last foothills face the Balkans, again on the Danube. Their first great elevation is reached where they separate northern Hungary from Galicia, in the broad chain, of very ancient rocks, of the Erzgebirge and the Hohe Tatra (over 8700 ft.), which are called the Northern Carpathians. Then the range turns southeastward, and becomes the Eastern or Wooded Carpathians—rolling ridges, rising to respectable heights, and covered with spruce and beech. Where they separate the Maramuresh and the Bucovina, great forests of larch give them the name of the Black Mountains (Mt. Hovârla, 6800 ft.); further south is the Rodna range (Mt. Pietros, 7500 ft.). Here is a much-used pass, the Shtiol (4600 ft.), leading from the Vishau valley to the upper Bistritza in Bucovina; and over the Körösmezö (Jablonitza) Pass run both highway and railroad from the upper Theiss valley to that of the Pruth in Moldavia. The next important range is the Ceahlau, which runs about 6500 ft.; here are several passes between Transylvania, the Bucovina and Moldavia; that of the Bârgăul is about 4000 ft. Further south the peaks do not much surpass 5000 ft.; the Penteleu (5800 ft.) is famous for the thousands of sheep which cover its pastures in summer. This region is full of passes; the

Trotush carries the railroad from Ajud, on the main line up the Sereth, to Ghemesh (2350 ft.), whence it descends into the Muresh valley. A side valley, that of the Oituz, leads over the Oituz Pass into the Szekler country in Transylvania. East of the main range of the Eastern Carpathians and extending as far as the Sereth, runs a parallel line of hills, occasionally reaching a height of 2250 ft., of schists and sand-stone; like the similar foot-hills in Wallachia, they are full of great pockets of salt and oil.

Just where the Carpathians approach nearest the lower Danube, they suddenly turn west, and skirting the Wallachian plain, reach the river finally at the Iron Gates. These Southern Carpathians in general form two parallel ranges of ancient crystalline rocks, the peaks of which have weathered off and are quite Alpine in appearance; hence the name of Transylvanian Alps. To me, they resemble more the Tuscan Apennines north of Lucca, or the lower Canadian Rockies. The peaks have no tree but dwarf juniper on their last 1000 feet, but a rich sweet turf, lode-stone of the Roumanian shepherds, grows everywhere among the rocks. The upper valleys are generally carved out into the likeness of the heel of a boot, and are called căldare (kettles); little Alpine lakes, fed by snow-banks which lie in sheltered spots till late summer, add to their beauty. Many of the peaks exceed 7000 ft., and the Moldovean and Negoiu are over 8300. Numerous deep defiles and passes give communication with Transylvania; the Bran (4000 ft.) is, according to tradition, the path over which (in 1330) the defeated Hungarian hosts of Charles Robert were pursued by Bessarab, ruler of Wallachia. The Predeal (3500 ft.), a few miles east, is the chief passage northward from the Wallachian plain, and the route followed by the railway; Sinaia, the summer palace, lies near the summit, in a charming region

of trout-brooks and spruce forests, behind which rise bleak
cliffs and sharp peaks; all this region is a favorite summer
resort, lying only a few hours from the metropolis. Further
west, the gorge of the Olt leads the railroad up from Wallachia to Sibiu (Hermannstadt) over the traces of a Roman
road; the deep ravine by which the Jiu pierces the Carpathians at Surduc (1750 ft.) is utilized by a highway, but
the railroad has not yet been carried through. Just as in
Moldavia, there is a line of foot-hills skirting the Carpathians to the south; these are of importance not only for
their deposits of oil and salt, but because the disintegrating
shales of their slopes make excellent farming and orchard
soil; the densest rural population of Roumania dwells upon
these hill-sides.

There are several other mountain groups on Roumanian
territory. The Eastern Banat has one, with peaks approaching 5000 ft.; it reaches the Danube at the Clisura Cazanelor
(cauldron rapids). This seems to have been the most popu-
lous region of ancient Dacia, and Roman roads run in every
direction; one of the best known is that from Caransebesh
to the Iron Gates of Transylvania, at Hatzeg. These mountains are notorious for horned vipers and scorpions, and for
a fly (musca culumbaca) which drives the cattle frantic in
early summer, and which local tradition says goes back to
the many-headed dragon whose den was at Columbaca, near
the Danube, and which was driven up into the mountains
and killed by Jovan Jorgovan (Hercules). These Banat
mountains spread out westward into wide low hills, which
drop off to the plain in gleaming cliffs of white marble.

The Carpathians hem in the Transylvanian plateau on
every quarter but the west; and on that side also rise mountain ranges, called the Western Mountains (Muntzii
Apuseni). They reach nearly 6000 ft. in elevation and are

dear to the Roumanian heart not only for the picturesque beauty of their narrow gorges and high cascades, but because they were the home of many distinguished patriots— among others, Nicola Ursu (Horia), head of the peasant uprising of 1784 against the Vienna government, and Avram Iancu, leader of the nationalist movement against the Magyars from 1848 on. They are rich in minerals—gold, silver, lead, copper, etc.—which have been exploited since Roman days; indeed, some of our most interesting Roman business documents, dating from the third century, were found in the Transylvanian mines.

Far off to the southeast, beyond the Wallachian plains and the Danube, we come across hills in the Dobrudja which belong to another system. In the northern Dobrudja they rise to 1600 or 1700 feet, and are thickly wooded with oak and beech scrub; they are remnants of the so-called Chimerical Mountains, to which belong scattered hills in eastern Moldavia, the Snake Island (Insula Sherpilor) out at sea, and the mountains of the Crimea. Further south in the Dobrudja we have a continuation of the Bulgarian uplands, rolling ridges of 1200–1300 ft., ending abruptly, both above the Danube and the Black Sea, in cliffs 300 or 400 ft. high. The region between Rustchuk and Balchik is largely covered with close thickets (hence the name Deliorman, bad woods) and deep coulees and arroyos, dry for most of the year; towards the sea the land is mainly bare, with only the vegetation of the steppe. It forms a bleak contrast to Roumania proper.

CHAPTER IV

PRODUCTS AND RESOURCES OF THE MOUNTAINS;
PETROLEUM

THE mountain-climber in Roumania comes upon the same plants and animals in the highest Carpathians that he would find in the Alps or the Rockies. The short sweet grass which grows to the foot of the cliffs is cropped even yet in remote fastnesses of the mountains by the chamois and mountain goat; deer and bear are still quite plentiful, and one hears of occasional wolves; foxes, badgers and smaller game are found everywhere. In the highest Alpine zone, the trees dwindle away to an occasional dwarf juniper; saxifrages and gentians brave the snow-squalls; wild strawberries, cranberries, bilberries, raspberries and blackberries solace the shepherd who brings up his flocks in summer from the plains along the Danube. Further down are magnificent pastures, used since time immemorial not merely for flocks but also for herds of cattle. Then come splendid forests of larch and spruce, the latter descending to about 2000 ft. These have been scandalously exploited near roads and water-courses, and the war caused much destruction, but the government Forestry Department is making progress with the situation. Below the spruce comes the beech belt; these forests descend to about 1000 ft. above sea level, and are so characteristic of the lower Carpathians that the district of the Bucovina gets its name from them. Hemlock, maple, birch, hornbeam, ash and other familiar trees of the temperate zone are mingled with the beech; in fact, I have never seen a forest

Photo, Fischer, Sibiu

A TRANSYLVANIAN PASTURE

Photo, Tzatzu, Bucharest

THE CARPATHIANS AT SINAIA

Photo, Fischer, Sibiu

THE NEGOIU

Photo, Fischer, Sibiu

SIBIU AFTER A BLIZZARD

or even a landscape in Roumania which could not be closely paralleled in one or another section of the United States.

The foot-hills and much of the plains were originally thickly covered with several different kinds of oak, interspersed with elm, linden, sycamore, ash, maple, hornbeam, hazel, alder, cornel, poplar and willow. But the need of firewood, particularly during the war, has made ravages in these forests; and the great extension of arable land during the last half-century has been largely at their expense.

In Roumania proper, 17% of the area (nearly seven million acres) was still timbered 25 years ago; this has now shrunk to about five million acres; about 40% of this is state property. In 1912, a typical year, 300,000 tons of wood were exported. Transylvania, the Banat and the Maramuresh have about nine million acres under forest, of which over half is beech; spruce and fir account for a quarter. In the Bucovina there are over 1,100,000 acres of woodland; Bessarabia has about 625,000 acres.

Thus one-quarter of Greater Roumania is under forest. There are about 500 saw-mills, employing 45,000 workers; several million railway ties are produced each year; firewood, planks and other lumber are exported to the value of (1928) 4⅔ billion lei, (1929) 4¼. German, Swiss, Italian and Czecho-Slovak capital finds employment in the Roumanian lumber business. The large lumber companies formed an export union with those of Jugo-Slavia in the summer of 1931 for joint marketing abroad of spruce, pine and other soft-wood products. The demoralization of the markets in Greece, Egypt, Italy and other importing countries had led to a cut-throat competition which this agreement is hoped to end.

In the spring the Roumanian hill-sides are white with the blossoms of the orchards, and sweet with the fragrance of the vineyards in bloom. It has the fruit possibilities of California; the cold winter prevents the growth of citrus fruits, to be sure, and other sub-tropical products, but gives a flavor and a tang which more than compensate. Roumanian grapes are famous, and the wine industry is susceptible of great development. A Rhine-wine expert says: "I have rarely seen in any country a vine so marvelous and rich as in Roumania. The vineyards are a picture that remind one of the Promised Land, of the prophecies of Joshua and Caleb. The clusters hang down compact, sweet as honey, marvelous in shape, size and quality." The table grapes are handsome and delicious. Unfortunately the phylloxera ravaged the country half a century ago, and the vineyards have never been entirely replanted. Still, Greater Roumania is the fourth wine-producing country in Europe, coming after Italy (10 million acres of vineyards, 31 million hectoliters of wine—a hectoliter is 26.417 gallons), France ($4\frac{1}{4}$ million acres, 56 million hectoliters) and Spain ($3\frac{3}{4}$ million acres, 17 million hectoliters). The former kingdom has some 315,-000 acres of vineyards; Bessarabia, which in the 'eighties lost half her vines from the phylloxera, has now 250,000 acres; it is interesting to note that though American vines occupy only $\frac{3}{8}$ of the total area, they furnish more than half the wine. The Bucovina has only 100 acres in vineyards; but the Banat has about 75,000, and Transylvania has about 43,000. In the Maramuresh (with which I customarily include the Crishana) there are about 45,000 acres. The total area, therefore, in vineyards in Greater Roumania is about 700,000 acres, with a production of 7,000,000 hl. in good years. Some excellent wines are made; but in general the Roumanian peasant clings to antiquated methods. In the summer of 1930, the planting of inferior varieties was forbidden, and the vineyards were brought under government supervision.

The characteristic fruit of Roumania is the plum; over 300,000 acres are given up to plum orchards; they are chiefly used for the tzuica, the plum brandy which is the favorite drink of the peasant; and the fragrance of fermenting masses of plums accompanies the autumn traveler everywhere among the hills. Fruit-canning and drying establishments are greatly needed; what can be done was shown by the Germans during their occupation of the country. As if by magic, four large establishments arose, employing some 1200 hands each, which turned these plums into marmalade for the German army. Some of the plums are dried into prunes in primitive fashion. Pears, peaches, apricots, apples and other fruits grow well, but need improved methods of growing and packing, and better sorts. In 1927, there were in Roumania nearly 50 million plum trees; 3½ million walnuts; nearly 8 million apple trees, and 3½ million pears; 8 million cherries, one million apricots, nearly a million peach trees, and over a million quince bushes.

The mountains and hills furnish Roumania not merely with pasture-land, forests, orchards and vineyards; they hold her wealth of minerals, salt and oil. Doubtless the mines were a great attraction for the Romans; at any rate, they developed them extensively, and connected them with the administrative centers by excellent roads. The gold mines were famous in early times, and are exploited even yet; there are two chief groups, one in northern Transylvania, and one down in the Metallic Mountains. They yield some 2000 kilograms (4400 lbs. avoirdupois) a year. The ore is crushed in a mill and carried over woolen blankets by a swift current of water; the particles of gold, which remain in the wool, are rescued by quicksilver. About 2500 kilograms of silver are extracted from the same and similar ores. There are important mines of manganese at Iacobeni in the Bucovina, large deposits of chrome in the Banat, and of lead in the Western Mountains. There are several copper mines, but their combined output does not begin to meet the needs of the country. It is iron and coal, salt and oil that form the mineral wealth of Roumania, and assure her future. The chief iron mines are at Dognacia, Moravitza, Bogsha and Nadrag in the Banat, and at Ghelar in Transylvania; they produce about 100,000 metric tons per annum. What gives these iron mines their value is that they lie next door to coal deposits; the combination has built up a number of great steel mills; there are five in the Banat, of which the largest is at Reshitza; here, and in Bucharest, even locomotives are built. Transylvania has six large iron and steel works. The Banat coal mines, producing a good quality of soft coal, turn out over 300,000 tons a year. In the upper Jiu valley over 1,200,000 tons of excellent lignite are mined every year; lignite of poorer quality is found in the upper Trotush valley; and in the Ialomitza and Argesh valleys they mine some 100,000 tons yearly of inferior lignite. The highest total production in recent years was three million tons (1928). There is one mine of excellent anthracite, at Shchela (in the county of Gorj), and another in the Banat, but the production is infinitesimal.

The Roumanian oil deposits lie mainly in three zones; the first, and by far the most important, extends from the Bucovina along the foot-hills down to the Dâmbovitza; the second is in the county of Vâlcea, bounded on the north by the Carpathians between the Jiu and the Olt, and on the south by the hills of Oltenia; the third is in the Maramuresh,

HER PRIDE AND JOY

A FAIR IN THE MUNTENIAN PLAIN

OIL WELLS AT CAMPINA

along the Theiss valley. In the former Kingdom, the chief producing district is that of Prahova, north of Bucharest, which produced 3,371,636 tons in 1929, of which half came from the new Moreni region; Câmpina, Bustenari, Tzintea and Baicoi are the other important centers. Moreni is famous for the burning well of the Româno-Americana Company, which caught fire in May, 1929, suddenly went out on Sept. 18, 1931, and caught fire again on the 28th. East of this lies the Buzeu district, with a production in 1929 of 86,405 tons. The Dâmbovitza region produced 1,290,641 tons in 1929; one of its centers, Schiuri-Razvad, was developed under the Germans during the war, to a daily capacity of 40 cars. The fourth important district is that of Bacău in Moldavia, producing in 1929, 78,598 tons. It is calculated that there are about 50,000 acres of oil-lands in Roumania, and 750,000 acres of probable oil-lands, of which only about six or seven thousand are exploited as yet. The oil is found in Tertiary deposits, in Wallachia in the upper layers of sand (Pliocene and Miocene), in Moldavia (where one must sometimes bore over 3000 ft.) in the lower strata of sandstone. The average boring is about 1500 ft.

These wells, now about 1800 in number, were not exploited till the middle of the 19th century, and it was not till 25 years ago that they reached international prominence; now Roumania has a total output of well toward five million tons. Before the war, the capital invested was about 530,-000,000 francs, of which only 33,600,000 (6.3%) was Roumanian; one-half was British-French-Dutch, 30.6% German or Austrian, and about 11% American. But the Germans had the best fields, notably the Roumanian Star (Steaua Română) property, at Câmpina. In the general destruction of the oil wells, carried out under British supervision during the German advance, to prevent their utilizing this resource, the Roumanian Star fields lay on the line of retreat of the Roumanian army. They were therefore used by the Roumanians to the last moment; the Germans came on so rapidly that there was no time for any but superficial wrecking; and within a few weeks the Germans had the property again in good shape. As the Roumanian Star was a German company, the Germans developed it greatly during their occupation; at the end of the war they had installed a new refinery which practically doubled its capacity.

Reconstruction was greatly delayed by the added expense of boring, etc.; the transportation crisis also greatly hampered rehabilitation. Nevertheless, by the summer of 1921 production had risen to over one-half the pre-war standard and is now far greater. The surplus goes to Egypt (in 1930, 538,190 tons); England (465,528); Italy (262,774); Austria (252,073); France (222,549); Germany (217,952); Hungary (204,749); Jugo-Slavia (174,335); and Czecho-Slovakia (124,180); total production in 1930, 5,792,311 metric tons. In 1930 an important contract was closed with the Spanish Monopoly. The world crisis in oil has hit Roumania hard, and it proved impossible to bring all of the companies into a restriction agreement, in view of the cut-throat Russian competition next door.

The destruction of the oil-wells during the war, and the defeat of Germany, which had so much capital invested in Roumania, raised problems solved in part by the San Remo Conference of April, 1920. As a result of this and later conferences, the territory is now exploited by various companies of which the leading are: The Astra Română (Anglo-Dutch), Steaua Română (Anglo-French-Roumanian), Sirius-Concordia (French-Belgian-Roumanian), Unirea (Anglo-Dutch), Credit-Minier (Roumanian), and Româno-Americana (Standard Oil of New Jersey). There are two pipe lines, of about 475 miles, connecting the fields with Constantza on the Black Sea, and Giurgiu on the Danube. Under the constitution of 1924, the state laid claim to the subsoil; later legislation confirmed this principle, but established a working agreement, on a royalty basis, with the oil companies. Almost all the product is refined in Roumania; the gasoline produced is of excellent quality, and motoring in Roumania costs as little as in California.

Natural gas is a side product of the oil area; it will shortly be piped to Bucharest. Great gas wells in Transylvania supply the factories in and about Turda; they produce about half a billion cubic meters.

The Roumanian state possesses an inestimable treasure in its great salt deposits; they were a state monopoly long before the days of the Kingdom. There are extensive beds in Transylvania; but the most famous mines are in the Carpathian foot-hills of Moldavia and Wallachia, especially near the great bend of the range; over 50 large deposits are known in these foot-hills. That of Turn-Ocna is about 2½ miles long, 1000 ft. wide and 350 ft. thick—a mass of about 250,000,000 metric tons, of which only one million has been extracted as yet. A visit of 1919 to the salt mines of Slănic, which are easily accessible from the capital, was most interesting. At the mine's mouth is a store-house, full of what seem to be large clear blocks of ice—so pure is the rock-salt. Down a couple of hundred feet in an elevator to a great gallery, from which a long staircase leads to the main gallery of these mines—a huge cathedral nave, some 450 feet long, 200 ft. wide and 250 ft. high! The ceiling and the walls are hewn out as carefully as if planned by an architect; the total effect was impressive in the extreme. Convict labor used to be employed, but was given up on account of its inefficiency. In the post-war currency confusion, salt and oil formed valuable commodities for barter; in 1919, I met a Vienna railroad man who had come up to accompany a train of 50 cars of oil and gasoline, which the Austrians were paying for with steel manufactures; and the Greek Government took salt in payment for Macedonian tobacco, purchased by the Roumanian tobacco monopoly. This salt might be made the basis of profitable chemical manufacture; as yet it is utilized almost exclusively for table and culinary purposes. About 350,000 tons a year are produced.

As might be expected, there are numerous salt springs; at Slănic is a salt lake which has resulted from the overflowing of a former digging; and there are also many mineral springs with other components, some radio-active. The best known are the hot springs at Mehadia (Baths of Hercules), which are over 140° and have a good bathing establishment. Roumania has also many excellent stone quarries, of granite, limestone, marble, cement rock, etc.

CHAPTER V

ROUMANIA's mineral wealth is immense, as we have seen; but her greatest treasure is the rich soil of her endless plains. These are the product of decomposition of soft and recent rocks, or of alluvial deposit. The famous black earth of the Baragan, the Burnas, the Budjac, the southern Dobrudja, and northeastern Moldavia and Bessarabia, as well as the plains of the Theiss, is the same that enriches the Ukraine; it is rich in humus, which rises to 8% of the total at Dorohoi, Covurlui and Buzeu; the Germans shipped out many carloads for the Berlin parks in 1918. Indeed, the peasant rarely uses artificial fertilizer, but merely alternates Indian corn and wheat. These same districts have (further to the south) a red soil (the so-called chestnut earth) which is nearly as rich; the soil of the hills and forests is a deeper red, full of iron oxide.

The black earth is the soil for cereals, *par excellence*. Wheat, barley, rye and oats have been grown here since time immemorial; and it has proved so suited to maize that corn meal mush is now the Roumanian national dish, as inevitable on the tables of aristocracy and peasantry as is oatmeal in Scotland. Four-fifths of all the farm land of Roumania is given up to these cereals; in summer, the billowy wheat-fields and the streamers of the corn give one the illusion of being in Illinois or Iowa. Wheat occupies over six million acres, producing over 100,000,000 bu. on the average; corn, about twelve million, and 240,000,000 bu.;

much fodder corn is grown also. Barley accounts for over five million acres, with a yield of 100,000,000 bu. Oats are grown almost exclusively in northern Moldavia, Bessarabia and southern Dobrudja; they occupy about three million acres. Rye used to be the staple grain of Bessarabia, in which lie ⅔ of the 750,000 acres devoted to its cultivation. Millet is grown and consumed almost entirely by the Mohammedan population of the southern Dobrudja.

This abundance of cereals gives Roumania a large surplus for export; here are the figures for 1928–30:

	Carloads exported	Average price f.o.b. per car	Total value, in thousands of lei (1000 lei = about $6)
		1928	
Wheat	2,792	91,300	255,000
Indian corn	47,314	75,500	3,575,000
Barley	41,455	68,650	2,846,000
Oats	1,686	66,420	112,000
Rye	3,452	74,740	258,000
	96,698		7,046,000
		1929	
Wheat	721	77,670	56,000
Corn	37,449	42,200	1,869,000
Barley	115,470	49,300	5,696,000
Oats	4,173	38,580	161,000
Rye	1,561	51,250	80,000
	159,374		7,862,000
		1930	
Wheat	33,647	43,017	1,447,000
Corn	118,080	32,909	3,886,000
Barley	144,313	24,823	3,584,000
Oats	9,405	24,511	231,000
Rye	2,911	24,688	71,000
	308,356		9,219,000

It is instructive to follow the recent fall in prices, in order to understand the difficulties of the Roumanian farmer:

INDEX PRICES OF CEREALS PER QUARTER-YEARS, 1929–30

	1929 Last Quarter	1930 First Quarter	Second Quarter	Third Quarter	Last Quarter
Wheat	104	104	92	75	56
Corn	104	79	72	87	64
Barley	106	74	60	55	45
Oats	93	80	71	65	54
Rye	111	77	68	56	53
Cereals, average	103	88.3	78.8	76	57.8

The destination of this grain is as follows (in ten-ton carloads):

Country of export	Wheat	Corn	Barley	Rye	Oats	Total
Germany	3,051	28,385	65,920	451	2,206	100,013
Italy	10,080	27,461	9,003	471	3,119	50,134
Holland	3,482	15,585	22,907	512	877	43,363
England	2,673	11,606	15,839	470	311	36,899
Belgium	4,266	4,455	12,968	284	667	22,640
France	3,933	7,261	6,337	285	371	18,187
Gibraltar	83	5,592	3,607	1	24	9,307
Czecho-Slovakia	1,632	4,956	101	14	277	6,986

It is striking to see how slight is the cultivation of other crops. The colza crop amounts to about a million bu.; flax, about 210,000 bu. of linseed; the five-year pre-war average was about 450,000. Peas cover about 30,000 acres. Hemp is raised in general only to supply local needs. The sugar-beet industry is growing rapidly. Tobacco being a government monopoly, may be planted only in certain restricted areas, totaling about 70,000 acres, where supervision is easy. Beans are grown chiefly in connection with corn; the average yield is about 5,000,000 bu., which allows a surplus for export. Alfalfa, clover and other forage plants are widely cultivated (a million acres) in the Theiss plain, Transylvania and the Bucovina; but the peasant in the former Kingdom, wedded to the culture of cereals, puts only about 300,000 acres into forage. Potatoes are widely grown in

Western Roumania (the Banat, Crishana, Transylvania and the Bucovina)—some 250,000 acres—but in Roumania proper they are not much raised except (like beans and pumpkins) in the corn-fields. Sunflowers are raised on a large scale for oil, almost exclusively in Bessarabia.

When we examine the yield per acre, it is evident that Roumanian agriculture, like that of the United States, can be greatly improved. In the former Kingdom, an acre of wheat yields only about one-half the number of bushels grown in England or Germany, and two-fifths the Belgian or Dutch product, and the proportion holds almost exactly for barley and oats. Bessarabia is in much the same agricultural stage; Transylvania and the Banat are much more advanced, getting 50 or 60 per cent more grain for the same area. Much is being done by coöperative buying of selected seed by municipalities and societies; but it is observed in Roumania, just as in Russia, that the cutting up of large estates, in which great economies of operation were possible, is followed by a lowering of the yield. Efforts are being made to offset this by combinations of individual small owners for the purchase and use of tractors, threshing-machines, etc. The principle of peasants' coöperatives, so widely developed in Russia, has made headway in Roumania also, especially in Bessarabia, where nearly 500 have been organized.

Taken as a whole, Roumania is an important stock-raising country; but the former Kingdom, which specializes in cereals, was far poorer in cattle than the new provinces before the war, and did not soon recover from the enemy's depredations; Czernin boasted that the Central Powers had stripped Roumania of 82% of all her cattle, all her sheep and all her horses. Some of this stock was left in Transylvania, which was actually richer in stock at the end of the

war than at the beginning. Hungary had long laid a tariff
embargo on Roumanian stock, in order to protect the Hungarian industry; and this measure had contributed powerfully to turn Roumanian agriculture into raising wheat and
corn rather than animals. Now there is an excellent opportunity to improve quality and increase the numbers of Roumanian stock. Only a century ago, Moldavian horses were
famous; the Porte specified that the Principalities should
send a considerable number of Roumanian horses along
with the tribute. Indeed, the Turks had a proverb: Persian
youths and Moldavian horses are the noblest. To-day it is
Bessarabia, the Dobrudja and the Wallachian and Theiss
plains which produce the best horses; there are about 2,000,-
000 head in Greater Roumania. The Roumanian Government maintains fifteen studs with English stallions of Arab
blood. There are an annual horse fair and horse races at
Constantza, and two racing seasons annually in Bucharest;
the excellent Jockey Club has maintained a studbook for
fifty years.

The Roumanian peasant prefers oxen to horses for the
work of the farm; the best picture of rural Roumania is
Alecsandri's Plugurile:

Noroc bun! Pe câmpul neted ies Românii cu-a lor pluguri!
Boi plăvani în câte shease trag, se opintesc în juguri,
Bratzul gol apasă 'n coarne; fierul taie brazde lungi
Ce se 'nshiră 'n bătătură ca lucioase negre dungi.

Treptat câmpul se umbreshte sub a brazdelor desime;
El resună 'n mare sgomot de voioasa argătzime,
Iar pe lanul ce în soare se svîntează fumegând
Cocostârcii cu largi pasuri calcă rar shi meditând.

Acum soarele-i l'amiazăzi; la pămînt omul se 'ntinde:
Cârd de fete shi neveste de la sat aduc merinde;

Plugul zace'n lan pe coaste, iar un mândru flăcăuash
Mâna boii la isvoare shi îi pashte la imash.

Sfântă muncă dela tzeara, isvor sacru de rodire,
Tu legi omul cu pămîntul în o dulce înfrătzire!
Dar lumina amurgeshte, shi plugarii cătră sat
Haulind pe lângă juguri se întorc dela arat.

TRANSLATION

Good luck! Over the level plain go out the Roumanians with
    their plows!
The blond oxen, six by six, pull, strain in their yokes,
The bare arm presses on their horns; the iron cuts long furrows
Which thread themselves on a woof like gleaming black
    stripes.
Gradually the plain becomes shadowed under the closeness
    of the furrows;
There resounds a loud clamor of the cheerful farm-hands,
While over the field which in the sun is drying itself, steam-
    ing,
The storks with long strides step far apart and ruminating.

Now the sun is at midday; on the ground man lays himself at
    length;
Bevies of girls and wives bring lunch from the village;
The plow lies in the field on a ridge, while a stout young fellow
Urges the cattle to the spring and sets them grazing in the
    pasture.

Sainted labor of the earth, holy spring of fruitfulness,
You bind man with the soil in a sweet brotherhood!
But the light is waning, and the plowmen towards the village
Singing beside the yokes return from plowing.

Transylvania is famous for its large handsome oxen, with wide spreading horns; they remind one of the Tuscan cattle. Another well-known breed is the Moldavian, raised in the region between the Pruth and the Sereth. In general, while Roumanian cattle are excellent for the work of the farm, there is room for improvement in the breeding of beef steers and milch cows. The milk problem is a serious one in all the cities of Roumania. The general condition of cattle raising is shown by the fact that in the former Kingdom, while there were 2,700,000 head of cattle in 1860, and 2,937,857 in 1916, the number had dropped to 1,990,556 in 1919; 87% belonged to the peasants. Bessarabia had a similar experience; the number of cattle and buffaloes, which had been 525,000 in 1905, dropped to 481,000 in 1910. The high point since the war in Greater Roumania was reached in 1922, with 5,745,538 head of cattle; since then, it has steadily declined, reaching 4,552,166 in 1927. This was due partly to increased local consumption from a higher standard of living, partly to the agricultural crisis, which forced farmers to sell surplus cattle.

The typical Roumanian through the centuries has been the shepherd; but the nineteenth century thrust his picturesque figure into the background, as sheep-raising and pasturing grew less and less important. To their neighbors, especially the Magyars, Roumania is still thought of as a nation of shepherds; but it is perhaps true to-day only of the scattered Aroumanians of the Balkans that the pasturing of flocks remains the chief national occupation. In Roumania itself, it has long since given place to agriculture. But the consciousness that during the invasions and the Middle Ages, these wandering shepherds preserved the Roumanian language and national feeling, is alive in every

Roumanian, and still invests them with romance, which is enhanced by their picturesque costumes.

There are about thirteen million sheep in Roumania; the best local races are the Bigaia (fine wool, 51 microns) and the Burcana (coarser, 56 microns). They produce about 25,000 tons of wool. This is largely made into home-spuns by the peasants; the distaff and spinning wheel are still to be seen in almost every cottage. In Roumania proper, there are only about a dozen woolen mills. In this as in other spheres, it is clear that Roumania, having passed from the pastoral to the agricultural stage, is standing at the threshold of a great industrial development, favored both by her position at the mouth of the Danube and the gates of Russia and the Near East, and by her wealth of willing and intelligent labor. She will certainly follow the path already trodden by her Romance sisters of the West, Spain and Italy, with whom she has so many points of resemblance.

To return to stock-raising: Roumania raises few goats (only about 400,000), but, like Russia, is a great hog-producing country, with perhaps four million hogs at the beginning of the war; the number is now nearer three million. Those of the mangalitza (charcoal) breed, with white and curly bristles, are quite comparable to York or Berkshire. Donkeys and mules are not so common as in Italy or Spain. Poultry-raising is in general merely an adjunct to the farmyard, and has great possibilities, shown by the recent marked increase in shipments of eggs to Northern Europe. It is reckoned that Roumania possesses 32,450,000 fowl; 4,200,000 geese; 6,300,000 ducks; 1,700,000 turkeys; 78,000 Guinea fowl; and 620,000 pigeons.

We must not leave the subject of agriculture without some mention of bee-keeping, which is widely diffused

IN THE WHEAT

A ROUMANIAN CORNFIELD

through Roumania, though not as it was a century or two ago, when Roumanian honey was famous, and the wax found a market as far west as Venice. The industry is better developed in the Banat than elsewhere in Roumania. It leads also in silk-culture, which is coming up since the war, thanks to government experiment stations; the largest is at Orshova. In 1928, 550,000 lbs. of cocoons were produced in the Banat.

CHAPTER VI

ROUMANIA arose from the waters about the middle of the Tertiary period; traces of man of the cut-stone period exist in Roumania. Recent excavations have brought to light remains of early stone age man within Bucharest city limits (Grădina Teului) and near-by, at Măgura Jilavei. The potsherds and tools are in general of the second Trojan period, but extend from very early handmade pottery to a time when bronze implements were being imported. The Municipal Museum of Bucharest now has an excellent little collection for the study of prehistory. In neolithic times, the civilization which flourished about the Ægean had already made its way here; and Cucuteni, near Jassy, has become famous for its painted potsherds and terra-cotta "owl's-head" statuettes. These are rough effigies of human beings, with the body often decorated with geometric designs. Similar figurines have been found not only in Serbia and Bosnia, but even in Asia Minor. Even at that early time, the primitive Roumanians were a mixed race; both long and short skulls were brought to light at Cucuteni.

Unfortunately, not enough material is as yet available to enable us to trace the early history of Roumania as we can of France, Spain or Italy. The lamented scholar Pârvan (see Bibliography) and his pupils have made a brilliant beginning. When we reach the period of the ancient historians, we find this quarter of the world occupied by the Thracians. The mountainous region was inhabited by taller

34

types; like the plain-dwellers, they had in general short, broad skulls, long-skulled individuals being very scarce even yet in Roumania. The primitive Roumanian would seem to have been of this tall brachycephalic Alpine subspecies, with a straight nose, and doubtless with dark hair and eyes; blonds are much rarer to-day in Roumania than in Bulgaria or Serbia—an incidental proof how little the ethnic type was affected by the Germanic and Slav invasions. The recent serological blood tests of Manuila, G. Popovici and others enable us to differentiate the plain- and mountain-dwellers, the former showing Oriental affinities.

The branch occupying the western Balkans and the Adriatic coast was the Illyrians; those north of the Danube, in Transylvania and the Carpathian region, were the Dacians and Getæ; while the Macedonians spread over the eastern Balkans. The Macedonians were early Hellenized, and under Philip and Alexander (who is claimed as a blood-relative by the Bulgarians and Roumanians) not merely conquered Greece itself, but carried Greek civilization in every direction. Greek traders had been active along the Black Sea much earlier. But, strangely enough, though this expansion of Macedonia made Greek the culture-language for Asia Minor and Egypt, so that Latin never could supplant it, the sturdy Dacians north of the river were never brought to accept the Greek tongue. They maintained their independence long after the new power of the Romans had subjugated the Illyrians and the Macedonians themselves; indeed, they defeated Roman armies, and Horace keeps begging Augustus to chastise them and wipe away the stain. But it was not till Trajan's day—the beginning of the second century of our era—that the brave Dacian king Decebalus was finally vanquished and slain, after two campaigns (101–2 and 105–6). Pârvan proves however that Roman elements had long been filtering into Dacia, and that Latin had already long been widely used. Roman colonists were now brought in from all parts of the Roman dominion, and Dacia—or rather the Dacias—became provinces of the Roman Empire. They covered just about the present area of Greater Roumania— the region bounded by Theiss, Dniester and Danube—but intense Romanization seems to have affected only the Banat, Transylvania and western Wallachia, to judge by the Roman inscriptions and relics of Roman roads. The present Dobrudja, which had been Hellenized along the coast, had come earlier under Roman sway; it was here that Ovid had been banished by Augustus to Tomi (Constantza); and his significant line

Hac arat infelix, hac tenet arma manu.
(Here plows the unfortunate, here he keeps holding his weapons in his hand.)

is a synthesis of the whole of Roumanian history, in its picture of the poor peasant's devotion to his plow in the midst of enemies. The important excavations (under Pârvan and Lambrino) at Histria, 30 miles up this coast from Constantza, carry us from its foundation, by Milesian Greeks in the seventh century B.C., well into Roman times. Histria is the Roumanian Pompeii.

For a century and a half, Dacia remained Roman, and the Latin tongue supplanted the old Thraco-Illyrian, while adopting some of its commonest words. Then under the emperor Gallienus (260–268), the Goths and other peoples north of the Black Sea began to move southwestward; and though Aurelian defeated them in 271, he yielded them Dacia north of the Danube, and withdrew the Roman legions, which had been concentrated in the Banat. The Roman colonists who wished to leave, he settled south of the river, in a province cut out of Mœsia and named Dacia Aureliana.

And now began a series of invasions which lasted a thousand years. We must imagine successive hordes of wandering barbarians, driven out of the Ukraine by similar movements up in further Russia and Turkestan, proceeding with their flocks and herds across the Moldavian and Wallachian plains, sometimes working westward along the Danube, sometimes following the Dobrudja and Bulgarian highlands southward into the Balkans. The Goths tarried long in the land; the marvelous gold treasure of Pietroasa gives some idea of their civilization. Then came the Huns (375–453), a Mongolian race, who established their chief domain between the Theiss and the Danube; the Gepids (453–566), of Gothic stock, who ruled Dacia as allies of the Eastern Roman Empire; and the Avars (566–799), relatives of the Huns, who came in first together with Slavs. The Slavs had been filtering into the Balkans for generations, and now arrived in dense masses, appropriating permanently most of the Balkans and the region northwest of it. In 679 another people related to the Huns, the Bulgars, descended upon Dacia from the Volga district, and laid the foundations of Bulgaria; in 840 and 890 came the Hunnish Magyars and in 900 the Turkish Petchenegs; the Cumans, another Finno-Ugric tribe, arrived in 1050; the Mongolian Tartars seized the coast regions in 1241; and in the beginning of modern times, all of this corner of Europe was seized by the Turks. Mircea the Old defeated their Sultan Bajazid in 1394 near Craiova, to be sure; but the Turks speedily recovered, and pushed steadily westward, till in the battle of Mohács (1526) Suleiman the Magnificent subjugated the Hungarians, and the Turkish Empire in Europe, whose extinction we are witnessing to-day, reached its greatest extent.

During these centuries of wild commotion, what happened to the Roumanian people? That is one of the puzzles of history, and there is a lively controversy over it. Few are the references during this period to the "Vlachs" or "Wallachs," as their neighbors called them—an interesting name, attached by Germans everywhere to the Romans and Celts, as is attested by the Welsh and the Walloons in the remote West. In 1774 a German scholar named Thumann, in his "Untersuchungen über die Geschichte der östlichen europäischen Völker," expressed the opinion that the Daco-Romans—this Romanized Thracian people—had fled before the invaders up into the Carpathians and maintained themselves there as shepherds and farmers. Seven years later an Austrian officer named Sulzer brought out a work entitled "Die Geschichte des transalpinischen Daciens" in which he tried to prove that all the Daco-Romans had withdrawn into Dacia Aureliana south of the Danube, living on in the Wallachian (Kutzo-Vlach) shepherds of the Balkans, and that it was only in quite recent times that they had spread northward again across the Danube. This thesis was eagerly seized by the Magyars, as it supported their contention that they were in possession of Transylvania and the Banat long before the Roumanians; there are some curious facts which apparently support their view—the absence of allusion to Wallachians in early documents, the presence of many Albanian words in Roumanian (which they would explain by the long sojourn of the Wallachians in the Albanian districts of the Balkans) and others. But Mommsen, Ranke and Kiepert came to Thumann's rescue, and it is to-day generally agreed (outside of Hungary!) that all through the southern Carpathian valleys Wallachian shepherds pastured their flocks on the mountain meadows during the summer, and drove them down to the plain in the winter, while their families dwelt in scattered farms and villages along the upper water-courses, and preserved their language, costume and traditions. That seems the easiest explanation of the astounding vitality of the Roumanian people, over which have rolled so many waves of invasion without affecting their most intimate characteristics. In the severe climate and harsh living conditions of these mountain fastnesses, they gained the temper as of steel which has at length enabled them to issue victorious as the leading people, both actually and in their possibilities, of south-eastern Europe.

The first documents which mention Roumanians in what later became the Kingdom, date from the 12th century—on the Galician border (1164) and down by the Black Sea (1166); a Byzantine chronicler tells us that in this latter year a Byzantine army was aided in a battle against the Hungarians by a "numerous host of Wallachs, ancient Italian colonists." Shortly afterward, two "Wallachian brothers," Peter and Asan, built up a powerful Bulgaro-Roumanian kingdom; the third brother, Ionitza (Jack), was recognized by the Pope (anxious to extend his power eastward) as Emperor of the Bulgarians and Wallachs, and succeeded in capturing Baldwin, Latin Emperor of Constantinople. But his successor, John Asan II, was beaten by the Hungarians in 1230 at Widdin, and Wallachia remained a fief of the Hungarian kings of the house of Arpád; under King Béla IV there is mention of a certain Seneslav as Voyevode of Greater Wallachia (Muntenia, east of the Olt); his grandson, Bessarab (Roum., Basarab) established a principality of Lesser Wallachia (Oltenia, west of the Olt), and later (1290) set his capital at Argesh. From 1301–08, Hungary was without stable government, and Bessarab was enabled to establish what became the Principality of Wallachia, under nominal Hungarian overlordship. In the middle of that century, a Voyevode named Bogdan came over from the Maramuresh and founded the Principality of Moldavia, extending from the Dniester and the Carpathians to the Black Sea. These two principalities are the first flowering forth of the Roumanian people; the shepherds of the mountains have become the masters of the plain.

CHAPTER VII

HOW THE PRINCIPALITIES ROSE, DECAYED AND REVIVED, TO BECOME THE ROUMANIAN KINGDOM

IN the outburst of national consciousness which followed the formation of the Roumanian principalities (with which we must not forget to count their cradle, the Principality of Transylvania, and the Banat), begins the heroic age of Roumania. Hemmed in by powerful enemies—Hungary, Poland, Turkey—they were inevitably drawn into their quarrels; but had they been able to keep from fighting each other, they might have advanced by centuries the day of their freedom. Mircea the Old of Wallachia (1386–1418) and Alexander the Good of Moldavia (1400–1433) began the series of able rulers; they were on good terms, and succeeded in fighting off their common enemies. Mircea was able to annex the Dobrudja to Wallachia, and defeat Bajazid in 1394; he had eventually to acknowledge Turkish over-lordship, but it seems to have been largely nominal. His fame was soon obscured by the rise in Moldavia of one of Europe's most remarkable rulers—Stephen the Great. During his entire reign (1457–1504), Moldavia was a powerful state; he vanquished the Hungarians at Baia, the Turks at Rahova and Rasboeni, the Poles at Cosmin; and his services in defending Christendom against the Turk were so conspicuous that in that age of great men, Pope Sixtus IV could nevertheless write him: "The victories you have gained with equal wisdom and bravery over the unbelievers, our common foe, have raised your fame to the point that

41

your name is on every one's lips, and all agree in exalting you." Impressed however by the power of the Turks, Stephen on his death-bed advised his son Bogdan to accept their suzerainty; it was a mild yoke, since the Turks did not interfere in the administration, insisting only on the payment of annual tribute. His Venetian physician tells us that Stephen was "much beloved of his subjects"; he built nearly 50 monasteries and churches, the decoration of which gave strong impulse to Moldavian architecture and art; the Chronicle of the monastery of Putna, which begins in 1470, inaugurates their historical writing; there is still in the abbey of Humor a Gospels given by Stephen, with a miniature portraying the ruler himself; and on Mt. Athos, in the Zographos monastery, were preserved two of his banners. He ruled over part of Transylvania, and founded there the convent Vadului (of the ford), which became the first Orthodox bishopric on that side of the mountains. At his death, his Venetian physician, writing the doge, remarks: "God forfend that the Turks occupy this country, for in that case Poland and Hungary will be crushed, and then Italy and all Christendom." A contemporary Polish chronicler, Matthias of Miechow, speaks of him as a "man victorious and triumphant, who gloriously vanquished all his neighbor kings; a happy man, who had in full all the gifts of fortune; those qualities which nature gives others only in part—to some understanding with shrewdness, to others the heroic virtues and justice, most eminent of all virtues, to others victory over their enemies—she presented him with these all, and in such measure that he shone above all others."

Wallachia twice tried to shake off the Turkish yoke; the first effort, under Vlad Tzepesh, was unsuccessful, though he defeated the Turks in the first battle; in 1462 they occupied the country and installed a rival favorable to them. But at the end of the sixteenth century, the Wallachian throne fell to the other great national hero, Michael the Brave (1593–1601). The Turks were then at the height of their powers; in 1526 they had completely subdued Eastern Hungary. Nevertheless Michael formed an alliance with the rulers of Transylvania and Moldavia against the Turks; he defeated their armies several times, and in the famous battles of Calugareni (1595) and Giurgiu, routed a far greater Turkish host, commanded by the Grand Vizier himself. That was the last time a Roumanian army defeated the Turks until the War of Independence.

Michael followed up the disaffection of his Transylvanian and Moldavian allies by occupying their territory; and for a moment, all Roumania was united under one scepter, as never again till 1918. But Michael had hardly entered Alba Julia (Karlsburg) in triumph in 1600, and received the allegiance of the Moldavian boyars (landed gentry) when he fell in 1601, at Thorenburg (Turda) by an assassin's dagger. In him perished the last of the Bessarabs. The church he built in Bucharest, in connection with his monastery of Mihai-Voda (1594), was the oldest important building in the city.

With the disappearance of Michael the Brave commences an era of decadence in the two Principalities. At first, the Turkish sovereignty reasserted itself mildly; but gradually the situation grew worse. Stephen Petriceicu of Moldavia (1672–1674 and 1683–1684) tried for independence, with Polish help, but in vain; and Gheorghe Duca of Moldavia and Sherban Cantacuzene of Wallachia even had to assist the Turks against Vienna (1683); they did refuse, however, actually to fight against fellow-Christians, and after his return from the defeat, Cantacuzene dealt with

the Emperor at Vienna, promising to recognize his over-
lordship if he would guarantee Wallachia autonomy, and
secure the Cantacuzene family (descended, on the female
side, from the Bessarabs) in the rule over the Principality.
But he died before the treaty was drawn up; and his successor, Constantine Brâncoveanu (Brancovan), had to court
the Turks, as did his Moldavian contemporary, Constantine Cantemir (1685–1693). However humiliating politically, it was a period of great artistic development; and
Brancovan covered Wallachia with handsome buildings, ar-
tistically decorated. The influence of western Europe was
growing greater; by the Peace of Carlowitz (1699), the
House of Austria gained all Turkish Hungary (except the
Banat and Transylvania) and became much interested in
the Principalities. Russia had also announced herself at the
Peace of Carlowitz as the official guardian of the Orthodox
Christians in Turkey; and in the Turco-Russian War of
1711, Demetrius Cantemir of Moldavia agreed with Peter
the Great to support him with troops in any war for Moldavian liberation, in return for autonomy and support of the
Cantemir dynasty. Brancovan also sent a secret mission to
Russia and offered to coöperate with a victorious Russian
army. But the Turks defeated the Russians at Stanileshti
on the Pruth; Cantemir had to take refuge in Russia; Brancovan and his sons were taken to Constantinople and executed—a fate which overtook also his successor Stephen
Cantacuzene. In his stead, and that of Cantemir, the Porte
appointed Turkish envoys; and the new régime of direct
Turkish exploitation had begun. This lasted from 1711
(1716) to 1821.

The Principalities were now governed by Christian officials sent out from Constantinople with a numerous retinue
of relatives and hangers-on; these governors had in general

only one ambition, to enrich themselves at Roumanian expense, and that speedily, since the Porte appointed them in quick succession, as the result of bribery of high Turkish officers. Most of them were Greeks, from the Phanar quarter of Constantinople, and the era is therefore called the Phanariote Period. It is true that the Principalities enjoyed far greater rights and privileges than did Serbia, Bulgaria, Greece or Hungary under the Turks; no Turkish pasha ever governed Roumania as they did Hungary for over a century; no Turkish cadi ever presided in her law-courts; the Turks never had even the right to settle on Roumanian territory, or build a mosque; there was always a local administration, local law-courts and a local law-code. But the government was corrupt at its head, and all manner of abuses flourished unchecked. Furthermore, the Principalities were now involved in the tremendous problem which has convulsed Europe even in our own day—how to get the Turks out of Europe, and what disposal to make of their dominions. On one side sat Austria, on the other, Russia, each offering help to the few Roumanian patriots, but at the price of domination.

Meanwhile the Turks constantly raised the tributes and increased disaffection. An occasional good ruler, like the Mavrocordats in Wallachia and Gregory M. Ghica in Moldavia, did improve the condition of the peasantry; the reforms of Constantine Mavrocordat, about 1750, which applied to both countries, allowed the peasant serfs to purchase their liberty by the payment of a sum of money, and limited the amount of produce and the number of days-work which their master might demand. Alexander Ypsilanti brought out in 1780, in Greek (which had become the language of administration and culture) and Roumanian, a law-code for Wallachia, which was done also in 1819 for

Moldavia. Nevertheless the excessive tribute demanded ($200,000 a year), and the huge sums paid by the Phanariote appointees for their nominations (over $100,000 in some cases; 38 appointments for Wallachia in 105 years, and 35 for Moldavia in 110!), plus special contributions constantly levied, drained the country; even the church and monastic organizations, which owned enormous estates, fell a victim to Greek cupidity. So the Principalities became a prey to the ambitions of the neighboring states. By the Peace of Passarowitz (1718), Turkey ceded Oltenia (Wallachia west of the Olt) to Austria, together with the Banat. In the war of 1736–1739, Austria tried to annex Muntenia also, as well as Moldavia, and thus acquire all Roumania; but she met Russia's firm determination to set up both Wallachia and Moldavia as independent principalities under Russian protection; indeed, the boyars (great land-owners) of Moldavia made formal acceptance of Russian suzerainty, on condition of autonomy, with exclusion of Russians, Greeks and other foreigners from high office.

But the vicissitudes of war and diplomacy proved the salvation of the Roumanians; in the Peace of Belgrade (1739), Austria had to restore Oltenia, and Russia Moldavia. In the war of 1768–1774, during which the Russian armies occupied Moldavia four long years, Russia considered this province surely hers; Austria nevertheless checkmated her, and in gratitude the Porte ceded (and this time till 1918) the northwest corner of Moldavia, called the Bucovina, with its holy city Suceava, which contains the monument of Stephen the Great. Moldavia suffered again in the war of 1806–1812, this time at the hands of Russia, who annexed the district between Pruth and Dniester, called Bessarabia, after the famous family of early rulers. Moldavia has never lost the tradition of the ruthlessness of the

Russian armies of occupation, who, as their general Kutusoff boasted, would leave the peasants only their eyes to weep with; and the Russian protectorate of the Principalities, which was formally recognized in the treaties of Kuchuk-Kainargi (1774) and of Bucharest (1812), proved still more oppressive and ruinous than the Turkish.

Matters came to a head in 1821. The peasants found the exactions laid upon them insufferable. The cultured classes, under the influence of the French Revolution and its literary sequel, had finally evolved an ambition for national existence, and at least to drive out the Greek Phanariotes, who were sucking dry the body politic. The Phanariotes themselves were engaged in a similar national undertaking, which looked to the liberation of Greece from the Turkish yoke; their leader in Roumania was Alexander Ypsilanti, son of the former governor. He entered Moldavia at the head of bands of Greek conspirators in February, 1821, and the governor joined him; they then entered Wallachia, whose governor had recently died, with the idea of making it their headquarters for the wresting of Greek independence from the Turk. But the fire they had lighted changed its direction and bore down upon them. The peasants as well as the upper classes rose against the Greeks; their leader was Tudor Vladimirescu, a peasant proprietor who had become a captain of gendarmes. From Oltenia he marched east at the head of several thousand adherents, and took possession in March of Bucharest. Ypsilanti tried to gain him over for the movement of Greek liberation, but received the reply: "The place for the Greeks is in Greece; Roumania is the home of the Roumanians." Tudor's uprising now became definitely a revolution for the improvement of the lot of the peasant and the expulsion of the Greeks. The latter were still too strong, and succeeded in capturing and executing him (May 27); but he was the martyr the cause needed, and his shade, at his centennial anniversary, must have exulted to see the final fruition of his reforms and his ambitions.

CHAPTER VIII

THE ROUMANIAN PRINCIPALITIES AND KINGDOM UP TO THE BALKAN WARS

THE Turks had no great difficulty in crushing what remained of Tudor's rebellious forces, and in driving Ypsilanti out of Wallachia; but they were impressed with the ugly temper of the country, permitted delegations from the Principalities to present their grievances at Constantinople, and actually asked them to nominate candidates for the governorship from among their own boyars. Thus the Porte restored native rulers to the Roumanians—Gregory D. Ghica in Wallachia, and John Alexander Sturza in Moldavia. At the very beginning of their rule, some ambitious spirits projected a constitution (1822) based on Western models, though it did restrict full citizenship to the landholding class (the boyars); but even that was too liberal for the Russians; and in 1826 they called a convention at Akkerman, to follow up the provisions of the Treaty of Bucharest, which had given them a certain protectorate over the Principalities. The Porte agreed to allow the Wallachian and Moldavian boyars to meet and choose their princes, to rule for seven years; and that their councils and they should at once approach constitutional government. The Russo-Turkish War of 1828–1829 led to a great extension of Russian influence. The Principalities were occupied by Russian troops from 1828 to 1834; the Russians made Ghica and Sturza retire, the Russian general Palin becoming governor-general, with the title of President of the

Divans (councils). A constitution elaborated at St. Petersburg was worked over and accepted by these councils—the famous "Regulament Organic." At the same time the councils petitioned the Russian Government to make the two Principalities one country, independent of the Porte; they asked for a prince neither Turkish, Russian or Austrian, but preferably from northern Germany; but this petition, repugnant to the schemes of all three neighboring countries, was laid on the table.

Fortunately for the Principalities, the administration of the new Organic Regulation was put in the hands of an enlightened Russian general, Kisseleff, whose influence was particularly felt in the improvement of the bureaucracy and the law-courts. He began also the organization of a Roumanian army. A legislative Assembly of boyars and clergy was created, and a special Assembly to choose the prince, in each country. Thus after five years of Kisseleff's government, in 1834, the Wallachians installed Alexander D. Ghica, brother of the last governor, as prince, and the Moldavians Michael Sturza. The tribute to the Porte was fixed at 6000 purses (about $120,000); and Russian councils were left at Bucharest and Jassy, nominally to advise, but really to keep sharp watch of the new governments.

There was from the start a strong Unionist party in both countries. They succeeded in 1846 in abolishing the tariff wall between Wallachia and Moldavia; and they tried to elect Sturza to the throne of Wallachia also, at the end of the first seven-year period. The Russians preferred, however, to keep up separate administration; they allowed Ghica to remain in Moldavia, but caused the election of George Bibesco in Wallachia. Luckily they did not object to Roumanian schools in the Principalities, as they did in Bessarabia; at the National College of St. Sava at Bucharest, founded by Gregory D. Ghica, were introduced courses in law, philosophy, literature, mathematics and science; and at Jassy was established the Academia Mihaileana (of Michael) for higher studies, out of which developed the University of Jassy. Elementary schools sprang up also all over the country. Prince Ghica introduced some ameliorations also in the condition of the Jews, who offered a serious problem in Moldavia. As a result of Russian and Polish persecution, they had been coming over the border for a couple of generations, but had proved an unassimilable element, keeping up their Yiddish tongue and living apart; while the Moldavian governors allowed them to come in freely, they denied them any greater civil rights than they had in their home lands, fearing that they would enter in enormous numbers if distinctly better treated. The result was that in the freer air of Roumania, enlightened Jews demanded equal rights; and Ghica took the first steps on a path the goal of which has only recently been reached. But the peasants' lot still remained hard, and the patriotic upper classes chafed under Russian overlordship as much as they had under Turkish.

1848 turned resentment into open protest. On March 27 a public meeting at Jassy adopted a memorial, to be presented to the Prince, demanding numerous reforms, chief among which were the expropriation of the church and monastery properties, the income of which went to Greeks, and an improvement in the lot of the peasants. Michael Sturza, under Russian prompting, refused to receive the memorial, and imprisoned or exiled various of the leaders, one of whom, Michael Kogălniceanu, published in the Bucovina a pamphlet on the ambitions of the National Party in Moldavia. These included civic and political equality of all citizens and union of the Principalities, with no Russian interference. Meanwhile a more radical movement in Wallachia had succeeded in proclaiming a new constitution; George Bibesco resigned immediately after signing it; a provisional government was formed, under the presidency of the Metropolitan; the national red, yellow and blue flag (a combination of the colors of the two Principalities) was unfurled for the first time; the Organic Regulation was burned in public before the Metropolitan Church. Russia, scandalized, demanded the armed intervention of the Porte; and a bloody encounter which ensued between the Bucharest firemen and Turkish troops (September 13) gave Russia the desired pretext for interfering. Russian and Turkish soldiers quelled the uprising, and its heads disappeared, to continue their agitation in Western Europe. This joint military occupation continued until 1851, and was followed in 1853–1854 by Russian occupation alone; during the Crimean War (1854–1856), Austrian troops controlled Wallachia.

Russia's defeat required a new solution of the problem; and the Congress of Paris (1856) provided for a joint protectorate of the Principalities by France, Great Britain, Prussia, Austria, Russia, Piedmont and Turkey; continuance of Turkish suzerainty, with local autonomy; that a European commission should regulate Danube navigation; and that Russia should return to Moldavia three Bessarabian counties along the Danube. In 1857 the Assemblies of the two Principalities voted separately in favor of union, under some prince chosen from a reigning family of northern Europe, and with a constitutional government, in which the parliament should represent all classes of the nation. In a conference of the Protecting Powers called at Paris the next year to consider these aspirations, the French and Piedmontese representatives favored all these requests; but

Turkey and Austria were successful in blocking the proposals for union and for the choice of a foreign prince. The tribute was reduced to $60,000 for Moldavia and $100,000 for Wallachia. Meanwhile a solution had occurred to the Roumanians themselves; and in January, 1859, the Moldavian Col. Alexander Cuza was chosen as Prince by the Assembly of each Principality. Turkey and Austria protested at this union; but Napoleon III and Cavour were in favor of it; and Cuza himself, in an interview with the Sultan in 1860, succeeded in getting his consent to a complete administrative union as well, at least during Cuza's incumbency. So on January 24, 1862, the Assemblies of Moldavia and Wallachia met in Bucharest as the first Parliament of Roumania; but Cuza remained "Prince of the United Principalities."

Cuza at once turned his hand to much-needed reforms. It is said that one-fifth of all the land belonged to the Greek clergy installed under the Phanariotes and who sent their revenues off to Greece and Constantinople. A decree of 1863 secularized the property of the monasteries, and their income reverted to the state. In 1864, Cuza and his premier Michael Kogălniceanu promulgated a temporary solution of the agrarian problem; the labor and tithes exacted from the peasant by the land-owner were abolished; in their stead the peasant was to make fourteen annual payments to the proprietor, after which he was to become the owner of the land he had been cultivating as a serf. This roused so much opposition from the boyars that Cuza resorted on May 2, 1864, to a *coup d'état;* he dissolved the Parliament, and called for a plebiscite on a new constitution, called (after Italian precedent) the Statute, which provided for universal suffrage and for a second chamber to the Parliament, to consist of a senate, partly nominated by the Prince. The adoption of this constitution was ratified by the Porte and the Protecting Powers; but Cuza took advantage of the interim before elections to issue a number of decrees—a favorite means of supplementing Parliamentary government in southern and eastern Europe. One carried out his ideas (and Kogălniceanu's) of reform in peasant ownership of land; another promulgated civil and criminal codes; another called for compulsory primary instruction and a graduated educational system culminating in the Universities of Jassy (1860) and Bucharest (1864). But the country lacked trained and conscientious men to carry out these reforms; the new Statute satisfied neither the conservatives nor the radicals; and the general dissatisfaction forced Cuza to resign on February 11, 1866. On the next day, the Parliament called Philip of Flanders (brother of King Leopold of Belgium) to the throne. The Porte and Russia protested; a meeting of the Protecting Powers was called at Paris March 10, 1866, to decide the question. John Bratiano the elder, Scarlet Fălcoianu and John Bălăceanu presented the Roumanian point of view; the Turkish and Russian representatives opposed the choice of a foreign prince; Austria and Prussia were indifferent; France, Italy and England supported the Roumanian wishes. Philip having declined, France proposed Prince Charles of Hohenzollern-Sigmaringen; England seconded the nomination; on March 14, Bratiano and Bălăceanu telegraphed the news of Charles' election to Bucharest, and it was soon confirmed by a plebiscite. Charles was a peculiarly suitable candidate, being a descendant of Frederick VI of Zollern, burgrave of Nuremburg and ancestor of the Prussian royal house, who had fought with Mircea the Old and Sigismund of Hungary in 1396 at Nicopolis against the Turks; his mother, Princess Josephine, was daughter of Grand-Duchess Stéphanie

Beauharnais of Baden, adoptive daughter of Napoleon I.

Bratiano accompanied the young prince (who was 27 years old on April 8, 1866) on his journey southeastward from Düsseldorf. As Austria and Turkey were opposed to Prince Charles, they traveled incognito, and entered Roumania in the second-class quarters of an Austrian Danube steamer, landing May 8 at Turn-Severin. The Porte refused recognition, and began massing troops on the frontier; Charles began mobilizing the new Roumanian army, which proved to be woefully short of munitions; no outside power would grant him a loan, so supplies had to be paid for with Treasury notes. But France exercised pressure upon the Porte, and the Austrian-Prussian War distracted attention. Charles appointed a strong cabinet—Lascar Catargi (Moldavian, Conservative), Premier, and Minister of the Interior; John Bratiano (Wallachia, Liberal), Minister of Finance; Peter Mavrogheni (Moldavia, Conservative), Foreign Affairs; John Cantacuzene (Wallachia, Center), Justice; Constantine A. Rosetti (Wallachia, Extreme Left), Cults and Public Instruction; Gen. John Ghica (Moldavia, Right Center), War; Demetrius A. Sturza (Moldavia, Center), Agriculture, Commerce and Public Works. They drew up a new constitution, which was submitted to a Constitutional Convention, called the 28th of April. This was based on that of Belgium, whose legal and constitutional influence has been great in Roumania; it was generally felt to be in advance of the times, since a country with a vast uneducated element could not be expected to handle Western political institutions; and the section dealing with the Jews at once led to trouble. The constitution provided that "religion should not be a bar to naturalization. As for the Israelites, a special law is to regulate their gradual admission to citizenship." Roumania had been a distinctively

Christian state, and Mohammedans, Jews and other non-Christians lacked civic rights. The constitution proposed in 1848 had indeed proclaimed the "emancipation of the Israelites and political rights for all compatriots of whatsoever creed"; and the National Party in Moldavia that same year demanded "the gradual emancipation of the Moldavian Israelites, by humane and progressive measures preparing them for the status of citizens useful to the commonwealth." But the rapid influx of Polish Jews—the number had grown from about 12,000 in 1800 to over 200,000 in 1866, and they had acquired a disproportionate share of large business, banking, and especially saloon-keeping and money-lending—had created bitter feeling. A howl arose all over Moldavia when this provision looking toward citizenship for the Jews became known; anti-Semitic feeling was skillfully inflamed by the opposition; and when the Constitutional Convention came to discussing this point, a mob wrecked the newly-built synagogue. A reaction ensued; a popular subscription was opened for the rebuilding of the synagogue, headed by Prince Charles with 6000 ducats; but the Convention deferred to the strong public sentiment which had been manifested, and voted that only foreigners belonging to Christian sects could acquire citizenship.

The constitution was soon ratified, and the coalition cabinet resigned; John Ghica, the new Premier, won the recognition of Charles as hereditary prince of the United Principalities (Turkey objected to the name Roumania); and with a formal visit in October, 1866, to the Sultan, who received him with exceptional honors, Charles (now Prince Carol I) entered upon one of the longest and happiest reigns of any European monarch. He began with a series of journeys through the country, in one of the earliest of which he confided to the poet Alecsandri his intention of covering Roumania with railroads; and he at once put his hand also to the reorganization of the army and to administrative and economic reforms. Ghica had to resign in consequence of elections which left him without a majority; in the new cabinet, Bratiano was the leading spirit, and had the satisfaction of signing the authorization for the first railroad in Roumania (Bucharest-Giurgiu, projected under Cuza, and built by an English company). This was inaugurated in 1869, together with that from Burdujeni to Roman, which was built by an Anglo-Austrian syndicate. Military reforms came to the fore with railroad building; and Charles now undertook his first formal journey abroad, beginning with a visit to Czar Alexander II at Livadia; the Czar was a connection by marriage, Charles' mother being a cousin of the Czarina. On his return he rode on the first Roumanian train to cross the Danube, and started north on the first steamer flying the Roumanian flag to pass through the Iron Gates. After visiting Francis Joseph at Vienna, he stopped at his ancestral castle of Weinburg, near Reineck; while there, he was offered the crown of Spain. On his declining to leave Roumania, the Spanish envoy Salazar took up those fateful negotiations with his elder brother Leopold, out of which developed the Franco-Prussian War.

Charles went on to Baden-Baden, meeting there Crown Prince Frederick, who urged him to marry Princess Elizabeth of Wied, then in her 26th year. After visiting Napoleon III at Saint-Cloud, he came to Cologne, where the princess was staying, and won her hand after a brief courtship. They were married at Neuwied November 3, 1869, and received in state at Bucharest on the 12th; the Metropolitan blessed them at the Metropolitan Church, and fifty peasant couples from different counties, married that same day, paraded before them in costume. The new queen, whom Europe was to know better as Carmen Sylva, at once established a fund from which every year on November 12 dowries are assigned to 8 poor girls, to celebrate this anniversary. The hold the Hohenzollern-Sigmaringen dynasty has on the affections of the common people of Roumania is largely due to the self-devotion and tact of Queen Elizabeth and Queen Marie.

King Charles also needed all possible tact. Roumanian politics is as turbulent as that of Spain or Illinois; the installation of urgently needed reforms left many discontented; and there was foreign encouragement of this discontent. The opposition tried to persuade the former ruler, Prince Cuza, to lead a movement against Prince Charles; and the French Ambassador at Vienna, in an interview at Döbling in 1868, promised him the support of France. His patriotism led him to refuse, and this danger was averted; but the Franco-Prussian War embarrassed Charles greatly. He was a German, of the same blood with the King of Prussia; but his Foreign Minister, P. Carp, replying to the Opposition on the government's attitude, said: "Unde este ginta latină, acolo este shi inima României." (Where the Latin race is, there is also the heart of Roumania.) The failure of a German company which had an important railroad concession, embittered feelings; the new ministry (ninth in five years!) under John Ghica and Demetrius A. Sturdza, was too weak to handle the situation; a mob wrecked the Café Capsha in Bucharest, where the German colony were toasting the Emperor on his birthday; and Charles decided to abdicate. He summoned Lascar Catargi, head of the commission which had welcomed him to Roumania, and notified him of his decision; but Catargi succeeded in dispelling his discouragement, and in forming a ministry which endured for five years (1871–1875) and installed a host of reforms. Stamp taxes and the tobacco monopoly (1872) greatly increased the revenues; Roumanian government bonds were finally listed in the Parisian and other stock exchanges (1875); the Rural Credit Bank (1873) and the Urban Credit Bank (1874) were founded, with local capital; the railroad crisis was solved by the formation of a company called the C. F. R. (Căile Ferate Române, Roumanian Railways), which took over the lines already in existence and the new construction; by 1875 there were two junction points with Austria and one with Russia; a third connection with Austria, over the Predeal Pass, was opened in 1879. Commercial treaties were made with both countries in 1875. A law establishing the Holy Synod (1872) gave the Church an independent organization. But the chief concern of the new ruler and his cabinet was the creation of a strong and well-equipped army; and the uprising of 1875 in Turkey gave speedy justification for their solicitude. Catargi's ministry fell at this time; but fortunately for Roumania, it was succeeded by one fully as strong, under the guidance of the veteran Liberal, John C. Bratiano.

Russia had long been preparing for a Balkan War to reëstablish her prestige. With Russian encouragement, in June 1876, Serbia and Montenegro openly declared war against Turkey. Turkish cruelty in Bulgaria, and the collapse in August of the Serbs, who were aided by Russian munitions and volunteers, portended Russian intervention. Bratiano went to Livadia late in September and consulted with the Czar and his Chancellor and Minister of War; it was agreed that Roumania should give free passage to a Russian army. At a council of ambassadors held at Constantinople, the Roumanians endeavored to induce the Protecting Powers to guarantee Roumanian neutrality, and urge the Porte to cede the part of the Danube delta which was once Bessarabian; but only Austria came to Roumania's support. Abdul Hamid tried to forestall action by the Powers, by promulgating a new constitution for Turkey. This spoke of Charles as the "head of a privileged province," thus reducing Roumania from the status earlier agreed upon; he at once broke off relations with Constantinople, and decided upon a military convention with Russia and the mobilization of the army. At a council of leading Roumanian statesmen, the majority proved diffident; Bratiano, Kogălniceanu and C. A. Rosetti were however in sympathy with the Prince; and Kogălniceanu, now Minister of Foreign Affairs, signed on April 4, 1877, a convention with Russia promising that Russian troops should receive friendly treatment during their passage through Roumania to fight Turkey, on condition that Russia would guarantee Roumania the full possession of her rights and "maintain and defend Roumania's existing territorial integrity." The Russians crossed the Pruth on April 12. On the 26th, Roumanian mobilization was complete, and Charles took supreme command of an army of 50,000 men with 180 guns. On that same day the Turks fired from Widdin on the Roumanian batteries of Calafat; and Charles superintended personally a counter-attack a few days later. The Russians at first refused to accept Roumanian coöperation except with complete subordination to the Russian high command; but after they had been twice defeated by the Turks in July at Plevna in Bulgaria, Grand-Duke Nicholas telegraphed begging Charles to come to his relief; and when Charles appeared before the Czar, the latter asked him to take command of the combined army before Plevna, where 60,000 Turkish troops under Osman-Pasha were well entrenched. Charles had 35,000 Roumanians, with 168 guns, and 30,-000 Russians, with 282. They began the attack on August

26, 1877; by an interesting coincidence, the numbers of the first two successful regiments—the 13th infantry and the 5th of the line—were those of the Roman legions (XIII Gemina and V Macedonica) that won and garrisoned Dacia under Trajan. On the 30th the redoubt of the Grivitza was theirs—the first victory over the ancient enemy for 282 years. The struggle continued for weeks; but on November 28, Osman-Pasha had to capitulate to Charles. Shortly afterward, the Roumanians attacked Widdin; but operations were interrupted by the Armistice of Adrianople (January 19, 1878).

The Peace of San Stefano (February 19) filled Roumania with indignation. It recognized Roumanian independence, to be sure, though after Montenegrin and Serbian; but it formed a Greater Bulgaria, destined to be the most important power in southeastern Europe, and gave Roumania to understand that Russia would appropriate the remainder of Bessarabia—a sacrifice which the Czar's special ambassador Ignatieff at once came to demand, holding out to Charles in compensation a possible nomination to the throne of Bulgaria, and annexation of the Dobrudja. Parliament and people came unanimously to the support of their sovereign in refusing this treacherous reward for Roumanian salvation of Russia; Bucharest was put into shape to resist Russian occupation; and to the threat from St. Petersburg that the Roumanian army would be forcibly disarmed, Charles made the proud reply: "The Roumanian army, which fought so heroically at Plevna under the eyes of the Czar, may be annihilated, but not disarmed." England and Austria prevented an armed conflict by demanding a revision of the Treaty of San Stefano, and Russia had, in the Congress of Berlin of 1878, to abandon her dream of a Greater Bulgaria; but the possession of Bessarabia, with control of the lower

Danube, seemed vital to St. Petersburg. The Congress sanctioned Russia's demand; Bismarck tried to persuade Bratiano and Kogălniceanu, the Roumanian delegates, to yield; they were given a hearing after the representatives of Greece (who, after non-participation, came in for a share of the spoils, as after the Great War; hence Lord Salisbury's ironic motion: "After hearing the delegates of a nation claiming provinces belonging to others, let us hear also the representatives of a country asking for territories belonging to it.") The Congress forced Roumania however to give all of Bessarabia to Russia, and receive the Dobrudja as far as Silistria and south of Mangalia, as conditions for Roumanian independence; and the French delegate, Waddington, succeeded in tacking to this a provision that Roumania must not allow religion to be a bar to citizenship or the practice of any profession or occupation. All this was exhumed, as we shall see, by the Paris Conference of 1919.

Thus Roumania was treated by the Powers in 1878—a precedent to be followed in 1918–1919. "In politics," remarked Lord Beaconsfield to Bratiano, "ingratitude is oftentimes the reward for the most distinguished services." With heavy hearts, the Roumanian Parliament sanctioned the Treaty of Berlin, on September 15; a fortnight later, the Roumanian officials left Bessarabia, for an exile of forty years. By November, the occupation of the Dobrudja began —460 years since it had been Roumanian, under Mircea the Old. A Constitutional Convention, called in January, 1879, voted that "difference of religious belief and confession shall not constitute a bar to the acquisition and exercise of civil and political rights"; it conferred citizenship *en bloc* upon all the Jews who had fought in the Roumanian army, some 900 in number, and provided that any non-Christian might petition Parliament for citizenship, by which means the entrance of the whole Jewish body into the electorate was delayed. We must remember that the Roumanian peasant had also no electoral status at this time. This withholding of civil rights from the peasants and the Jews, while doubtless inevitable under the peculiar conditions, was a serious handicap to the new state, both in acquiring sympathy in western democracies, and in borrowing money from the great financial houses; and it has returned to plague Roumania many times later.

The death of Princess Maria, only child of Charles and Elizabeth, brought up the question of succession. The Constitution provided that in the absence of a direct male heir, the eldest brother of the prince, or his descendants, should succeed, in order of primogeniture. Charles' brother Leopold resigned in favor of his children; the elder, Ferdinand, became Crown Prince; Charles himself, on March 14, 1881, was proclaimed King Carol; on May 10, before a distinguished gathering, the King put on the Crown of Roumania, fashioned of the steel of a Turkish cannon captured at Plevna.

The 'eighties saw rapid progress. Bratiano formed a ministry which lasted seven years, the Conservatives having become demoralized. A National Bank and National Savings Banks were established in 1880; Farmers' Credit Banks began operations in 1881; the State took over the railways (1882); there was great development of building and of public works; Bucharest was fortified after plans of Gen. Brialmont; and a fortified line was drawn (under German plans) from Focshani to Galatz—evidently against Russia. At the Congress of Berlin, Bratiano had complained to Bismarck of Roumania's helplessness and isolation; "Don't come to me," said the Iron Chancellor. "Go to Vienna and offer them guarantees; make a treaty of alliance with them, and matters will right themselves." In 1883, Charles made a secret treaty with the Austrians, by which Roumania became an adjunct of the Triple Alliance; it provided, e. g., that if Russia attacked Austria, Roumania should dispatch her armies to assist the Hungarian forces; in case Russia invaded Roumania, Italy should dispatch 40,000 troops to the Carpathians. As with Italy, agreement with Austria and Germany certainly contributed to the peace of Europe, distasteful as it was to both countries to enter into friendly relations with Austro-Hungary, oppressor of hundreds of thousands of their own compatriots.

Bratiano retired in 1888. Under the Conservative ministries of Theodore Rosetti (1888–1889) and G. Manu (1889–1891), the Treasury, under M. Ghermani, succeeded in reaching a gold basis, and Roumanian currency now circulated at par throughout the Latin Union. The status of judges was also raised by confirming them in their tenure of office. In 1889, the last stretch of private railroad passed into government hands. Lascar Catargi presided over another Conservative ministry for four prosperous years, retiring in 1895. Bratiano had died in 1891; Catargi lived until 1899. Roumania was fortunate that such distinguished men headed her leading parties during this troubled period.

To trace the history of the next twenty years would be a tabulation of great material and intellectual progress; but these matters fall rather under other heads. The new men that appear in politics—Carp, Marghiloman, John J. C. Bratiano, Take Jonesco—will receive attention later. Financial reforms and the commercial outlook, must be considered in their entirety. The new educational institu-

A MODERN GARAGE IN BUCHAREST

A MODERN BANK BUILDING
(BY GEORGE CANTACUZENE)

"TURKS IN BRAILA," PAINTING BY J. STERIADE

tions are intertwined with the history of the literature. But we cannot close this chapter, which is designed to give a general idea of progress up to the Balkan Wars, without mention of the most remarkable phenomenon in Roumanian commerce and business life in the beginning of the twentieth century—a phenomenon visible (as so often) in Italy also— the sudden growth of German trade and influence. Here the official figures tell their own story:

	Imports into Roumania from Germany (in lei)	Percentage of total imports	Exports from Roumania into Germany (in lei)	Percentage of total exports
1883	43,886,724	12.20%	4,560,118	2.07%
1888	83,224,501	26.81%	6,515,142	2.54%
1893	117,878,929	27.38%	130,997,326	35.33%
1898	110,535,081	28.35%	12,545,366	4.45%
1903	78,446,863	29.06%	14,588,402	4.10%
1908	140,810,539	34.01%	24,566,838	6.47%
1913	238,000,000	40.33% (1912)	42,536,432	6.62%

The imports from Austro-Hungary, which formed almost exactly half the total for the period from 1875 to 1885, fell to about a quarter for the period 1903–1913. Together, Austria and Germany furnished half or more of the imports into Roumania from 1878 on; and in recent years the proportion ran ⅗ or ⅔. German enterprise was powerfully seconded by the Jewish wholesalers, bankers and retailers of Bucharest, Jassy and other centers. Their connections were with Vienna, Frankfort and Berlin. German commercial travelers were accompanied by German writers and scholars; Berlin granted subventions to German schools, which speedily became fashionable; and Roumanian engineers, officers, professional men and scholars acquired the habit of studying in Germany rather than in Paris. The visitor to Roumania finds German almost as useful to him as French, and it was striking to me, on my first trip in 1919, to note how frequently scientific and professional men—in the museums, salt-mines, oil-fields and even the army—changed with relief from French to German as soon as they found I spoke both.

CHAPTER IX

GEOGRAPHICALLY, Roumania is not a Balkan country; ethnographically, she is; for several hundred thousand Roumanians live south of the Danube, and many an Albanian and Macedonian village counts a majority of "Aromâni" (as these Balkan Roumanians call themselves). They count as Greeks in Greek propaganda literature, and have proved a fertile field for Hellenization; many a wealthy Greek trader, like the banker Averoff, a poet, like Valaorites, a scientist like Prof. Lambros, not to speak of patriots like Marco Bozzaris, were Macedonian or Albanian Kutzo-Vlachs, as the Greeks call them. But among themselves they cling to their Latin dialects, which we find all the way from the few thousand Cici of Istria (for whom Italy has restored Roumanian schools) to the compact scores of thousands of Kutzo-Vlachs in the Pindus Mountains. They were mentioned at some length by Kogălniceanu in his history of the Roumanians (1837); and after 1848, a number of the banished liberals went down into Turkey, and came to know their Macedo-Roumanian brethren. The poet Bolintineanu and the leading littérateur Eliade Rădulescu were pioneers in bringing home to the Roumanian public the fact that down in the Balkans, under Turkish political oppression and Greek educational influences, were hundreds of thousands of Roumanian-speaking farmers, shepherds and business men. Indeed, there are two Roumanians in the 1931 Albanian Parliament. Bolintineanu presented a memorial to the Grand Vizier asking that these Roumanians might have schools in their own language; an item for schools in the Balkans was inserted in the budget of the United Principalities; and the first school was opened soon at Tirnova, near Monastir. By 1910, this number had grown to 120 primary schools, three colleges (lycées or gymnasia), a commercial college, and a girls' normal school. There are also Roumanian churches, of which the finest, at Coritza (Korcha), collapsed in the great earthquake of 1931. In another, at Moscopole, worshiped the Shagunas, Gojdus and Mocionis, whose sons were to achieve distinction in Transylvania later. Among the other educational problems of Greater Roumania is the maintenance of these Macedonian schools; the teachers' salaries are now totally inadequate.

Besides these Albanian and Macedonian Roumanians, there are perhaps 250,000 Roumanians incorporated into Serbia in the Timok Valley, and Bulgaria has about 25,000 along the Danube. We shall be under the mark in stating that when the Balkan Wars of 1912–1913 broke out, half a million Roumanians in the warring countries looked north across the Danube for sympathy and help in securing their rights.

Roumania's situation was difficult. According to the principle of compensation, if European Turkey fell to pieces, and Greece, Serbia and Bulgaria absorbed this half-million of Roumanians, she had the right to be reimbursed. It was clear that this compensation should come in the form of a cession of part of the Bulgarian Dobrudja, predominantly settled by Turks; thus the transaction would not be objectionable on the score of nationalities. But the war began without Roumania being consulted; during the diplomatic negotiations, Mr. Bourchier, Balkan correspondent of the

London *Times,* states that he failed to convince Premier Maioresco that he must clear up the situation before Bulgaria mobilized. Not till the autumn of 1912 did a Bulgarian diplomat, Mr. Daneff, come to Bucharest. There the Roumanian position was made clear to him. He asked to have further dealings in London; and perhaps the most experienced and capable man in the Roumanian diplomatic service, the late Mr. Mishu, was transferred from Constantinople to London to treat with him. But the Bulgarian victories turned the heads of the military party in power, and before the dream of the revival of the Bulgarian Empire of the Middle Ages, all sense of realities faded.

Meanwhile, the situation grew more complicated. Austria, ever ready to pounce upon Serbia, began sounding Roumania, just as (thanks to Giolitti and Tittoni) we know she was sounding Italy. Gen. Conrad von Hötzendorff, the Austrian Chief of Staff, who later failed so dramatically on the Asiago Plateau, visited General Averesco, the brilliant Bessarabian soldier who was then Chief of Staff and later Premier, to discuss military coöperation against the Serbs; but he got small encouragement. One of the Archduke Francis Ferdinand's intimates, an Austrian high official named Riedl, came to offer Austria's services in negotiations with Bulgaria—at the price of customs union with Austro-Hungary. He was perfectly frank with Take Jonesco in outlining the Teutonic program. Europe, he said, is divided up into three classes of nations. England and France are predatory; they must be eliminated from European commerce. Russia is Oriental; she must be driven out of Europe and away from the Black Sea and the Baltic. There remain the Scandinavian countries, Germany, Austro-Hungary, Holland, Belgium, Switzerland, Italy, Spain, Roumania, the Balkan countries and the new states to arise from the ruins of Russia—Finland, Courland, Poland, the Ukraine. These must all form a customs union with Germany and Austria. The partition of Russia was Bismarck's scheme, and he was willing to come to an understanding with Great Britain in order to realize it.

Take Jonesco, who was a member of the Ministry, tells us that he conceived the idea of offering Bulgaria three Roumanian army corps for the reduction of Adrianople, to make the Bulgarian cession easier; but when he went to London in January, 1913, to confer with Mishu and Daneff, he found the latter unresponsive. However, a conference of ambassadors at St. Petersburg awarded to Roumania the town of Silistria and a 3-kilometer zone about it. Just then occurred the break between Serbia and Bulgaria. It was clear that every eventuality would now have to be faced. The decree of mobilization was ready for the King's signature—he was opening a mosque at Constantza—when Czar Nicholas' telegram arrived asking all the Balkan sovereigns to compose their differences. Immediately upon Take Jonesco's return to Bucharest, he received a telegram from Venizelos asking if, in case of a new Balkan War, he could count on Roumanian aid for the Greek Army. Jonesco replied affirmatively on his own initiative. Austria was suspicious; Prince Fürstemberg, the Minister, warned Jonesco that Austria was determined to support Bulgaria against Serbia, and that if Roumania came into the war against Bulgaria, she would soon find herself fighting Austria; but, he added, you will get such concessions from the Bulgarians that you will have no incentive to fight them.

The concessions did not materialize. The Bulgarians attacked the Serbs and Greeks, and a huge popular demonstration against Bulgaria took place in Bucharest. Mobilization was decreed. A note was sent to Sofia stating that since

Bulgaria, in spite of the warnings of Roumania, had re-opened the Near Eastern question, the Roumanian Government had given orders to its troops to enter Bulgaria. But the Daneff government at Sofia telegraphed to Sazonoff that Bulgaria was willing to submit her differences with Serbia and Greece to the arbitration of the Czar. Sazonoff therefore wired the Russian Minister at Bucharest to notify the Roumanian Government that any Roumanian advance into Bulgaria would be considered by Russia an unfriendly act, but that Russia guaranteed Roumania a new Dobrudja frontier (Turtucaia-Balchik). Take Jonesco persuaded the Minister to telegraph back to St. Petersburg for further instructions before presenting these. Meanwhile, orders were sent the Roumanian commander to cross the Danube. Two days later, the Daneff cabinet fell, and the pro-Austrian ministry of Radoslavoff came in; now Russia asked Roumania to advance into Bulgaria, and the Austrian Minister asked that the advance be stayed! Austria also was willing to guarantee the Turtucaia-Balchik line. Both of Roumania's powerful neighbors felt this was a minimum compensation.

Bulgaria saw she was doomed, and accepted an armistice before any clash with Roumania. The Peace Conference was held at Bucharest, resulting in the Treaty of July 28, 1913. This sanctioned the new line, which leaves the Danube just above Turtucaia, and runs to a point on the Black Sea coast between Balchik and Varna. By a secret annex, Serbia, Montenegro, Greece and Roumania guaranteed each other their new boundaries until they should be officially ratified by the Bulgarian Sobranje—which has never occurred! This was the clause invoked by Serbia for Roumanian and Greek aid early in the World War, and considered morally binding by Take Jonesco and Venizelos.

This sketch of the development of Roumania will prepare the reader to appreciate the difficulty in choosing sides in the World War. On the one hand an admiration, even an affection, for France, the intellectual home of all cultivated Roumanians; esteem and sympathy for Belgium; a great respect for England; a fellow-feeling for the "Latin sister," Italy; recent coöperation with Serbia against Bulgaria; and an agreement with the ideals of the Allies, especially as voiced by President Wilson. On the other, a deep, well-grounded fear of the Russian colossus; a treaty with Austria, and an economic dependence on Austria and Germany, with most seductive offers on the part of the Germans if Roumania would only stay neutral. What turned the balance was (as with Italy) the unredeemed provinces; and we must consider them before we can understand the situation.

CHAPTER X

THE "Beech Forest," as the name Bucovina indicates, is of only some 3850 square miles (less than Connecticut), and nearly half of that is woods of beech and pine; but its population (800,098 in 1910, 854,000 in 1930) is a strange mixture of Roumanian, German and Slav (Ruthenian). Before 1774 it formed the northwestern extension of Moldavia into Poland and Russia; and the rulers of Moldavia several times subjugated considerable districts in those countries, while the Bucovina hills formed a shelter for generations for the raiders of whom the Polish writer of the Life of St. Cunigund (about 1400) speaks: "Valachorum . . . natio, rapto vivere assueta, in pecore pascendo et ove nutrienda occupata, agmine facto ex Alpibus quae Hungariam a Poloniae Regno determinant, in quibus suas exercent pasturas tenentque cubilia, frequenter in oppidum Antiquae Sandecz hostiliter nocte . . . insiliebant"—"the tribe of the Wallachs, accustomed to live on rapine and busied in pasturing their herds and feeding sheep, used to raise bands and sweep down from the Alps which separate Hungary from the Kingdom of Poland and in which they pasture their flocks and have their shelters, often making night raids upon the town of Old Sandecz." Indeed, there were Roumanians scattered all over nearer Galicia, and in Lemberg they had their own Chamber of Commerce, their quarter, market-place, church, "Pons Valachicus" and "Via Valachica" (Roumanian Bridge and Avenue). But the increasing power of Poland

and then of Austria turned the tables, coinciding with the continual decadence of the Principalities under the Phanariote régime; conditions of life, especially for the peasants, were much easier in Moldavia, and there was constant emigration of Ruthenians (Ukrainians, Little Russians) into the border districts.

The Poles, who were short of labor, made every effort to stop this; a typical episode is this of 1742: four cart-loads of Ruthenian peasants had surreptitiously crossed the border, but were followed by mounted Polish frontier-guards, who fired upon them and wounded several till driven away by the nearest Roumanian villagers; the local governor made a formal demand upon the Poles for the punishment of these guards who had violated the boundary. But the infiltration kept on, till all the districts nearest Galicia had a large proportion of Ruthenians. Meanwhile Austria, her appetite whetted by the Partition of Poland which had given her Eastern Galicia, applied to the Porte for the strip of land next adjoining in order to have a corridor from Galicia to Transylvania. Prince Gregory Ghica protested against the cession, but in vain; and in 1775 the Austrians took over this Roumanian territory. They found it probably at least three-quarters Roumanian, and at first made use of that language, with German, as official, together with some use of Ruthenian. A very interesting contemporary description by an Austrian officer says: "The original inhabitants of the Bucovina are just the same as the majority of those in Turkish Moldavia, descendants of the Wallachian or Roman colonists . . . one finds many Hungarian, Transylvanian, Armenian and especially Jewish families in the country. The general language . . . is the Wallachian, which is composed of a corrupt Latin; various other tongues are spoken, however, by the tribes which have settled in the country, especially the Old Russian or Ruthenian. There has even been a bountiful sowing of the German language, since the lamented Maria Theresa founded German schools throughout the country, to the benefit of all the inhabitants, but especially of German veterans' children."

This passage brings up two of the most interesting problems in connection with the Bucovina—the religious question, and the school situation. While Moldavian, the Bucovinans had belonged to the Oriental Greek Orthodox Church; and this organization, which had very valuable property, was at first left untouched by the Austrians, though they dipped more and more into its income, and at the beginning of the World War seized all its fluid assets as a loan. The Ruthenians, however, belonged to the Greek Catholic (Uniate) Church, ever since the Pact of 1595 with Pope Clement VIII; their rite and belief coincide in general with those of the Greek Orthodox Church, but they owed allegiance to Rome. As these Galician Ruthenians crossed over into the Bucovina, where there were no Greek Catholic churches, they naturally joined the Orthodox congregations; and Rome saw with alarm the constant increase of the schismatic Oriental Church, at the expense of the Catholics of Greek rite. In 1780 the Papal Nuncio at Vienna was besought to appoint Greek Catholic priests and found churches for the Bucovina; the Council of War disapproved of the step; but in 1806 the Greek Catholic Archbishop of Lemberg in Galicia addressed a memorial to Emperor Francis I, informing him that the Ruthenians of Greek Catholic rite who had entered the Bucovina in such numbers, would not join Catholic churches of Latin rite, but went instead to the Oriental churches, and begging him to use the Bucovina religious funds to establish Greek Catholic worship there—but again in vain. Proselyting went on, and in

1848 one of the counts against the government on the part of the Roumanian liberals was that they had countenanced the activities of missionaries from Galicia. Meanwhile the Ruthenians had discovered that their aim of becoming the predominant element in the Bucovina was better served by wresting the control of the Greek Orthodox Church from the Roumanians; in this the Austrian government gave them every assistance. Their policy was to eliminate Roumanians as rapidly as possible, from fear of Roumanian irredentism, and give Ruthenians every possible privilege, with a view to effect in the Ukraine—Austria's dream being an expansion to Odessa, quite as much as to Saloniki. The Ruthenians therefore began a campaign to control the Greek Orthodox organization and funds in the Bucovina, and gave scant assistance to the Greek Catholic propaganda, which, beginning in 1861 with the founding of a Greek Catholic community in Czernowitz (Cernăutzi), has had very slight success.

The Orthodox authorities had early given special privileges to the Ruthenians in their church services; in 1789, the new Bishop of Czernowitz, Daniel Wlachowicz, a Serb by birth, permitted them to use Church Slavonic instead of Roumanian in their services, and even imported Ruthenian priests from Galicia and the Ukraine. In time, they demanded (and received in 1906) a Ruthenian Orthodox bishopric in the Bucovina; and at the beginning of the war it was understood that there should be a Ruthenian successor to the venerable and distinguished Archbishop of Czernowitz, Vladimir de Repta, whom I had the privilege of seeing both in his magnificent palace at Czernowitz, and in the first Parliament of Greater Roumania, where it was reserved for him, as protagonist of the Roumanians outside the kingdom, to be the first presiding officer of the Roumanian Senate. I shall never forget his ascetic figure, in brilliant purple robes, as he listened to King Ferdinand's inaugural address, with the tears running down his cheeks. His dearest prayer had been answered before he was gathered to his fathers.

Austria had also utilized the schools as a method of suppressing the Roumanian element. Austrian methods were however far less arbitrary and severe than Hungarian. Any one who traveled in Transylvania and then in the Bucovina, noted the difference at once. With the Roumanian occupation of Transylvania, one saw the exultation over Hungarian oppression in a hundred little ways; the railway stations, for instance, which had, under Magyar jingoism, borne only the Hungarian name of the town, immediately blossomed forth with only the Roumanian name, which however more melodious than the Magyar designation—one need only compare Nagyvárad with Oradia Mare—is equally unintelligible to a Westerner who knows the town only as Grosswardein. But in the same month (November, 1919) I was amused to find the main square in Czernowitz, the capital of the Bucovina, still called the Franz-Josefsplatz, and the street-names (German in large type in the center, Roumanian in small type above and Ruthenian below) still untouched. But apparently the live and let live methods of Austria were none the less effective—far more so than the brutal Hungarian system, which fanned Roumanian resentment to a flame; in the Bucovina, Roumanian national feeling was gradually dying out before this slow, unimpassioned encouragement of Ruthenians in religion and German in schools, and before the social privileges which the Austrians never failed to accord to the Roumanian landed gentry in the Bucovina, to keep them contented.

The Austrians found a few Roumanian schools and one

theological seminary in the Bucovina when they took over the province in 1774. These they closed and replaced with German schools, which they declared in 1815 Roman Catholic confessional schools depending on the Archbishop of Lemberg. That automatically excluded Roumanian Orthodox teachers. It was not till 1844 that permission was given to open Roumanian confessional schools also. In 1869 the schools ceased to be confessional and became governmental—which meant German. All the courses in the Czernowitz Normal School were given in German. In 1911 the census gave 82 German schools, 12 Polish, 126 Ruthenian, 179 Roumanian, 5 Magyar and 127 bi- or tri-lingual!

The University of Czernowitz (Cernăutzi) was founded in 1875, for the centennial celebration of the incorporation of the Bucovina into Austria. Its avowed purpose was to become an outpost of German culture in southeastern Europe; indeed, it was some years before it contained even a chair of Roumanian language and literature! The University has an excellent library, of well toward 300,000 volumes, which luckily was spared under the various Russian occupations of the war; and it succeeded in attracting a number of distinguished scholars. I had the good fortune, in lecturing in 1925 and 1927 at Czernowitz, to make the acquaintance of a number of non-Roumanians in the faculty; they tell me they are given every facility for their work by the Roumanians. But unfortunately the financial crisis hampers all scholarly and university activity. The University Library allowance for the purchase of books and periodicals hardly suffices to pay for the renewals of periodicals alone! And the teacher crisis, which is enough of a problem even in the United States, is in the highest degree embarrassing in the Bucovina. It is true that in the gradual decay of culture which we are witnessing all over the world,

60% of American teachers have never graduated from high-school; but where is the Roumanian government to find its teachers for the Bucovina, where (according to a Roumanian author) thanks to the long Austrian embargo on Roumanian higher schools, 80% of the Roumanian population could neither read nor write?

Of the 854,000 inhabitants of the Bucovina, nearly one-quarter live in the city or county of Czernowitz. The city lies fan-shape upon the steep hills running down to the Pruth, and is quite Austro-German in its appearance and construction. Its business is largely in the hands of the 50,000 Jews and 15,000 Germans who live there; most of the Polish population of the Bucovina is concentrated there also. I found it possible to make myself understood everywhere on the streets and in the shops with German or Roumanian. Its population (1930) is 111,600.

Politically, Roumania has had a serious problem, as in Bessarabia, with Bolshevistic agitation among the Jews and Ruthenians. The latter, being Slavs, are fertile soil for Communistic propaganda, like the Russians and Bulgarians; while the Roumanian peasant, being a hard-headed Latin like an Italian or Spaniard, is not at all receptive to Bolshevism. I had ocular demonstration of this the evening of November 17, 1919, in Czernowitz; Ruthenian soldiers who formed half of a regiment newly formed by the Roumanians out of returned war prisoners from the Bucovina, were tampered with by local Bolshevistic sympathizers, who persuaded them to mutiny and return to their homes; they shot up the town, seized a train and were nearly home when overhauled. The Roumanian half of the same regiment remained loyal!

According to the census of 1910, of the 800,098 inhabitants of the Bucovina, 273,254 used Roumanian as

"Umgangsprache" (customary spoken language), 305,101 Ruthenian, 168,851 German, 36,210 Polish, 10,391 Magyar, 1005 Bohemian, 80 Slovak and 5206 Russian and other languages. The first Roumanian census (1919) gave the Roumanians 378,859 and the Ruthenians 227,361. About 68% of the population is Greek Orthodox, 13% Hebrew, 12% Roman Catholic, 3% Greek Catholic, 3% Protestant. The farms are prevailingly tiny; this applies particularly to the Roumanian element, who occupy three-quarters of all the individual farms; but their farms make up only one-eighth of the whole farm area.

The Bucovina is a small district, neither wealthy nor fertile; and the joy over its return is disproportionately great in Roumania. It is much as if the State of Maine had been held by the British for over a century, during which it became half French-Canadian, and were then returned to us. The Bucovina has always been a favorite theme with the Roumanian poets; the Bucovina littérateur, S. F. Marian, has published a collection of the ballads and other poems which circulate among its Roumanian peasantry. One of the best of Alecsandri's poems is that dedicated to the Bucovina:

Dulce Bucovină,	Sweet Bucovina
Veselă grădină	Blithe garden
Cu pomi roditori	With fruitful trees
Shi mândri feciori!	And proud sons!
Cuib de păserele	Nest of birdlets
Albe, sprintinele,	White, quick,
Care 'n ochii lor	Which in their eyes
Au foc răpitor.	Have ravishing fire.
Tu ce eshti o floare	Thou who art a flower
Căzută din soare	Fallen from the sun

Photo, Tzatzu, Bucharest

TURKISH FORTRESS, SOROCA, OVERLOOKING THE DNIESTER

MAP OF BESSARABIA

Cu trei alte flori,
A tale surori!
Ele cătră tine
Privesc cu suspine,
Shi tu le zimbeshti
Cu zimbiri cereshti.

Dulce Bucovină!
Vîntul ce înclină
Cu aripa lui
Iarba câmpului
Nashte prin shoptire
Scumpa amintire
De-un trecut frumos,
Mare, glorios.

Fii în veci voioasă
Pre cât eshti frumoasă!
Fie traiul tĕu
Dupa gândul meu!
Ah! Cine te vede
Chiar în raiu se crede.
Cine-i trecător
Te plânge cu dor.

With three other flowers,
Ah, such sisters!
They toward thee
Look with sighing,
And thou smilest at them
With heavenly smiles.

Sweet Bucovina!
The wind that bends
With its wing
The grass of the field
Rouses by its whisper
The dear memory
Of a beautiful past
Great, glorious.

Be ever happy
As thou art beautiful!
Be thy life
After my plan (for thee)!
Ah! he who sees thee
Actually believes
Himself in Paradise.
He who is a passer-by
Mourns for thee with longing.

CHAPTER XI

THE Bucovina shows how Austria handled a Moldavian province; in Bessarabia, we see the result of Russian dominion in a larger section of Moldavia, detached a few years later. Russian policy, under Catherine II, aimed to absorb both Moldavia and Wallachia, as a step toward Tsarigrad (Constantinople); and in 1810–1811 the time seemed ripe. But Napoleon's invasion of Russia altered the situation, and Russia succeeded in taking possession of only Bessarabia, and that by the bribery of Turkish officials, who were later executed by the Porte. After the Crimean War, three of the Bessarabian counties were returned to Roumania, but for only twenty years, as Russia obtained their retrocession by the Treaty of Berlin in 1878.

When Russia took over Bessarabia in 1812, she found a homogeneous Roumanian country, in which the only foreign elements worthy of remark were recent Bulgarian colonies in the southeast. Alexander I organized the new province in liberal fashion, preserving the Roumanian laws and customs; he appointed as governor a Roumanian boyar, Scarlat Sturza, and as Metropolitan the Roumanian bishop Gabriel Banulesco Bodoni. The population was exempted from taxes for five years; and there was no recruiting—a beatific state which lasted till 1874! He provided for a legislature, which was naturally Roumanian in majority; and Roumanian remained a state language, on a par with Russian. Bessarabia was really autonomous, and remained so till the accession of the autocratic Czar Nicholas I, late in 1825. He suppressed the State Council of Bessarabia in 1828; reorganized the courts on Russian models with the provision that only Russian might be used in them; and commenced the insidious process of Russification. Already in 1824, it had been provided that all teaching should be in Russian, the study of Roumanian being allowed only in addition to that of Russian. In 1841, the Marshal of the Bessarabian nobles, John Sturza, succeeded in having Roumanian introduced as language of instruction in a few schools; but it was soon superseded by Russian; and the Archbishop Paul Ledebef, who began his ministrations in 1871, succeeded in driving the last use of the language out of the churches, although the vast bulk of the worshipers knew no other. A favorite story tells of a priest, Ruthenian by origin, who had to conduct services one day and found he had forgotten his prayer-book; he could quote the prayers by heart (in Church Slavonic, the language of the cult), but not the gospels. He always carried with him a little volume of the works of the Ruthenian poet Kevchenko; taking it out, he read in place of the gospel selection, with the utmost unction, the poem, "Dumi moi, dumi" (thoughts, my thoughts), to the full satisfaction of his Roumanian hearers.

The Russians encouraged immigration from the Ukraine and Russia itself, and also established German, French, Swiss and Bulgarian colonies, all of which prospered. They made room for many of these immigrants by inducing Roumanians to emigrate to other parts of the Empire, especially Siberia and the Caucasus; several hundred thousand of these Roumanians and their descendants are now scattered where they can never again form part of Roumania. With the predominance of Russian law, bureaucracy and education, the city bourgeoisie became prevailingly Russian; this tendency was helped by the introduction of the Russian zemstvo system, largely administered by Russians. Commerce was mainly in the hands of the Jews, who ordinarily speak Roumanian and Russian in addition to Yiddish.

Bessarabia was therefore superficially Russified when the war broke out; but the Roumanian peasantry had been untouched. Many were reconciled to the lack of schools, which allowed them to exploit the children on the farm; to government negligence and the zemstvo system, because they were not taxed for expensive roads, railroads, sewers, etc.; to the police system, because for a few rubles they could bribe the gendarmes to overlook illegalities. It speaks volumes for the devotion of the few Roumanian intellectuals that they won the conservative peasants over to a new régime which means heavier taxes, schools that will take the children out of farm-work for much of the year, and a higher standard of law-enforcement.

The Russian Revolution of March, 1917, was immediately followed by the formation in Kishineff of the National Democratic Moldavian Party, which aimed at complete autonomy for Bessarabia, like that of the Ukraine and other parts of Russia. On April 6–7 was held a Congress of Members of Coöperatives, which sent up to the Provisory Government a demand for the continuance of the war against the Central Empires; for Bessarabian autonomy, with Roumanian as official language; and for the organization of a Sfat or Divan (council), for all local matters. Next came an Ecclesiastical Congress (April 19–25), which also demanded autonomy and a Divan, to be chosen by a National Assembly, the Sfat; these demands were repeated at a later assembly of priests in August. Over ten thousand Bessarabians who were at Odessa held a meeting on April 18, which voted not merely for autonomy for Bessarabia,

but also for a local militia, of Bessarabian soldiers in the
former Russian army, to help defend the Roumanian line
against the Germans, and protect the district itself from
marauding bands of Red soldiery. The Ukraine having secured its autonomy in June, endeavored at once to appropriate Bessarabia; meeting followed meeting in Kishineff;
the Moldavian Military Committee, representing 190,000
Bessarabian soldiers in the Russian army, protested ef-
fectively at Petrograd; and on October 20–27, 1917, 989
delegates of the Bessarabian soldiers met at Kishineff, voted
the autonomy of Bessarabia unanimously, and decided upon
the calling of a Sfat (assembly) for November 21. This
met in the midst of wild enthusiasm; John Inculetz, a young
law professor, was elected president (and later the first
Minister for Bessarabia in the first Ministry of Greater
Roumania); speeches were made in favor of autonomy by
Mayor A. C. Schmidt, of Kishineff; Judge Luzghin, head
of the Russian District Court; Dr. Lutzenko, delegate of
the Ukrainian Rada; the representatives of the Jewish Nationalist Societies (Stern and Fischer), the Polish Club
(Pomorski), the Ukrainian Club (Mitkevitch), the Greek
Club (P. Sinadinos), the Bulgarian Club (Stoyannoff), the
Jewish Social Revolutionaries (Cohen), the Jewish Social
Democrats (Grünfeld), the Bund (Covarsky), the Kishi-
neff Barristers (Kircoroff), the Press Club (German), the
Zemstvos (Muzhichikoff and Podlesny), etc.; I have speci-
fied in order to show the manifold elements in Bessarabian
politics, and would refer to my "Bessarabia" (New York,
Dodd, Mead & Co., 1927) for greater detail.

The menace of Bolshevism spurred them on to rapid
effort; on December 2, 1917, the Sfat declared Bessarabia
a Democratic (Moldavian) Republic, and endeavored to
organize a militia to stop the pillaging of the country by

the disorganized bands of Russian soldiery. But in the general anarchy it proved impossible; even the Russian Commander-in-Chief had had to ask for a Roumanian body-guard; and on January 13, 1918, yielding to repeated demands, the Roumanian government entered upon a campaign to rid Bessarabia of Bolshevist bands. Meanwhile the Ukrainian Rada had proclaimed the independence of the Ukraine, and the Russians of Bessarabia who wished to keep up dependence on Moscow found themselves completely severed from Great Russia. On January 24, 1918, the Sfat followed suit, and unanimously declared Bessarabia independent. But it was impossible to find money with which to finance the new state; and as the Ukraine remained a constant threat, on March 27, 1918, the Sfat voted by 86 to 3 (36 abstaining) that from that day forth, the Democratic Moldavian Republic of Bessarabia was united with the mother country, Roumania. This Sfat had 85 of the peasant class, of its total membership of 138; 5 deputies of the large land-owning class, who feared the Roumanian agrarian laws, had withdrawn early. There were 103 Moldavians, 13 Ukrainians, 7 Russians, 6 Jews, 5 Bulgarians, 2 Germans, 1 Pole and 1 Armenian; much the same proportion was preserved in the first and second elections for the Roumanian Parliament.

The last important work of the Sfat, before it disbanded, was to pass an agrarian law expropriating all large land-owners of all their estate surpassing 250 acres; vineyards, gardens and orchards were not affected. Payment was to be made for the land expropriated. All forest land was to be taken over by the State, under conditions to be determined later.

Thus Bessarabia became Roumanian. The large land-owners of Russian nationality and sympathies, the Russian office-holding and professorial classes, and certain Jewish interests, protested at once to the Supreme Council and the press of the world; and the Supreme Council characteristically took advantage of the situation to apply pressure to Roumania. It is worth while to study dates. On March 27, 1918, the National Council of Bessarabia passed its resolution of union with Roumania, with certain reservations. On November 27, it repeated the resolution, this time unconditionally.

The Supreme Council was deluged with reports unfavorable to the new régime in Bessarabia. It appears that in Bessarabia (as in the Bucovina with the Germans), many Russian office-holders and professors, who did not know Roumanian, resigned and left for Russia; otherwise, the Bessarabian judges and college professors retained their positions, as was the case, e. g., at the University of Czernowitz. I must confess that, at the risk of doing injustice to Mr. Krupensky, Mr. Schmidt and other unreconcilables, I cannot help grouping them with the very delightful and persuasive Russian land-holders who have become permanent exiles from their country in consequence of agrarian reform. The first Bessarabian elections, in November, 1919, brought out 385,630 voters, of the 505,393 registered; 5% of the ballots were declared void. The election was an overwhelming victory for the Peasants' Party, which elected 72 candidates; the Workingmen's Democratic Party had 3, the Nationalist Conservative and People's League 4, and the Independents 9. There were elected not only Roumanians but also Ruthenians, Germans, Bulgarians, Gagaoutz, Greeks and Jews. The province took hold of Roumanian politics with apparent gusto.

In the second election, in the spring of 1920, the Peasants' Party, which had shown receptivity to Bolshevist agitators,

lost ground. Like the other new provinces of Greater Roumania, which taken together outweigh the former kingdom,
it is in little danger of the carpet-bagging which has been the
curse of Jugo-Slavia.

The province of Bessarabia derives its name from the
Turks, who so called it from the ruler, Bessarab, under
whom they first came to know it. Its area is about 17,000
square miles, a little under Vermont and New Hampshire
combined. It lies between the Pruth and the Dniester as
they flow down to the Black Sea from the Carpathians; in
the northwest it is hilly, but most of it is the famous black
earth steppe of Southern Russia, wonderfully suited for
wheat-growing. Its population depends directly or indirectly
almost entirely on agriculture; there is only one large city,
Kishineff (Chishinău), of over 116,000 inhabitants, of
whom about one-half are Jews. Hotin, Soroca, Baltz, Ismail
and Akkerman are about 30,000 each. According to the
census of 1908, the population was 2,344,800, of whom the
Russians claimed 28%, giving less than 54% to the Roumanians; in 1930, the population was 2,848,000; according
to a recent Roumanian estimate, the percentage is 64%
Roumanian, 12½% Russian (or Ukrainian), 10% Jewish,
5½% Bulgarian, 4¼% German; 3% are Protestants, 10%
Hebrew, 1% Roman Catholic, 3% Mohammedan, the rest
Greek Orthodox. The railroads cover only about 530 miles,
and of improved highway there are only about 60 miles! The
Pruth is navigable up to Leorda (150 miles) for grain-boats,
and 2½ million hectoliters of grain have been so transported in one year, and the Dniester, which is a slow winding
stream, is navigable for over 500 miles. With the lack of
communications goes a lack of schooling; in 1908, 35%
only of the men could read and write Russian, and 23%
of the women. The Roumanians estimate that less than

20% of the men can read and write Roumanian, and less than
5% of the women. The Russian Government had forbidden
the importation or possession of Roumanian books and
newspapers, and when the Bessarabians began publishing
in Roumanian after the declaration of autonomy, they used
the Cyrillic (Russian) letters, which have been discarded
in Roumania for half a century. Imagine the school problem which results! I must add that I have never had more
crowded and appreciative audiences, nor more adequate re-
porting in the papers, than in my lectures of 1927 in Kishineff.

Bessarabia is almost entirely agricultural. Recent droughts
have been disastrous to the farmers; and when at last (in
1929 and 1930) they had good harvests, the sudden drop in
the price of grain completed their discomfiture. They are
heavily burdened with debt, on which they have had to pay
exorbitant interest (up to 40%); and since money-lending
is mainly in the hands of the Jews, anti-Semitic sentiment
has been roused by agitators. Like our Western farmers, they
have sold much stock to pay taxes and interest; horses, cattle,
sheep and hogs, which totaled 4,020,000 in 1923, had dropped
to 2,684,373 in 1929. Here are the figures for 1930:

	Area in hectares (2.47 acres)	Production in metric tons
Barley	806,393	846,248
Wheat	632,788	695,881
Indian corn	935,197	674,062
Potatoes	37,978	245,180
Sugar-beets	12,779	162,682
Rye	136,342	135,025
Oats	134,945	117,875
Wine	64,784 *	19,390,954 hectoliters
Beans	20,249	51,999
Plums	6,839	16,115
Rape-seed (colza oil)	30,025	14,198
Flax	8,247	5,634
Hemp	5,997	3,087

* Plus about 25,000 hectares in table grapes.

It is interesting to compare this with pre-war production. Prof. N. Maghiliansky, in his "Cereal Production in Bessarabia," Kishineff, 1916, gives the following 1902–1911 averages:

	Area in hectares	Production in metric tons
Indian corn	704,865	663,767
Wheat	785,339	595,282
Barley	534,261	442,473
Rye	211,537	182,620
Oats	72,799	73,733

There has been an enormous increase in cultivation in Bessarabia since Russian days; and as 1930 was an abundant year, the Bessarabian farmer looked forward to paying his debts and making a fresh start. But alas, the price of barley dropped 31%, that of wheat 31%, corn 30% and rye 50%. On the entire cereal crop of 1930, it is calculated that the Bessarabian farmers received $37,000,000 less than if 1929 prices had prevailed. 1931 crop prospects are good. The areas (in hectares) sowed in 1931 to the various grains are (preliminary figures of June 1931):

Indian corn	876,108
Barley	684,732
Wheat	194,129
Oats	114,651
Rye	4,604

Grain mills and vegetable oil mills are the chief industries, there being 60 of the latter, many of which make soap also. There are various small establishments—woodworking plants, woolen mills, knitting mills, brick-yards, etc.—employing altogether only a few thousand hands. Wooden windmills are conspicuous in the landscape.

Industrially, therefore, Bessarabia is backward, and offers an inviting field to the capitalist. The present situation there shows much friction, caused by the natural mistakes of a new administration, the slow improvement in transportation facilities (their greatest need), Soviet and other Russian propaganda and even terrorism; and too much politics; but we can trust the innate conservatism and love of order of the Roumanian peasant to surmount all these difficulties and make Bessarabia a land not merely of plenty but of contentment and progress.

The negotiations between the Great Powers and Roumania over the Bessarabian Treaty dragged on till late October, 1920. France and Britain insisted as a condition that Roumania should compensate their citizens in full gold value for land expropriated in Bessarabia. The policy of the Wilson Administration forbade recognition of the smaller Western states which seceded from Russia; and this policy has been continued by the State Department as regards Bessarabia, so that this treaty is not yet accepted as valid by the United States, alone of the Great Powers. The Soviets do not recognize Bessarabia as Roumanian; indeed there are officially no relations between Roumania and the Soviets; but a mixed Russo-Roumanian Commission, with several local subcommittees, has been meeting for several years and settling questions of extradition, repatriation, etc.

We must not take leave of Bessarabia without some mention of the great mass of Roumanians who live the other side of the Dniester, in the rich black earth regions of Podolia and Cherson. According to the Russian census of 1897, the number of persons speaking exclusively Roumanian in these districts was about 225,000. They form a homogeneous continuation of the Roumanians of Bessarabia, having the same dialect, songs, ballads, costumes and customs. In the break-up of Russia after Kerensky's fall, they endeavored to be annexed to Bessarabia, and sent delegates to Kishineff; but the political difficulties involved were too great.

The Soviets have organized the Roumanian-speaking district across the Dniester into a Moldavian Soviet Republic, with Balta as its center and several Bessarabian political refugees in its administration; Roumanian is a state and school language beside Russian and Ukrainian. From this vantage-point they disseminate Bolshevist propaganda through Bessarabia; but in spite of the hard times they have had little success. Three chapters of my "Bessarabia" describe these Communist machinations (up to 1927); and as the Soroca trial of 1931 showed, the same organizations are still hopefully active.

CHAPTER XII

AMONG the interesting interviews which I had in Buda-Pesth in late 1919 was one with a giant Magyar, a minister of Friedrich's, whose conversation was a mixture of whining over the dismemberment of Hungary by the Entente, and chauvinistic bombast over its futility. "All these subject nationalities," said he, "Serbs, Slovaks, Roumanians, whom the Supreme Council is cutting off from our body politic, must inevitably return; for they are naturally subordinate, and we are naturally the masters. But," he added, "you can't be expected to understand that, for you are Indo-European, Aryan, and we are Turanians!"

That, in brief, is the Magyar attitude. It injects an element of greater partisanship into the Transylvanian question; it has been bolstered up abroad by an admirable propaganda service (the very day of the armistice, three pro-Hungarian articles appeared in London newspapers, and through the Protestant religious weeklies they succeeded in maintaining a remarkably active campaign for sympathy and funds); indeed, the Magyars have had a favorable press abroad ever since Kossuth's day; and the attractive members of the Hungarian aristocracy and officialdom in Buda-Pesth succeeded in making active partisans out of British and American correspondents and other visitors. So it is difficult to take a detached attitude, even in discussing purely historical matters; I never knew the truth harder to get at than in Buda-Pesth in late 1919; while reading Roumanian and

Hungarian histories is like studying the War of 1812 in Canadian and American accounts!

At any rate, there is no doubt even from Hungarian statistics that the Magyars have been in a minority in Hungary as a whole, and still more so in Transylvania. By Transylvania (Ardeal in Roumanian, Erdély in Hungarian, Siebenbürgen in German) we mean the region bounded by the Carpathians or their outrunners on the north, east and south, and on the west by the Crishana and the Banat. It forms a hilly and well-watered plateau, with a landscape and climate much like that of the middle Appalachian region of the United States; at Sibiu (Hermannstadt), during the 5-year period 1906–1910, the lowest temperature recorded was —28.4 C. (—19° F.), and the highest 34.3° C. (95° F.); the mean December temperature was 32°, and for January 25°; for July and August just under 68°. Politically it comprises 15 counties of the former kingdom of Hungary with an area of about 22,220 sq. miles, somewhat smaller than the state of West Virginia, but with over twice its population. According to the Hungarian official figures, Transylvania contained 2,166,236 inhabitants in 1869, and 2,678,367 in 1910. Eighty-seven per cent. of this population is rural; in fact, there are no large cities in Transylvania. The last Hungarian census assigned the Roumanians 55% of the total, 34.3% to the Hungarians (in which figure were incorporated 64,000 Jews, 2.4%), and 8.7% to the Germans. The Hungarians were lumped in 5 counties, which together showed 612,000 Hungarians (exactly 2/3 of the whole) and 277,000 Roumanians. Four of these counties form a linguistic island in far eastern Transylvania, next the Carpathians; these Magyars (the Szeklers) are isolated in a Roumanian sea, and their economic interests have always united them with their Roumanian neighbors on both sides of the Carpathians, while they have had little to do with the Hungarians of the remote plain beyond the Theiss.

There is no doubt the Hungarians padded these figures to their own benefit, the question asked having been: "Which language do you speak by preference?" A closer approximation is offered by the tables of religious affiliation. The Roumanians were almost exactly divided between the Greek Oriental and Greek Catholic (Uniate) Churches. These two had 1,542,268 communicants, from which must be deducted 1759 Ruthenians, 225 Bulgarians and 421 Serbs; and we must add 6249 Roman Catholics. That gave the Roumanians 57% of the population of Transylvania. The Greek Oriental Church had 29.6% of the whole, the Greek Catholic 28, the Roman Catholic 14, the Reformed 15, Evangelical 8½, Unitarian 2½, Jewish 2½. Recent Roumanian figures for Transylvania and the Banat record 59% Roumanians, 25% Hungarians, 10% Germans and 3¾% Jews, in a total of 5,487,966; this had risen in 1930 to 5,563,000.

We have already mentioned the long-standing controversy whether Magyars or Roumanians are the older race in Transylvania. The pro-Magyar argument rests largely on the use of *desertum* (wilderness) in an early document to describe this region—from which they draw the hardly warranted deduction that it was without inhabitants—and on the lack of explicit mention of Wallachians here till some time after it is known that there were Magyars in this district. But as far back as the twelfth century we find Voyevodes in Transylvania. The Voyevode was the military chief among the ancient Slavs; during the long period when Slavs and Roumanians were intermingled, the Roumanians adopted this institution and term, as they did many others; the Slav unit, e. g., was the valley, and the Roumanians are designated as Oltean, Bistritzean, etc., from the river valley they inhabit. As with the Slavs, the family bulked large with the Transylvania Roumanians; numerous are their villages whose names end in -eshti, which means the descendants of, co-members of a family with. These institutions seem to date from that early period when Slav and Wallach formed one people in Transylvania, and to have survived the devastation of the Tartar invasion of the middle of the thirteenth century, in which almost all written documents must have been destroyed. We do not even possess any of the twelfth and thirteenth century patents of the Saxon colonies in Transylvania, who had every possible government aid. The early Slav and Roumanian place names have been preserved all over Transylvania, just as in Wallachia.

It would appear reasonable then that these German colonists who were settled through Transylvania at the end of the Middle Ages and even founded Câmpu-Lung (Langenfeld) in Wallachia, entered a region settled, even if sparsely, by Roumanian shepherds and farmers. That these Roumanians had an organization is shown, e. g., by a document of 1222 giving the Teutonic Order certain privileges, which speaks of a "terra Blachorum" next the "terra Siculorum"—a land of the Wallachs next that of the Szeklers. Pressure upon these Wallachs led them to emigrate; the Voyevode of Făgărash crossed the Carpathians not long after 1300 and founded the Principality of Wallachia; in 1365, the last Roumanian Voyevode of the Maramuresh, Bogdan, led his forces over the mountain passes and established the Principality of Moldavia.

The Magyars were now installed as rulers of Transylvania. They had brought with them the feudal system, and the burdens of the Roumanian peasantry, now reduced to the status of serfs, grew heavier and heavier. In 1526 the Turks

TRANSYLVANIAN PEASANT TYPE (NEAR SIBIU)

Photo, Fischer, Sibiu

A TRANSYLVANIAN GERMAN FAMILY IN COSTUME

defeated the Hungarian army at Mohács, killing the last King of Hungary, Ladislaus II. Hungary was extinguished. The Hungarian plain, the Banat and Croatia passed under direct Turkish administration; a Turkish pasha ruled at Buda-Pesth; the north and northwest were assigned to the Hapsburgs; Transylvania, the Crishana and the Maramuresh became an independent Principality, governed by a prince chosen from among the Magyar landed aristocracy. He had to pay a small tribute to the Sultan, but was otherwise practically undisturbed. Under Michael the Brave, all Transylvania became for a couple of years part of Roumania; and Peter Raresh united a large share of it for several years to Moldavia. But the Hapsburgs coveted the province; Austrian generals tried in vain in 1545 and 1601 to conquer it; in 1687 Duke Charles of Lorraine was successful. Transylvania was given a constitution, called the Diploma Leopoldinum, from the Emperor; this was accepted on January 10, 1691, by the Diet of Transylvania, and the Emperor took the title of Prince of Transylvania. This constitution lasted till 1848, during all of which time the province was autonomous under Austria, with no connection with Buda-Pesth.

The Hungarian mastery of Transylvania dates from the Kossuth movement in 1848. He aimed at a Greater Hungary, independent of Austria, and was successful in incorporating both Transylvania and Croatia for a few months; but with Russian aid, Francis Joseph crushed the movement for the moment, and Transylvania regained a certain autonomy, with some rights for the Roumanians, who had previously had none at all. But Austria grew weaker before the Prussian and Italian menace; Bismarck gave powerful aid to the Magyars; and in 1865 the Transylvanian Diet, meeting at

Cluj (Klausenburg, Kolozsvár), voted (against unanimous Roumanian protest) annexation of Transylvania to Hungary.

It was only a couple of generations since the Hungarians had "discovered" the Magyar tongue. Despised as the language of the peasantry, unintelligible to any Western European, the Hungarian aristocracy had neglected their own melodious speech, with all its wealth of popular literature and of poetry. Latin was the language of the Parliament at Buda-Pesth; not till 1830 was Hungarian used for the reply to the Address from the Throne. Count Stephen Széchenyi was the leader in this campaign to rehabilitate a noble language; he was successful beyond his wildest dreams. Enthusiasts at once began insisting that Hungarian should be used to the exclusion of all other vernaculars throughout Hungary; and Széchenyi, in his inaugural as first President of the Hungarian Academy of Sciences, in 1842, warned against the excesses of this "Magyar zeal." One of the most thoughtful of the Germans of Transylvania, High Commissioner Joseph Bedeus of Scharberg, writing to his sons about the events of 1848 and the ambitions of the Magyars there disclosed, says very truly: "The verse applied by a clever historian to the Hungarians: *nec iugi patiens, nec libertatis capax*, has been brilliantly justified by them from the earliest times; they never would bear the yoke, but they cannot stand freedom. . . . The motive which drove the Magyars to union was vanity and national pride; they were hurt at the unobserved disappearance among the other much smaller provinces, of the Hungarian crown-lands, which form the largest and strongest component of the Austrian monarchy; at their appearing as an appendage to unimportant Austria; at their being ruled by a foreign German ministry. Accordingly they wanted to fuse Hungary and Transylvania completely and make a large and compact body, for which to secure a separate government, independent of Austria and the Germans. That was the ostensible aim of their efforts; but the initiated went much further with their plans. They wanted to unite and strengthen the Hungarian element scattered over both countries, and then with their united forces suppress all other nationalities and languages throughout the country, fuse their representatives with themselves and turn them into Hungarians, thus claim supreme sway for Magyarism, then form a separate united indivisible self-sufficient independent Hungarian intermediate state, and finally cut this loose from Austria."

This severe judgment has been only too well carried out by the event. The Hungarians have been in the habit of pointing to the liberal provisions of their constitution, as proof that the Roumanians in Transylvania were not justified in their protests. One need not go over the ground so admirably traversed by Mr. Seton-Watson; suffice it to point out that the Hungarian Law of Nationalities prescribed that in the counties where the Roumanians were in the majority, the prefects and other officials should be Roumanian— whereas there never was in these counties one prefect or vice-prefect of that nationality! It prescribed that in these counties, Roumanian should be the language of the courts and public administration—a regulation also never carried out; indeed, one saw only Hungarian street-signs in towns almost exclusively Roumanian. The climax of disingenuousness is reached in the Hungarian propaganda documents by quoting the number of elementary schools—3500 in 1905—in which Roumanian *was* the language of instruction—as proof of the thoughtful care of the Hungarian State for its Roumanian wards! These schools were founded and maintained at their own expense by the Transylvanian Roumanians themselves;

but once established, the central government stepped in and insisted (1879) that the instructors should learn Hungarian, so as to be able to teach in that language; in 1907 Count Apponyi ruled that the schools where the instructors had not made sufficient progress should be replaced by Hungarian schools; in 1917, he closed the Roumanian normal schools; but the ferment started by the Russian Revolution caused their reopening. He did, however, succeed in that year in banishing Roumanian altogether from the primary schools. The net result of this anti-Roumanian campaign has been, not a falling-off in the use of Roumanian as a colloquial language, but a far greater illiteracy among the Roumanians of Transylvania. There was one gymnasium (lycée) in their own tongue for every 25,000 Germans in Transylvania, and one for every 25,000 Hungarians; for the Roumanians, one for every 585,000! and this in spite of the urgent appeal of the Roumanian church authorities to be allowed to open more at their own expense! Accordingly, the percentage of illiteracy in the Roumanian counties of Transylvania ran as high as 65 and 70 per cent!

We have just mentioned the solicitude of the Roumanian church authorities. They have been among the leading champions of their race, and we must sketch briefly the religious history of this province.

The Roumanians of Transylvania remained with the Oriental Church after the Great Schism, like their congeners in the Danube provinces; but during the first Hungarian period, ending with the battle of Mohács, there was a strong proselyting influence exerted by the court toward Roman Catholicism. Intercourse with Rome had a powerful effect on the young Roumanians who went to study there, and discovered they were Latins, with affiliations in the West, and not Orientals. Still more vital was the influence of the Refor-

mation, in that it led to the beginnings of Roumanian literature and of that self-consciousness which the possession of
a literature brings with it. The Hussite movement had prospered among the Slovak peasants next the Maramuresh;
many of them passed over into tolerant Moldavia to escape
the persecution of the Catholic Emperor Sigismund, who
had burned Huss at the stake in Constance. In 1416 at Trotush in Moldavia they translated the Gospels into Hungarian; and later in the century they began translation into
Roumanian; the most famous MSS are the Psalter of Scheia
and the Gospel Codex of Voronetz, both Transylvanian and
ancient and dignified in style.

In 1557 the Lutherans won recognition from the Diet; in
1564 the Calvinists; in 1571 the Unitarians. In 1544 appeared at Sibiu (Hermannstadt) the first Roumanian printed
book—a Lutheran catechism. About 1560 a Wallachian dea-
con named Coresi established a Roumanian press at Brashov
(Brasso, Kronstadt) in Transylvania. He brought out a
Roumanian Gospels in 1561; then a Prayer Book and the
Acts; in 1564 a Commentary on the Gospels; between 1565
and 1577 three editions of the Psalms; in 1580 the Gospels,
with Church Slavonic parallel text; in 1581 a new Orthodox
Commentary on the Gospels. This proselyting roused the
Orthodox elements in Wallachia; under Michael the Brave,
in 1595, the supremacy of the Greek Orthodox Metropolitan
of Târgovishte in Wallachia was recognized for all Transylvania. This formed a link with Roumania proper of the
highest importance.

The victory of the Hapsburgs over the Turks renewed the
Roman Catholic propaganda in Transylvania—this time
under a very able Jesuit, Baranyi. In 1697 the Roumanian
bishop Theophilus and his synod accepted in principle the
supremacy of the Pope; his successor Athanasius wanted to

renew affiliation with the Metropolitan of Wallachia, and
Constantine Brancovan encouraged him in this direction;
but the Vienna government had sanctioned the arrangement
made by Theophilus, and Athanasius and his clergy passed
over to the Roman communion. They preserved, however, all
the Orthodox rites, ceremonial and usages, together with the
Julian calendar (which has been abolished in Roumania
proper only recently), so that a service in the Greek Catholic
(Uniate) Church is almost indistinguishable from one in
the Greek Orthodox. The peasantry made no objection; and
the Roumanians in Transylvania enjoyed one advantage,
that their church administration was in close connection with
Vienna and with Rome. The Vienna government always
looked favorably on the Roumanian Catholics; and as the
Roumanian peasants were always devoted to the Emperor,
whom they considered their champion against the exactions
of the Hungarians, relations were far more cordial with
Vienna than with Buda-Pesth. From their intercourse with
Rome, the budding priests derived full knowledge of the
liberties and progress of the western world, as well as the
consciousness of their Latin origin. As half the priests and
communicants remained with the Orthodox Church, relations with Roumania itself maintained the feeling of Roumanian solidarity which was to become a great bugbear for
the Hungarian government. Thus Transylvania and the
whole Roumanian race were greatly benefited by this religious competition; it caused the foundation of the two
Principalities, the beginnings of the literature, the cultivation of the language, the awakening of national consciousness. With post-war union, a movement sprang up to combine the Greek Catholic and Greek Orthodox Churches; by
1931, this had reached the point of a public appeal for re-

ligious unity in the Blaj "Unirea," official organ of the Greek Catholic Church.

Meanwhile, the sufferings of the downtrodden Roumanian peasant had led to various efforts to lighten the burden. A bloody revolution broke out in 1437, and the nobles were forced to accept the Agreement of Kolos-Monostor (Cluj-Mănăshtur) of July 6, which made an exact enumeration of the obligations of both master and serf, on terms quite liberal to the latter. In an attempt to avoid their obligations, the Magyar, Szekler and German nobles met immediately afterward and formed the famous *Unio Trium Nationum*—an association of the privileged classes to avoid granting the concessions just exacted. That led to another peasant uprising, again successful; this time, the serfs gained the right to change masters, once their debts were paid up. But again the Union of the Three Nationalities refused to keep faith; the peasants rose a third time, but were crushed in January, 1438. Another revolution broke out in 1514, under Doja, who had distinguished himself against the Turks; this time the small land-holders took part also against their lords, and the Roumanians were only the most numerous nationality in Doja's army. But he lost the day, also; and the nobles gained the right of life and death over their serfs, together with an increase of the tithes and labor due from the serf. There was a brief improvement under the Roumanian King of Hungary, John Hunyádi, and his famous son Matthias Corvinus; but in general the attitude of the ruling classes is well summarized by the declaration of the Transylvanian Diet in 1576, in the midst of the Protestant propaganda to convert the Roumanians: "The Roumanian nationality has no political rights whatever, for it is foreign, together with its religion, and is tolerated in this country only temporarily, so long as it pleases the Prince and the citizens of the realm."

Even the conquest of Transylvania by a Roumanian prince, Michael the Brave, brought no relief; and the Thirty Years' War (1618–48) saw no improvement. The courageous Bishop Innocent Klein (Micu) of the Greek Catholic (Uniate) Church, in 24 petitions he addressed to the Emperor Charles VI between 1730 and 1740, reminds him that not only have the schools promised to the Roumanians by the Act of Union, never been granted, but that children of Roumanians are forbidden to go to school, are not received as apprentices, may not hold public office, "may not buy, may not inherit, have no desire to plant vineyards or cultivate gardens for others to come and ruin, have no water or forest rights, nothing but many heavy burdens to bear, by the fulfilment of which they not merely get no consideration as sons of their country, but are not even tolerated." The Emperor transmitted these complaints to the Transylvanian Diet, which replied in 1735 that there was no real Union, "for these Wallachs are altogether ignorant and confirmed schismatics. . . . They cannot be called a nationality, for they are nothing but a horde of peasants, all serfs, tramps, fugitives, half-savage if not altogether so, given over to all evils and crimes, hostile to the Catholics and the Catholic faith, and with an opportunity would be the greatest persecutors of this faith. Their nobility is weak, not capable of filling public office. They are not even true believers. In the uprising under Rákoczy, they were all in his camp, and committed every kind of misdeed against the nobles, burning their castles, stealing their cattle and ruining their crops. The bandits, of whom the country is full, are chosen from among them, and the land-owners are constantly terrorized by these stiff-necked fugitive serfs, under threat of fire and sword. They fear neither God nor man. . . . This Bishop of theirs has no comprehension of politics, is no statesman, has no solicitude for the law. He is not even able to deliver a speech in Hungarian. He cannot be acknowledged to have any right of speaking for his nationality, for this nationality does not exist. These vagabonds have no territory of their own, but are scattered among the rest. To admit to the Diet this incompetent in the name of a people of savages would be an affront to the chief families of Transylvania and even to the Catholic priesthood. Let the Bishop rather look to his priests and suffragans, who are a set of villains. To lead them out of their darkness would be beyond the powers of ten bishops and theological advisers."

Micu was met with the same manner of insults when he later asked of these crusted old Junkers some of the rights guaranteed by the Diploma Leopoldinum; and when he appeared before the Diet in 1737, to speak "in the name of the Roumanian nationality of Transylvania," he was interrupted by the combined cries of Magyar and German: "There is no Wallachian nationality! There is only a Wallach rabble! Down with him! Take back your words! Out with him! Beg our pardon!" They even tried to make Micu ban Roumanian from church services for Latin. He decided to wake up the national consciousness, and called an assembly in 1744 at Blaj, to which he explained the promises of Vienna, the Diploma Leopoldinum, and the attitude of the Hungarian gentry. He failed; but the institution of three Roumanian regiments of boundary-guards was a powerful stimulant to national feeling. Maria Theresa made some slight improvements, also, in the condition of the serf; he now had three days a week for himself, did not have to feed his master's stock for nothing, and a woman serf might not receive more than 24 strokes of the lash! Enlistment put an end to all these exactions; the peasants flocked in to join the army;

when the nobles, in alarm, stopped the recruiting, a veritable revolution broke out (in 1784), under Nicholas Ursu, called "Horia." He demanded the abolition of aristocratic privileges, the distribution of the estates to the peasants of the estates, equality of taxation, and the supremacy of the Orthodox religion. He was successful in his contest against the Hungarians and Austrians, for many months; but in December his aide Closhca and he were captured, and put to death on the wheel.

Another courageous bishop arose to continue Micu's work—George Shincai. With his friends, Samuel Klein (Micu, a relative of the bishop) and Peter Maior, he devoted himself to education. Klein and he got out a Roumanian grammar, using Latin and not Cyrillic letters, and a series of school-books for the church schools which the enlightened Emperor Joseph II had finally sanctioned. Joseph had been shocked by the abuses brought to light by the Horia revolution, and in 1791 received favorably the famous memorandum of Roumanian wrongs which is called the "Supplex Libellus Valachorum." This claimed that the Roumanians were the oldest inhabitants of Transylvania, having been found there by Trajan; that by the census of 1760 they formed two-thirds of its population, being a million in number in 1790; that they should therefore have the same rights with the rest of the population. Clergy and laity, whether Orthodox or Uniate, should be treated on a par with Hungarians or Germans; in Roumanian districts there should be Roumanian officials in proportion to the population; the language should be used exclusively in altogether Roumanian districts, and concurrently in others; and there should be a Roumanian assembly. This document was not unwelcome at Vienna, but was rejected by the Transylvanian Diet; the only important improvement to which it led was

Joseph's decree of August 22, 1785, abolishing serfdom. That is, when George Washington had just been inaugurated, the Roumanian serfs of Transylvania received the right of calling themselves persons in law, of buying and selling the land on which they had grown up like slaves; but their economic and intellectual slavery was not to be abolished by a mere imperial fiat. However, the influence of the French Revolution tended to improve conditions in Transylvania, as elsewhere; and the distinction between Uniates and Orthodox, artificially stimulated by Vienna and Buda-Pesth on the immemorial principle of "Divide et impera," began to disappear before the consciousness of Roumanian unity.

The great figure in this movement during the nineteenth century was Andrew Shaguna. His people were Kutzo-Vlachs from Moscopole in Macedonia. He began his career as a Greek Catholic, but went over to the Orthodox Church, in which his talents advanced him rapidly; and in the crisis of 1848 he became Bishop of Sibiu (Hermannstadt). Just consecrated by the Serb Patriarch, head of the Orthodox Church in Austro-Hungary, he was the most prominent figure at the great meeting of 40,000 Roumanians at Sibiu on May 3, 1848—a meeting in which were Cipariu and Laurian, future leaders of Roumanian intellectuals in Transylvania, as well as the poet Alecsandri, and the future Prince Alexander Cuza. The chairman, Prof. Barnutz, revived the claims of the Supplex Libellus, and demanded recognition of the Roumanians as an autonomous nationality of Transylvania, as free as the others. Shaguna, in a modest speech, begged all to remember that whether Uniates or Orthodox, they were brothers; and he reminded them of the interest which the Emperor took in them. The new Emperor, Francis Joseph, had good reason to be grateful to Shaguna, for the latter went down to Bucharest with the German representative

Gottfried Müller and induced the Czar's generals to intervene against Kossuth to save the Austrians. On February 6, 1849, Shaguna had his first interview with the young Emperor, at Olmütz, and found him favorable to granting the Roumanians the rights long promised them; but the Hungarians always succeeded in blocking the way, and in 1861, when Shaguna had almost reached his goal of a co-ordinate Orthodox church organization in Transylvania (the Uniates had succeeded in obtaining a Metropolitan in 1853), he wrote sadly à propos of delays: "I am struck with the complete similarity with the circumstances of 1848, when they were still giving us fine words. But what was the use? They stayed words, and even after a dozen years they have failed to take on form. We foresee that after another dozen years we shall be lying still deeper in the ditch." Shaguna did have the satisfaction of being named Metropolitan of the Orthodox Church in 1863; but his last days were depressed by the increasing Magyar persecution, of which we must now present some examples.

Gerrymander is an American word; but Hungary gave classic specimens of the art, by the use of which (and of other electoral devices) the Hungarians succeeded in electing some 400-odd delegates, and the non-Hungarian *majority*— Serbs, Slovaks and Roumanians—7! One of the neatest was the famous "half-hour law," which provided that if only one nomination had come in by the end of the first half-hour after the opening of the polls, that candidate was declared elected. Under Magyar management of the polls, that simplified elections enormously. The few Roumanian newspapers were constantly prosecuted and suppressed. The *Tribuna* of Sibiu in 1903 figured up that in the previous ten years it had paid 57,000 crowns ($11,400) in fines, and its editors had been condemned to 17 years' imprisonment! The writer

Aurelius Popovici was given four years' imprisonment for a pamphlet in which he had inveighed against Magyar chauvinism; his defenders, the well-known authors Slavici and Rusu Sireanu, had also to take a year's imprisonment. In 1911 the poet Octavian Goga, who was to represent Transylvania in the first Parliament of Greater Roumania, received eight months' imprisonment for patriotic poems. The total penalties laid upon Roumanian newspapermen of Transylvania for the period 1896–1916 came to over 250,000 crowns, and one hundred years in prison! The Hungarian gendarmes carried on a petty persecution in every direction, comparable to those of the Austrians at Riva, or the Germans in Schleswig. At Hanarade, the wife of the local Roumanian priest was fined and imprisoned for offering Dr. Julius Maniu (later Premier of Roumania) a bouquet tied with the Roumanian tricolor ribbon.

The war redoubled Magyar vigilance, for the sympathy of the Roumanian intellectuals was strongly with France and Italy; and after Roumania came in, the pressure was increased. But the Russian Revolution, and the menace of the Hungarian proletariat, brought about a reform movement at last. Poor Charles I, in a still greater crisis than that in which his great-uncle had received Shaguna, demanded electoral reform from the Hungarians. Count Tisza resigned; Count Esterhazy seems to have made genuine efforts to carry out the new Emperor's wishes; but the Hungarian Junkers blocked his path, and he made way for Baron Wekerle. He evolved a law taking an educational qualification as criterion; only males over 24 able to read and write should have the suffrage; and his secretary naïvely states that in Transylvania "of the 64 election districts, there would be, according to the latest statistics, only four where the Roumanian element would be in the majority"! The Hungarian Government had spent millions of crowns colonizing Hungarians in Transylvania, from 1906 on, just as the Prussian Government did in Poland; and after the war began, they increased their effort. To revenge themselves upon the Transylvanian Roumanians, who had fraternized with Roumanian troops during the Roumanian invasion of Transylvania, they passed an edict forbidding all Roumanians of the border region to buy or sell property—evidently with huge colonization projects in mind.

Transylvania offers then the same sad spectacle as in Alsace-Lorraine, in Poland, in Bessarabia—the effort of a government to crush nationality and language. That is revolting even when nationalities and language are no more widely separated than German and French, or German and Polish; but it is especially sad when a people kinsmen of the Italians, Spaniards and French, with a language whose melody impresses every listener, is oppressed by an Oriental oligarchy, who still keep even their own lower orders in political subjection. It is still more depressing to reflect on the part played by religious persecution, under the ægis of Protestantism and Roman Catholicism, in this unhappy province; and it is disgusting to hear the whining of the former masters, now that the tables are turned. We have had the amazing spectacle of appeals addressed to us through our religious press from "Hungarian victims of Roumanian religious persecution." To this appeal it is a sufficient answer that the Roumanian Government, after the annexation of Transylvania, confirmed every Hungarian and German prelate in his former dignity! What a contrast with the procedure of the French in Alsace-Lorraine, and of the Poles in Posen! Where the shoe really pinches is that the Roumanian agrarian reforms were applied to Transylvania, and the churches (which had their wealth largely in landed property) have to see the despised Roumanian peasantry in possession of the broad acres they had been tilling as farm laborers. The churches are compensated, to be sure, but in small annual installments; and as the Hungarian Government had seized all their liquid funds for the prosecution of the war against us, they are left empty-handed for the moment. It is a typically Hungarian procedure to try to convince us that it is all the fault of the Roumanians. The charge of persecution of Hungarian Catholics in the Banat was even brought up in June, 1921, by the Abbé Wetterlé in the French Chamber, at the ratification of the Trianon Treaty, and gave occasion to both Premier Briand and Mayor Herriot of Lyons (who had just returned from Roumania) to testify to the "correct attitude of the Roumanian Government, which is fully meeting its obligation to protect the ethnic minorities." For further discussion, I would refer to Chapter XXIX.

CHAPTER XIII

THE BANAT, CRISHANA AND MARAMURESH

THE Banat of Temeshvar is the region opposite Belgrade, bounded by the Danube, the Theiss, the Muresh, the Transylvanian hills and the Carpathians. It covers some 11,000 sq. mi., being larger than Vermont and smaller than Maryland. Under the Romans it was the heart of Dacia, with a net-work of Roman roads, and an active business and administrative life. Submerged by the invasions, it disappears till we come upon mention in the Hungarian chroniclers of the twelfth and thirteenth centuries, of "Romanorum coloni et pastores" (Roumanian peasants and shepherds) in these parts; and the famous "Notarius Regis Belæ" (secretary of King Béla) tells us of Hungarian victories over the combined Bulgarian and Roumanian troops of a Duke Glad, ruler of this territory. The natives were Greek Orthodox in belief. In 1233 we find mention of a Hungarian ruler (Ban) of the Banat of Severin—the first use of the term; Ban is one of those designations, like Voyevode, which came into Roumanian from the early Slav. His subjects were "Valachi schismatici," i. e., Roumanians of the Oriental Church. They kept a considerable autonomy; Hungarian documents up into the sixteenth century speak of their enjoyment of their own law ("antiqua lex districtûm Valachicalium"), and of their having their own judges ("judices vel kenezii," the latter term, cnez, also being Slav); a charter of 1493 says: "Semper ab antiquo, quo memoria hominum comprehenderet, tali libertate usi fuissent" (they had always enjoyed such

112

freedom from ancient times, so far as the memory of man recollects).

Like Transylvania, the Banat passed under Turkish control as a result of the Battle of Mohács (1526); and when the Austrians finally drove them out, the Turks carried off many of the population as slaves. Vienna imported great numbers of German colonists, largely Suabians; and there were also several waves of Serb immigration from the South, beginning in 1389, after the Serb defeat of Kossovo, and 1459, when the Serb state disappeared; King Matthias Corvinus, in a letter to the Pope, even represents their numbers as 200,000; but this would appear to be a pious exaggeration. The bulk of the Serb population probably dates from the movement of 1690 on, when 30,000 families crossed the Danube to accept Emperor Leopold's offer of land and privileges if they would help expel the Turk. They went at first into Southern Hungary, but then began dribbling over the Theiss into the Banat, especially after 1718. Hungarians, who had always been scarce in the Banat, came along with them; and the Germans poured in, after 1720, in ever-increasing numbers; indeed, had they not been decimated by malaria, to which, as we have seen, the Roumanian race is singularly resistant, they would probably have become the dominant race in the Banat.

Meanwhile the Roumanian nobility had largely become Roman Catholic; the Serbs captured the Orthodox Church organization, and for 150 years the Orthodox Roumanians were subordinated to the Serb Patriarch of Carlowitz, and had to worship in Church Slavonic. Not till 1865 were the Roumanians granted the right to have two Roumanian Orthodox Bishops (at Caransebesh and Temeshvar), subordinate to the new Roumanian Metropolitan in Transylvania; there was already a Uniate (Greek Catholic) Bishop at Lugosh. From the political point of view, they had much the same experience as the Transylvanians; from 1869 to 1881, they had a few representatives in the Hungarian Parliament, among whom were the Mocsonyis (Mocionis) (a Macedonian Kutzo-Vlach family), two of whom were elected to the first Parliament of Greater Roumania. In 1881 they adopted the policy of parliamentary inaction which had prevailed several years in Transylvania, and did not vote till 1906, except that in 1888 they elected Gen. Trajan Doda, though he was not officially a candidate. He declined to accept the post so long as Roumanians were deprived of full political rights—a criticism which cost him a condemnation to two years' imprisonment!

The Banat always formed a political unit; for administrative purposes it has been divided into three counties, the Torontal, Temesh and Carash-Severin. The Torontal is the western plain and marsh country, given up to grain-raising and vineyards, with a population (in 1910) of 615,000; it is an extraordinary conglomeration of Germans, Magyars, Serbs and Roumanians; the two former dominate in the towns, while Serbs prevail in the western country districts, and Roumanians in the eastern. In Temesh, part plain and part hills, there are half a million inhabitants; the farmers are mainly Roumanian, except in the two southern districts opposite Belgrade, which are mainly Serb. In Carash-Severin, the eastern county, we find mountains reaching 7000 ft. and over; the population, some 470,000, are overwhelmingly Roumanian. According to the Hungarian census of 1910, the total population of the Banat was 1,582,133; of these, the Roumanians were 592,049 (37%); the Germans, 387,545 (24½%); the Serbs, 284,329 (18%); the Magyars, 221,-509 (14%); the Jews, 20,643 (1.3%); there were also 22,-131 Slovaks, 4872 Croats and 2392 Ruthenians.

The Banat thus presented an inextricable confusion of nationalities. Of the 36 districts, the Roumanians formed more than half the population in 18; the Germans in four; the Serbs in three; the Magyars in one. If a line be drawn from Biserica-Alba (Féher-Templom) to the Muresh, at the junction of the Torontal and Temesh, east of this line 55% of the population is Roumanian; west of it, no nationality has a majority (Serbs, 34%; Germans, 26%; Magyars, 20%; Roumanians, 14%; Slovaks and others, 6%).

The indivisibility of the Banat was recognized by France, Great Britain, Italy and Russia in the Treaty which they drew up with Roumania before she entered the war. According to that treaty (Art. 4), the western boundary of Roumania was to run "from Algyö . . . along the thalweg of the Tisza (Theiss) down to its confluence with the Danube," and then "the thalweg of the Danube down to the present frontier of Roumania. Roumania binds herself not to erect fortifications opposite Belgrade." It was, therefore, definitely agreed by the Powers that the Banat was to become Roumanian, without any division. But at the Peace Conference the French policy of a Greater Jugo-Slavia prevailed, and found powerful reinforcement in the United States Delegation, who hastened to apply their principle of the self-determination of peoples. Mr. Wilson's pronouncement against recognition of secret treaties to which the United States was not a party; the disappearance of Russia as a factor; Roumania's signing the separate Treaty of Bucharest, a technical infringement of the agreement—all these furnished easy excuses for disregarding the inconvenient promises made in the hour of extremity. Delegations of Serbs were heard in support of their claims to the western and southern part of the Banat; a subcommittee of the American Delegation drew up a line of division between Serb and Roumanian based upon numerical preponderance, without any consideration of historical, geographical or economic criteria; and the Peace Conference sanctioned this line of division, which in several cases ran between the village and the school, the farm-house and the out-buildings, and cuts off the Roumanian up-country of Transylvania and the Banat from its natural and immemorial river and canal outlets! I asked a secretary of this subcommittee what he would think of a permanent line between the United States and Canada, or the United States and Mexico, based exclusively upon the census preponderance at any given moment of French Canadians in northern New England, or Mexicans in the southwestern border states. He had no answer.

It took a mixed commission several years to straighten out this line; and not till 1931 did the two countries settle the problems raised by the divided water-courses of the Banat. This new line has already caused deep dissension between Roumanian and Serb—two nationalities who have never fought in the past; and as for the Germans of the Serb Banat, they were aghast at being surrendered to Belgrade. The Serb Banat contains 100,000 Roumanians, while there are only 40,000 Serbs in the Roumanian Banat. There is a special injustice in the transaction, in that a considerable district of Serbia, south of the Danube, has a large Roumanian population. In the four districts of Kraina, Poyarevatz, Timok and Morava, which cover 4700 sq. mi., the Roumanians form either the vast majority or a large proportion of the total population, which was 635,286 in 1900; of these, the Serb census recognizes 122,429 as Roumanians; curiously enough, this is almost identical with the figure of 1859 —122,593—when the four districts had only 282,378! Competent outsiders consider that there are between 200,000 and 250,000 Roumanians in this Timok region of Serbia, in spite of the persistent efforts of the Belgrade government to Serbize them. The Serbs endeavor to denationalize them just as they do the Bulgarians; one of the most distinguished of the Roumanians of Serbia, Dr. Athanasius Popovici, was forced to adopt this latter Slav name, instead of his own, which was Furnica (the Roumanian word for "ant"). It is interesting to compare the methods of the Hungarians, which we have studied in Transylvania, and of the Serbs, who made their most chauvinistic statesman out of a boy born Bulgarian, in a recently annexed valley (and I say nothing of Greek methods), with the easy-going tolerance of Roumania. The Roumanians even allowed Hungarian propaganda schools, in Hungarian, among the Szeklers who live over the line in Moldavia; and they always welcomed the German schools in Bucharest, Jassy and elsewhere.

The Serbs even have another group of Roumanians under their control, but at a distance from the frontier—down in Old Serbia and Macedonia. In another chapter we have discussed these interesting Wallachians of the Balkans, the Kutzo-Vlachs or Aromâni. In the vilayets of Monastir and Kossovo, especially in the former, live many thousands of these Kutzo-Vlachs. According to Roumanian statistics, they would total nearly 100,000. I think there can be little doubt that there are altogether at least 300,000 Roumanians in Serbia, so that the Roumanians were somewhat justified in their feeling that the annexation of 285,000 Serbs in the Banat would form a suitable counterpoise—especially as the Serbs of the Banat retain under Roumanian government the right to the use of their own language in church services and schools—a right denied for generations to the Roumanians in Serbia. Much of the Serb insistence upon a share of the Banat is due to the great possibilities of this province, which is not only wealthy agriculturally, but has large manufactur-

ing establishments. The Banat will be the industrial nucleus
of Greater Roumania, and will lead in making an industrial
state out of the present agricultural conditions. Its present
population (1930) is 932,675.

The Crishana and the Maramuresh were the other Hungarian territories prevailingly Roumanian, and assigned to
the new Roumania by the treaty with the Powers. The Crishana (so called from the river Crish, Hung. Cörös) has the
Maramuresh and Hungary to the north and west, the Banat
on the south and Transylvania to the east. The Maramuresh
(Hung. Marmoros, from the river Muresh, Hung. Moros)
is bounded on the north by Galicia, on the south by Transylvania and the Crishana, on the west by the Crishana and
Hungary, and on the east by the Bucovina. The western
Crishana is plain country; it becomes hilly as one goes east,
and the Maramuresh is prevailingly mountainous.

The Crishana is composed of nine counties; of these only
three come under our consideration as prevailingly Roumanian—those of Arad, Bihor and Salagiu, plus four adjoining communes of other counties. This region comprises
a little over 8000 sq. mi., or nearly the area of New Jersey,
with a population (in 1910) of 1,316,981, of whom, according
to the Hungarian religious census, 486,014 were Greek Orthodox, 208,737 Greek Catholic, 204,298 Roman Catholic,
337,806 Reformed, 22,713 Evangelical, 625 Unitarians and
52,769 Jews. Subtracting from the combined Greek Orthodox and Catholics the Serbs, Ruthenians, etc., we have 694,-
129 members of these churches who were not Slav, and,
therefore, Roumanian—52.7% of the total population of this
region of the Crishana.

The Maramuresh contains three counties, part of one of
which (Ugocea) is on the right bank of the Theiss. Taking
the two other counties (Maramuresh and Satul Mare), to-

gether with the eight communes of Ugocea on the left bank of the Theiss, we have an area of 6232 sq. mi., a trifle larger than that of Connecticut, with a population of 766,666. Applying the religious test to the Hungarian official figures of 1910, we have a total of 278,284 non-Slav Greek Orthodox and Catholics (i. e., Roumanians), or 36.3%; 219,731 Hungarians, or 28.7%; 159,585 Ruthenians, or 20.8%; 96,396 Jews, or 12.6%.

These districts of the Crishana and the Maramuresh (population in 1930, 1,412,213) have in general had a similar development and history with Transylvania and the Banat. About 73% of their population is agricultural, and 11% dependent on industry. In the break-up of the Austro-Hungarian Empire at the close of the war, these districts united with Transylvania and the Banat in a great Roumanian demonstration, with 40,000 participants, at Alba-Julia (Karlsburg); and on November 18, 1918, this Roumanian National Assembly, under the presidency of Dr. Stephen C. Pop, who had had to suffer Magyar persecution when a Roumanian Deputy at Buda-Pesth, voted

"the union of these Roumanians and of all the territories which they inhabit, with Roumania. The National Assembly proclaims in particular the inalienable right of the Roumanian nation over the entire Banat, as comprised within the courses of the Muresh, the Theiss and the Danube.

II. The National Assembly reserves, for the above-indicated territories, provisional autonomy, up to the meeting of the Constitutional Convention elected on the basis of universal suffrage.

III. In consequence, as fundamental principles for the constitution of the new Roumanian State, the National Assembly proclaims:

1. Complete national liberty for all the peoples dwelling with the Roumanians. Each people is to receive instruction,

administration and justice in its own tongue, from persons chosen from among its own representatives, and each people shall have right of representation in the legislative bodies and in the government of the country, proportional to the number of persons constituting each people.

2. Equality of rights and complete autonomous confessional freedom for all the religious confessions of the State.

3. The definitive institution of a purely democratic régime in every field of public life. Universal direct secret communal proportional suffrage for both sexes, from the age of 21, for representation in the communes, departments or Parliament.

4. Absolute liberty of the press, of association and of public meeting; liberty of propaganda for all human ideas.

5. Radical agrarian reform. A census of all estates shall be made, particularly of the large estates. In accordance with this census, with cancellation of the *fidei-commis*, and on the basis of the right of cutting down large estates according to the needs, the peasant will be given the possibility of creating for himself a property (agricultural, in pasturage or forests) at least in such measure that his family and he can work it. The principle directing this agrarian policy is on the one hand the progress of social levelling, on the other the increase of production.

6. Industrial workers are assured of the same rights and advantages as are given them by the law in the most advanced western industrial states.

IV. The National Assembly expresses the desire that the Peace Congress create a League of Nations, free in such wise that right and liberty may be assured for all nations, small and great, equally, and that in the future, war may disappear as a means of regulating international relations.

V. The Roumanians united in this National Assembly salute their brethren in the Bucovina, who have escaped from the yoke of the Austro-Hungarian Monarchy, and are united with their mother-country, Roumania.

VI. The National Assembly salutes with love and enthusiasm the liberation of the nations which have up to the present supported the yoke of the Austro-Hungarian Monarchy—the Czecho-Slovak, Austro-German, Jugo-Slav, Polish and Ruthenian Nations. . . .

IX. For the further direction of the affairs of the Roumanian Nation of Transylvania, the Banat and Hungary, the National Assembly decides upon the institution of a Great National Roumanian Council, which shall have all authority to represent the Roumanian Nation in all circumstances and everywhere, before all the nations of the world, and to take all the steps it shall judge necessary in the interests of the Nation."

On December 11, 1918, King Ferdinand of Roumania issued the following decree:

"Art. I. Provisionally and until the final organization of completed Roumania, we charge with the direction of the public services in the territories designated in the decree-law no. 3631, the Directing Council appointed by the National Assembly of Alba-Julia, of the 18th November (1st December) 1918.

II. The Royal Government shall however administer foreign affairs, the army, the railroads, posts, telegraphs, telephones, fiduciary circulation, the customs, public debt and public security of the State.

III. The territories united to the kingdom of Roumania by the decision of the National Assembly of Alba-Julia of the 18th Nov. 1918, shall be represented in the government by Ministers without portfolio.

IV. For operations affecting these territories there shall be nominated by royal decree in the ministerial departments, on the proposal of the Ministers without portfolio, special counselors.

V. The Directing Council has as its first mission to present to us, within the shortest possible time, for the territories over which its administration extends, the bill for electoral reform on the basis of universal suffrage, and the bill for agrarian reform.

VI. Our President of the Council of Ministers is charged with the execution of the present decree-law.

Done at Bucharest, Dec. 11, '18

FERDINAND.

The President of the Council of Ministers,
JOHN J. C. BRATIANO."

This was followed in January by a unanimous vote of the Germans (Saxons) of Transylvania in favor of union with Roumania. Meeting at Hermannstadt (Sibiu) on January 8, they resolved as follows:

"World events have created for the territory in which the Saxon people of Transylvania have established their homes these nearly 800 years, an unprecedented situation. King Ferdinand of Roumania, in his decree of Dec. 27, 1918, has proclaimed and established Roumanian dominion over this territory. The people which is the most numerous in Transylvania and the adjoining parts of Hungary has decreed, in the National Assembly of Alba-Julia, its union with Roumania. By this union of Transylvania and the parts of Hungary inhabited by Roumanians, with Roumania, will be created a common territorial unit, founded on an ethnographic basis. In the presence of these facts, and with the conviction that it is a world event, the Saxon people of Transylvania, resting on the right of peoples to dispose freely of themselves, proclaim their union with the kingdom of Roumania, and transmit to the Roumanian people their fraternal salutation and their cordial wishes for the complete realization of their national ideal.

In this, the Saxon people of Transylvania take account not merely of historical evolution, but also of the fundamental rights of the Roumanian people to unite and form one state, and declare that they expect confidently that the Roumanian people and the Roumanian State, at whose disposal the Saxon people put their hereditary virtues, will be animated towards them by the highest sentiments of justice. The Saxon people, who for centuries enjoyed an autonomous constitutional administration of which they were deprived illegally and in contradiction with solemn and legal affirmations, expect furthermore that never in the future will they be hindered from asserting and developing the consciousness of their political and national unity, and that the new State will offer and grant them voluntarily in the future everything that they consider indispensable for their existence." After quoting the bill of rights enunciated in the Resolutions of Alba-Julia, they conclude: "Fully cognizant of the importance of their resolve, the Saxon people consider themselves henceforward as a part of the Roumanian State; they consider their sons and daughters as citizens of this State. They pray God to guide fruitfully and to bless this step full of responsibilities which they have felt themselves obliged to take.

At Mediasch, Jan. 8, 1919.

The National Saxon Assembly,
The National German-Saxon Council for Transylvania,
Dr. Schullerus, Pres.
Dr. Hans Otto Roth, Secr."

Transylvania had been ably represented at the Peace Conference by Dr. Vaida Voevod, one of her leading politicians, who had had to suffer several times at the hands of the Hungarian masters of the province. After Bratiano, and later Mishu, returned to Bucharest, he represented Roumania also, and held out manfully against the whole force of the Entente endeavoring to make him sign the Minorities Treaty. I was present at an interesting conversation in Paris in October, 1919, in which Vaida, replying to the advice of an American diplomat that he sign the Treaty at once, spoke

eloquently and forcefully; he said the Hungarians had put
him in prison for his defense of Roumanian rights, and he
would cut off his hand before he signed the Treaty in its
present shape.

In November, 1919, I saw Dr. Vaida again at Bucharest,
with Dr. Julius Maniu, perhaps the most distinguished of the
Roumanians of Transylvania. Each later became Premier.
Meanwhile in Transylvania the Roumanians had unearthed
two Hungarian plots aiming at an armed rebellion. They
were engineered in each case by former officers and officials
of the Austro-Hungarians, and were helped unfortunately
by high church officials; I am informed that the highest dig-
nitary of one church was involved. One can imagine what
would have happened to him, on mere suspicion, at the hands
of the French in Alsace, or the Poles in Posen; the Roumanians merely let him know that they were apprised of his
participation, and left him untouched in his church jurisdiction! That was their general procedure; they found six different systems of law in their new dominions, and spent
many years in replacing them. Would we had been as reasonable in Porto Rico, where we tried to introduce American
law overnight!

These plots were not confined to Transylvania. During
French occupation of the Banat, Hungarians there worked
up a scheme to declare a republic, later to be joined to Hungary, and thus keep the mineral and agricultural wealth of
the province under Hungarian control. Explicit rumors connected Béla Kun, who was prominent in this scheme, and
certain Allied financiers. It is even alleged that the severing
of the Serb section of the Banat from Roumania, was not
so much due to solicitude for the self-determination of
peoples as to the greater complaisance of the Serbs to out-

side concession-seekers—an explanation given also for the Fiume episode.

We have now traced the development of the Principalities and of the Roumanian Irredenta, up to the World War. For completeness' sake, we have sketched the process by which various segments of the Irredenta became fused with Roumania later. Now we shall return to 1914, and try to give the essentials of the part Roumania played in the war.

CHAPTER XIV

ROUMANIA IN THE WORLD WAR

MUCH interesting testimony to the preliminaries of the war comes from Roumania. Nicholas Flondor, at that time Secretary of State of the Bucovina under the Austrians, and in 1919 a representative of that province at Bucharest, noted that on March 17, 1914, the officers and men of the Austrian Landsturm received written orders from the military authorities which told them to which branch of the service they would be assigned in a general mobilization, and where they should report. Flondor was greatly impressed, since nothing of the kind had taken place even after the capture of Scutari by the Montenegrins. In May, 1914, he went down to Vienna to negotiate a loan of eight million crowns for the Bucovina administration, and interviewed Baron Popper, president of the Wiener Bankverein. He refused to accede to the request, and when pressed by Flondor for a reason, confessed that he was providing Bulgaria with 20 million crowns for military expenditures. "You know," Baron Popper continued, "we are on the eve of a world war. That is why we must enable Bulgaria to enter the war as our ally, to counterbalance the power of Roumania, a neighbor we cannot rely on in the case of a general conflict."

On June 26, 1914, the day of the funeral of the Archduke Francis Ferdinand, Flondor happened to be again in Vienna, and ran across Brig. Gen. Karl von Perztyansky, military commander of Buda-Pesth. Flondor was on his way to Holland, and asked for information from his military friend.

The latter said to him: "The war against Serbia cannot be avoided; in fact it has been prepared for months" (as we know from Italian sources) "and worked out to the smallest detail. It will be just a military walk-over. The assassination of the Archduke provides the pretext we needed for declaring war. But if the Archduke had not been murdered, we should have found another pretext, as, e. g., the question of the Oriental railroads. Our aim is to end the Pan-Slav agitation, which threatens the very existence of Austria."

Flondor at once objected that neither Russia, France nor England was likely to stand idly by and watch the annihilation of Serbia. Von Perztyansky replied: "If Russia should help Serbia, from the very opening of hostilities she would find herself threatened with a revolution in the Ukraine. The ground has been carefully prepared there by our military agents, who would instantly block any action from that quarter. As for France, the French Socialists would never let their country go to war for a Balkan question. England has only a small army, and on that account is not in the least to be feared. Her navy would find the German navy ready to oppose it everywhere. In case of a European conflict, the chances are, as you see, that Germany and Austria would win the war. We should then take Saloniki, which we need for our Eastern trade, and Germany would appropriate Antwerp, thereby gaining control of the North Sea."

This interview shows that the Austrians did not reckon on Roumanian coöperation, in spite of Roumanian relations to the Triple Alliance, her economic dependence on Germany and Austria, and her German King. Their scepticism was quite justified. A Crown Council, presided over by King Charles, decided on neutrality, and notified Vienna (as did Italy) that there was no obligation of aid under the Treaty, since Austria's action was aggressive, not defensive. King

Charles' sympathies were largely with his native land; he was an old man in delicate health, and the shock of the war was too much for him; he died in October, 1914. As Carmen Sylva and he had no living children, he was at once succeeded by his nephew, Ferdinand, who had now lived for many years in Roumania. King Ferdinand deserves the greatest praise for his whole-souled devotion to Roumania. A German born and bred, educated at the Düsseldorf Gymnasium and the University of Leipsic, speaking both English and Roumanian with a German accent, he nevertheless turned a deaf ear to the appeals of his German kinsmen. The King was immeasurably aided by the extraordinary ability and attractiveness of Queen Marie; her many months of work as a hospital nurse during the war, in real privation, have never been forgotten. I have never seen more genuine enthusiasm than the wild cheering that followed the mention of her name at the opening of the first Parliament of Greater Roumania; and when the historian Professor Iorga proposed a cheer for Queen Marie, "Mama rănitzilor" (Mother of the wounded), the whole assembly leaped to its feet in a demonstration of profound admiration and devotion for the stately woman who stood blushingly bowing her acknowledgments beside the King. The King's services to his country and the Entente stand out in all the higher relief when one observes the course of other German royalties in southeastern Europe.

The first few months of the war were accompanied by great confusion in Roumanian politics. Some of the most distinguished of the older generation of Roumanian statesmen, like Peter Carp and Alexander Marghiloman, had always been anti-Russian or sympathetic toward Germany, and felt that German capital and enterprise had been of the greatest

KING FERDINAND

KING FERDINAND AND QUEEN MARIE, (IN LOCAL COSTUME), GREETING TRANSYL-
VANIAN PEASANT GIRLS, MAY 25, 1919

benefit to Roumania. Take Jonesco, Roumania's most brilliant lawyer, had had close affiliations with German interests. Fear of the Russian colossus and resentment for the seizure of Bessarabia neutralized much of the enthusiasm for France and the sympathy with Belgium. Nevertheless Roumanian public sentiment was distinctly behind Bratiano, whose policy looked toward participation in the war on the side of the Allies, if Roumania could be assured of the help she needed in money and munitions; she had no arsenal, and her army chiefs were aghast at the new requirements of warfare, disclosed as the struggle progressed. The Germans and Austrians maintained an expensive propaganda, buying newspapers and corrupting various of the lesser fry of politicians; and toward the end, when they saw Roumania was probably coming in against them, they made desperate overtures in return for continued neutrality. Marghiloman told me that he was promised by the Germans, if Roumania would only stay neutral, the whole of Bessarabia; the southern Bucovina, including Suceava but not Czernowitz; and immediate autonomy, with their own Diet, for the Roumanians of Hungary—a concession the Germans had extorted from the Hungarians. From the coldly calculating point of view, this would seem to have been the better bargain, since the Germans would doubtless have been beaten eventually without Roumania's assistance, the Transylvanian Diet would have voted annexation just as did the similar Assembly of Alba-Julia, and Roumania would have been spared the Calvary she had to undergo; while the example of Greece shows how lukewarmness in the Allied cause won extensive rewards from the Solons of the Paris Conference. But sympathy with Serbia and France and later the highly influential example of Italy (with which country Roumanian affiliations have always been close), combined with distrust of Germany and Austria, and bitter dislike of Hungary, Bulgaria and Turkey, turned the scales.

The Entente had had no reason to complain of Roumania's neutrality; she had cut down her grain exports to the minimum required for the arms and munitions she was buying from her only available source. She facilitated transport of material for Serbia, and refused to transmit that for Turkey. These and other manifestations of friendly neutrality were acknowledged by Russia in an agreement of October 1, 1914, by which Russia promised to support Roumania's claims to the Roumanian parts of Austro-Hungary. In the spring of 1915 the Entente asked Roumania to enter the war; the Roumanian Government pointed out that it would be necessary first to specify distinctly the boundaries which would be given Greater Roumania in case of victory; that Roumania must be assured of sufficient arms and munitions immediately; and that measures must be taken to protect Roumania from a flank attack by Bulgaria. These considerations, which must appear elementary to any one who has studied the history of Roumania's relations with the Great Powers, particularly Russia, and which appear furthermore almost prescient of the Paris Conference, gave certain of the Allies pause, and diplomatic effort was concentrated on Bulgaria and Greece, with lamentable results.

We have a dramatic account of the decisive Crown Council in "La Roumanie" (Take Jonesco's organ) of March 6, 1921, based on notes made at the time by "one of the participants." King Ferdinand sat at the center of the table, with Premier J. J. C. Bratiano opposite him, to his right Crown Prince Carol, and to his left ex-Premier Theodore Rosetti, ex-Premier Titus Maioresco and Premier-to-be Alexander Marghiloman. Ex-Premier Peter Carp, the veteran Conservative and Germanophile, sat next the Prince; to Bratiano's right were his Ministers; to his left Speaker Ferechide, Senate Vice-President Robescu, the party chiefs Take Jonesco and Nicholas Filipescu, ex-Speakers Cantacuzene-Pashcanu and Olanescu. The King was under the stress of deep emotion; having made up his mind that Roumania should intervene on the side of the Allies, he had argued with Maioresco the night before, but to no avail. The Italian Minister had also pleaded with him, telling him that as a Transylvanian he might hope to be Minister in the first Government of Greater Roumania. But Maioresco, impressed with Germany's strength, held out for neutrality.

King Ferdinand opened the session by saying that he had summoned the country's leaders, not to ask their advice, for he had come to a decision, but to request their support. Neutrality was no longer possible; Roumania must side with the Entente against the Central Powers. Being a Hohenzollern, he had suffered greatly in coming to this view, and had had to conquer himself; his victory was to him the proof that he had chosen the right path for his country. He begged their united support of him, a good Roumanian. Still, he would ask all who held contrary views to state them, and called first on Carp. Carp, however, said he saw no reason to call this council, since its decision was already made, and refused to speak; whereupon the King called on Bratiano. The Liberal Premier felt that Roumania could no longer stay neutral without moral bankruptcy; since Roumania had an ideal, national unity, she should take advantage of the occasion to realize it. Roumania had recovered her liberty of action, as regards the Triple Alliance, just as Italy had; he had already pledged her assistance to the Entente, and taken military steps to relieve the Roumanians across the Carpathians. Carp again refused to speak; Take Jonesco congratulated the Sovereign, and promised his party's support. Marghiloman was apprehensive, in view of the Germans' strength, and the blow he had learned they were preparing against the Russians. He felt that the country was not in favor of war, and that the Roumanians in Hungary were not anxious to come into the Kingdom. The definite result of Roumanian success with the Allies would be the installation of Russia at the Dardanelles, with the consequent choking of Roumania. "But," interrupted the King, "admitting that the Russians take Constantinople, which will be preferable for us, to be their friends or enemies?" Filipescu recalled that the understanding with Russia of October 1, 1914, had been approved by Marghiloman, and he pledged the unanimous support of his party.

And now Carp broke his silence. This war can only result, he said, in German or Russian supremacy. The latter would be fatal to Roumania, for she would bar Russia's way to Constantinople, and fatal to the dynasty, for Russia would install some family friendly to her. Carp was so convinced that Roumania should enter the war on Germany's side that in contrary case he would pray for defeat, as the only means of her salvation, though his three sons were in the army. The King and Bratiano protested, but Carp said he had come to that decision only after long reflection, and abode by it.

At a question from Maioresco, Bratiano stated that he was already bound to the Allies, and that in his judgment the country also was morally bound. He had postponed entry into the war as long as possible, but he had just learned that the Allies were about to treat with Hungary. Maioresco said he felt the issue was still too doubtful for Roumania to take sides; furthermore, his information was that the Roumanians of Hungary wanted to remain under the Hapsburgs, and have German protection against the Magyars. Both Bratiano

and Take Jonesco protested against this, Bratiano adding
that he had letters from Vaida and other Transylvanians diametrically opposed to Maioresco's understanding. Nevertheless, said Maioresco, what Roumania should have done
was to negotiate with the Hungarians to better the lot of the
the Transylvanian Roumanians. Here the King protested
again, saying that both before and after the declaration of
war he had begged both Germany and Czernin to make the
Magyars give the Transylvanians at least as much freedom
as the Czechs of Bohemia enjoyed, and that before the war
Emperor William had gone to Vienna on this very errand,
but without success. The King added that he was convinced
that Germany could not gain this from the Hungarians; he
had made many efforts, but in vain. Maioresco, however,
still objected, finally asking to have elections held on the
issue of war or neutrality—the only suggestion that brought
a smile. To a statement of Costinescu, one of Bratiano's
ministers, that whether Russia or Germany held the Straits,
it was a misfortune for Roumania, the King remarked that
he was not afraid of Russia, but if he were, he would much
prefer a Greater Roumania to undertake the anti-Russian
defense. Take Jonesco brought out an interesting bit of history, that in 1911 Vaida and other prominent Transylvanians
proposed to Roumanian leaders that national unity should be
achieved by all entering the Hapsburg Empire, as the only
practical method of realizing the national ideal; but since
1914 their views had changed, and they were now convinced
all should act together against the Central Empires.

In a moving peroration, Bratiano said that like his father,
he was a Roumanian only, not a Russophile or a Germanophile. Those who opposed war, overlooked the moral question involved. He did not feel certain of victory, but even
though conquered, they might rest assured of national unity;

Italy was defeated at Novara, but union arrived soon afterward. Michael the Brave was the national hero, because he had crossed into Transylvania; it would be the same with King Ferdinand. The Hohenzollern dynasty was no longer foreign, but after the King had passed the Carpathians, the question would never be raised again. This the King confirmed; and in closing, he pleaded for their united support, since the responsibility would fall on them all.

All difficulties were now overcome; and on August 16, 1916, the Allies and Roumania signed the secret Treaty of Bucharest. This is a document of such importance that I reproduce it here in full:

Art. I. France, Great Britain, Italy and Russia guarantee the territorial integrity of the Kingdom of Roumania in the total extent of its present boundaries.

II. Roumania binds herself to declare war and to attack Austria-Hungary in accordance with the conditions stipulated by the Military Agreement; Roumania promises also to discontinue all economic relations and commercial exchanges with the enemies of the Allies, as soon as she declares war.

III. France, Great Britain, Italy and Russia acknowledge Roumania's right to annex the territories of the Austro-Hungarian Monarchy stipulated and set by Article IV.

IV. The limits of the territories mentioned in the preceding article are set as follows:

The line of delimitation will start on the Pruth at a point of the present frontier between Roumania and Russia near Novosulitza and will ascend this river as far as the frontier of Galicia at the confluence of the Pruth and the Ceremos. After that it will follow the frontier of Galicia and Bucovina, and that of Galicia and Hungary, up to the point Steag (hill 1655). From that point it will follow the line of separation of the waters of the Theiss and the Viso until it reaches the Theiss at the village of Trebuza up-stream from the spot where it unites with the Viso. Starting from that point it will go down along the thalweg of the Theiss to a distance of 4 kilometers down-stream from its confluence with the Szamos, leaving the village of Vasares-Nemény to Roumania. It will then continue in a SSW direction to a point 6 km. east of the town of Debreczin. From that point it will reach the Crish (Körös) 3 km. down-stream from the union of its two affluents (the White Crish and the Swift Crish). It will then join the Theiss on a line with the village of Algyö, north of Szegedin, passing to the west of the villages of Croshaza and Bekessamson; 3 km. from the latter it will make a slight curve. From Algyö the line will descend the thalweg of the Theiss down to its confluence with the Danube, and will finally follow the thalweg of the Danube down to the present frontier of Roumania.

Roumania binds herself not to erect fortifications opposite Belgrade in a zone to be later delimited, and to keep in that zone only the forces necessary for police service.

The Royal Roumanian Government binds itself to indemnify the Serbs of the region of the Banat who might want to abandon their properties and emigrate within a space of two years from the conclusion of peace.

V. Roumania on the one hand, and France, Great Britain, Italy and Russia on the other promise not to conclude a separate peace or general peace except conjointly and simultaneously. France, Great Britain, Italy and Russia bind themselves as well that at the Peace Treaty the territories of the Austro-Hungarian Monarchy stipulated in Art. IV shall be annexed to the Crown of Roumania.

VI. Roumania shall enjoy the same rights as the Allies in all that concerns the preliminaries of the peace negotiations, as well as the discussion of the questions which will be submitted to the decisions of the Peace Conference.

VII. The contracting Powers bind themselves to keep the present convention secret until the conclusion of the general peace.

Article II of this secret Treaty of Bucharest speaks of a Military Convention entered into at the same time. To understand the extent to which Roumania was misled by the representatives of the Allies, it is essential to study this document also:

Art. I. Following the Treaty of Alliance concluded on the 4/17 August, 1916, between France, Great Britain, Italy, Russia and Roumania, Roumania binds herself by mobilizing all her forces on land and sea, to attack Austria-Hungary at the latest on Aug. 15/28, 1916 (eight days after the offensive of Saloniki). The offensive operations of the Roumanian Army will begin on the day of the declaration of war.

II. As soon as the present agreement is signed, and during the mobilization and concentration of the Roumanian Army, the Russian Army undertakes to act in a specially energetic way along the whole Austrian front so as to ensure the above-mentioned Roumanian operations. This action will be especially offensive and energetic in the Bucovina, where the Russian troops will have at any rate to maintain their present positions and effectives.

Beginning with the 12/25 August, 1916, the Russian fleet will have to ensure the security of the port of Constantza, prevent the disembarkation of enemy troops on the Roumanian coast, and any incursion on the Danube up-stream from the mouths of this stream.

On her part Roumania will acknowledge the right of the Russian Black Sea Fleet to utilize the port of Constantza and take the necessary measures against the enemies' submarine fleet.

The Russian warships which will use the Danube for protecting the banks as well as for giving aid to the Roumanian Army and Fleet, will be under the command of the Commander-in-Chief of the Roumanian Armies, and will cooperate on that stream with the squadron of Russian monitors. The details of this coöperation will be settled according to the articles of the present Agreement.

III. Russia binds herself at the moment of the mobilization of the Roumanian Army, to send into the Dobrudja two infantry divisions and one cavalry division to coöperate with the Roumanian Army against the Bulgarian Army.

The Allies bind themselves to precede by at least a week the entry of Roumania into the war by a determined offensive of the Armies at Saloniki, in order to facilitate the mobilization and concentration of all the Roumanian military forces. This offensive will begin on the 7/20 August, 1916.

If, during the military operations, the Allied Powers, after an agreement between the respective General Staffs, should be induced to increase their military forces coöperating with the Roumanian Army, this increase of forces will not modify in anything the stipulations of the concluded agreements.

IV. France, Great Britain, Italy and Russia undertake to furnish to Roumania munitions and war material which will be transported by Roumanian or Allied vessels and transited through Russia.

These deliveries and transports are to be executed so as to assure the arrival in Roumania as continuously as possible of a minimum of 300 tons per diem, calculated at one month of transport.

Should the Allies have at their disposal new ways of access facilitating the transit of ammunition, Roumania may have the benefit of them.

V. The Allies undertake the engagement as well of furnishing to Roumania, within the limits of possibility, the horses, tires, medicaments, articles of subsistence and equipment which she may ask for in the quantities and categories which shall be fixed by mutual agreement.

VI. The Allies will put at Roumania's disposal the technical personnel necessary for the manufacture in that country of ammunition and war material.

VII. As soon as the present agreement is concluded, the General Staffs of the Russo-Roumanian Armies, as well as the General Staffs of the Armies of Saloniki, will come to an agreement for determining the exact form of their coöperation.

The accord during military operations of the Russo-Roumanian Armies or any change, elucidation and supplement with a view to establishing a permanent liaison, will be settled at respective Headquarters, as stated lower down.

VIII. The coöperation of the Allied Armies does not imply the subordination of one of the contracting parties to the other, it implies only the free acceptance of the dispositions or modifications due to the general situation, to the necessities of the object aimed at, and to brotherhood in arms.

IX. Generally speaking, the Royal Roumanian troops and the Imperial Russian troops retain their own Command, their distinct zone of operations and complete independence in the conduct of operations. The line of demarcation between the two armies will run from Dorna Vatra through the Bistritza and Chaio and Samesh valleys to Debreczin. The principal objective of the Roumanian action, as far as the military situation south of the Danube will permit, will be through Transylvania in the direction of Buda-Pesth.

The Russian troops provided by Art. III, intended to coöperate with the Roumanian Army, will be under the Supreme Command of the Roumanian Army.

In case the Russian contingent operating south of the Danube should be considerably increased, so as to be of equal or superior strength to the Roumanian troops with which it will coöperate, this contingent may form upon exit from Roumanian territory an independent army which will be placed under the Supreme Russian Command.

In this event, that Army when operating outside Roumanian territory must have a distinct zone of operations, and will be conducted under the orders of the Russian Supreme Command, though it must act in entire accordance with the plans of the two Headquarters, on the bases established above.

If, in view of the object aimed at, military operations with combined Russo-Roumanian forces should take place, the command of this force would be indicated by the respective zone of operations. All orders and instructions regarding the direction of these operations will be drawn up in Roumanian and in Russian.

X. In principle, the armies of the one contracting party may not enter the national territory or occupied territory of the other, except if the general interest and the common object should demand it, and only with a written preliminary agreement in each particular instance.

XI. On each occasion when during the operations the Allied Armies may be obliged to use a railway or railways on the territory of the Allied State for transporting troops, provisions and military requirements, their use will be determined in each particular case by the Delegates of General Allied Headquarters. The administration and organization of transports and revictualling from local resources will fall in each instance to the territorial authorities.

XII. The prisoners, war booty and trophies taken by one Army will belong to it.

The war booty taken in common engagements and on the same battlefield shall be divided proportionately to the participating effectives. Nevertheless, in order to facilitate the provisioning of the Roumanian Army, the Imperial Russian Command will deliver up the war material and ammunition included in this common booty, of which the Roumanian Army may have urgent need.

XIII. In order to coördinate the activities of the Roumanian, Russian and Allied Armies, and to carry out with greater assurance their military aims, a representative of the Roumanian Army, assisted if necessary by a certain number of aides, shall be present at Russian and Allied Headquarters at the moment of the opening of Roumanian military operations.

In like manner representatives of the Russian and Allied Armies and their aides shall be at General Headquarters of the Roumanian Army.

The Headquarters of the coöperating armies shall inform each other at the proper time with regard to military conjectures, division of forces and the course of operations.

XIV. If during operations, situations should arise demanding new measures and raising questions not foreseen in the present agreement, these questions will be discussed at each headquarters with the delegate of the Allied Army, but no final action will be taken except with the agreement of the Supreme Commands.

XV. In order to take preparatory measures in time at the beginning of operations, the contracting parties shall come to an understanding with regard to the plan of military action, before the day on which the Roumanian Army opens hostilities.

XVI. The question of armistices shall be decided by common agreement of the Supreme Commands of the coöperating Armies.

XVII. The present Agreement shall remain in force from the day of signing up to the general peace.

Made in five copies at Bucharest
Aug. 4/17, 1916.

The Roumanians entered the war therefore with definite promises of military aid from the Allies; they were to strike westward through Transylvania towards Buda-Pesth, while the Russians should divert Austria by operations in the Bucovina, and Sarrail's offensive from Saloniki should be already a week under way. They were also to receive at least 300 tons daily of war material through Russia.

Mobilization took place rapidly and efficiently, and over 850,000 men were gathered together, 200,000 forming a reserve. This material made 366 battalions of infantry, 106 squadrons of cavalry, and 327 batteries of artillery. There were also four armored monitors, one protected cruiser and several gun-boats and patrol-boats. The land forces made up 23 divisions, with two cavalry divisions. They had only 440,-000 rifles for these 850,000 men, and of this total only 330,-000 were Männlicher rifles (6.5 mm.); the rest were old Martini Henris, and Bulgarian rifles taken in 1913. There were only 1400 field guns, mostly antiquated, and only 500 machine-guns! The Roumanians lacked heavy artillery; were without modern aëroplanes and anti-aircraft guns; had no mountain artillery, grenades, gas-masks, gas shells, helmets, etc., and were very short of automobiles, telephones and other technical material, and modern outfits for officers and soldiers. The Allies were exactly informed of these deficiencies, and also knew how unlikely it was that missing material could be rushed through Russia in time. Roumanians now realize that they were encouraged to come in quite coldbloodedly; that all competent persons in Paris knew that they would be sacrificed, but that the Germans would have to let up the murderous pressure on the western front and send some divisions down to Roumania—which did come about. Indeed, we now have Ludendorff's testimony that it was Roumania's entry that made the Kaiser issue orders stopping operations at Verdun, and thus saving the French. It must also have been known in Paris by the military authorities, if not by the diplomats, that Sarrail would not be able to issue forth from Saloniki, and that the Russians had already become an uncertain quantity.

Of all these engagements entered into by the Treaty and Military Agreement of August, 1916, none was fulfilled but the Roumanian. Their First Army, of six divisions (140,000 men), occupied Oltenia and the mountain frontier up to the sources of the Argesh. The Second, which was the best, had four divisions, with 120,000 men; they guarded the frontier from the Argesh to the Putna Valley. The Northern (or Fourth) Army held the mountains of Moldavia, with three infantry and one cavalry division, totalling over 110,000 men. The Third Army, of six infantry and one cavalry division, with more than 140,000 men, covered the Danube from the Iron Gates to Turtucaia, and then the boundary of the Dobrudja up to Balchic. A strategic reserve, of two divisions with 50,000 men, protected Bucharest on the north and south.

Mobilization began August 14, the eve of the declaration of war, and was practically completed in five days. It called out immediately 13% of the population—a higher proportion than had been reached so quickly anywhere in the West. King Ferdinand's proclamation eloquently expressed the thought of every patriotic Roumanian as he went to his nearest barracks: "After endless periods of misfortune and of painful efforts, our fathers succeeded in founding the Roumanian State on the Union of the Principalities, on the War of Independence, on their tireless labor for the rebirth of the nation. To-day it is given to us to complete their work, building for all time what Michael the Brave fashioned for but a moment—the Union of the Roumanians on both sides the Carpathians. It depends upon us to-day to deliver from foreign oppression our brethren beyond the mountains and in the highlands of the Bucovina, where Stephen the Great sleeps his eternal sleep. In us, in our virtues, in our bravery rests the power of restoring them their rights, so that, in a Roumania that shall be complete and free, from the Theiss to the Sea, they may progress in the peace that is due the destinies and the aspirations of our race. . . . On with God, the Lord!"

Alas, with all this enthusiasm and energy, the failure of

the Allies to act paralyzed all Roumanian initiative. The Russians in the Bucovina gave no signs of life; Gen. Sarrail continued his automobile drives down the boulevards of Saloniki. Marshal Joffre had telegraphed him August 17 to begin the offensive on August 20, as planned; and full light has never been thrown on the reasons for his hesitation. Thus Joffre's masterly plan of utilizing Roumania as an essential factor in the blow to be dealt the Germans that summer, broke down under Russian and Greek lukewarmness. Yet as Ludendorff confesses in his Memoirs, "In spite of our victory over the Roumanian army, we had become on the whole still weaker."

The Roumanian General Staff did not understand this lack of coöperation; but they had obligated themselves to strike westward, and at the very moment that the declaration of war was presented at Vienna, the troops covering the frontier dashed across into Transylvania, striking confusion into the Hungarians. Within a few days they were in possession of the Cerna valley, the coal mines of Petroshani, the plains south of Sibiu, with their center at the village of Shelimberg (Shelimbăr) where Michael the Brave had defeated the Hungarians in 1599, Brashov (Kronstadt) ·and the upper Olt valley. But on the 17th of August, three days after the decree of mobilization, the consequences of Sarrail's defection became painfully evident south of the Danube; the Bulgarians struck at Turtucaia. Under Fieldmarshal Mackensen's leadership, a force of over 120,000 troops, admirably equipped, had gathered along the frontier from Rustchuk to Varna, with a strong concentration between Rustchuk and Rasgrad. They found opposite one good Roumanian division, the 9th, and two inferior, the 17th and 19th, which had some militia battalions, and old 75's and 87's. Mackensen had the 217th German Division, the 1st,

4th, 6th and 12th Bulgarian (a Bulgarian division had 24 battalions, about double the Roumanian number), one Bulgarian cavalry division and one German-Bulgar. He had abundance of armored automobiles, aëroplanes, dirigibles, and captive balloons; the Roumanians had practically none. With 80,000 men he attacked Turtucaia; and after 6 days of desperate fighting, on the afternoon of August 24, the Roumanians began a retreat toward Silistra. Mackensen had struck also further east in the Dobrudja, at Bazargic; and on the 24th the Roumanians here (19th) had to give up, and effect a junction with the remnants of the 9th division, retreating towards Caraomer.

This disaster south of the Danube at once endangered the whole Roumanian southern flank; the victorious advance into Transylvania had to be arrested. The 2nd, 5th, 12th and 15th Divisions were sent back through the mountains to join the 9th and 19th—the 17th had been captured or cut to pieces by Mackensen—in a defense of the Dobrudja line; at least three Russian divisions arrived to help them, with one of Russian cavalry, and one of Czechs and Jugo-Slavs, former Austrian soldiers, captured by the Russians and formed into a Russian division. These combined Russo-Roumanian forces were formed into the Army of the Dobrudja, under a Russian generalissimo, but under the orders of the Third Army commander, who now had charge from the Olt to the Black Sea. The First, Second and Fourth Armies were much weakened by the loss of these divisions, but maintained their name and organization intact. Strategy however was much hampered by the fixed idea of the Russian staff that the Wallachian salient must be abandoned, and the line withdrawn to the Sereth.

The situation was now serious, but not yet critical. By the first of September German troops began appearing in

Transylvania, drawn from both Western and Russian fronts, and from the reserve formed to expel the Russians from the Bucovina. Falkenhayn was put in command of these well-outfitted troops. There were now massed against the Russo-Roumanians 10 German divisions, 7 Austro-Hungarian, 4 Bulgarian, 2 Turkish, with 5 cavalry divisions (2 of them German). Toward the end of November the number had risen to a total of 42½ divisions, of which 21½ were German (5 of them cavalry). By January 1, 1917, Roumania with its 28 divisions, was confronted by 58 enemy divisions!

The new Roumanian Dobrudja army amounted to nearly 100,000 men, of heterogeneous elements—there was one division of mounted Cossacks, of highly debatable value, according to the Roumanians—with only 6 machine-guns to a regiment, and no heavier artillery than 5-inch guns. They had no aviation. Opposite them were 7 German-Bulgarian-Turkish divisions, with 2 of cavalry—some 130,000 men, with 12-inch guns, hundreds of machine-guns, plenty of aviators and two Zeppelins. These advanced steadily till finally held at bay along the Rashova-Tusla line, which cover the Cernavoda-Constantza railroad. Indeed, the Roumanians made in early September a powerful counter-attack which broke up the Bulgarian right wing, and yielded them several thousand prisoners and much equipment.

This attack was also designed to distract attention from a bold maneuver planned to outflank the enemy in the Dobrudja. Five divisions were secretly concentrated along the Danube between Turtucaia and Rustchuk, and on the evening of September 17 a bridge of boats was rapidly thrown across the river at Flamânda; by evening of the 19th the 10th Division was already across, and most of two other divisions. Again the lack of accessories was fatal; Austrian monitors coming down the river and finding

neither torpedoes, mines nor heavy artillery, bombarded the
bridge at will; German and Austrian aëroplanes dropped
tons of bombs on the troops waiting to cross, without having
to guard against anything but rifle fire; and finally Austrian
floating mines blew up the bridge simultaneously in five different places! The whole maneuver had to be abandoned;
the troops were hurriedly brought back to the north bank
over the hastily repaired bridge, and were rushed up into the
mountains to the relief of the Second Army, which was
already being driven down the Câmpulung and Prahova
valleys.

In their advance into Transylvania and the Banat, the
First Army had occupied Orshova and the whole Cerna valley; Petroshani; the heights above Hatzeg; and the plain of
the Olt between the mountains and Sibiu. The Second Army
had seized Făgărash and was enveloping Segesvar (Sigi-
shoara) with its right wing. The North Army had gone down
the Muresh and Tarnava valleys, and had occupied the western outlets of mountain valleys north of the Olt. They had
had no difficulty in beating back the Austro-Hungarian
troops, and had been enthusiastically received by the Roumanian population; but they had had to send back many regiments for the Dobrudja episode, and the Germans at once
took advantage. Gen. von Arz, later commander on the
Italian front, organized an Austrian army at Cluj (Kolozsvár), and Gen. Falkenhayn formed the Ninth German
Army east of Arad. At the end of August they fell upon the
First Army, and for ten days a battle raged for the possession
of the coal mines at Petroshani, which passed into the enemy's hands on September 7. The Roumanians however still
held the ridges which commanded Petroshani. But they were
outflanked by a daring German Alpine corps, which had
started climbing at a point 20 miles west of Sibiu, and for

four days had clambered among the heights of the Carpathians without running across a Roumanian patrol, there being a gap here between the Olt and the Jiu forces. Thus they succeeded in reaching the Olt at Lunci, and actually occupied the trenches, facing northward, which the Roumanians had dug to protect their march forward when they made their way into Transylvania. The Germans now commanded the only channel by which the Roumanian Olt corps could communicate with Roumania. At the same time the enemy's cavalry surrounded the Olt corps on the right, cutting their communications with the Second Army in Făgărash; and the Germans opened a furious frontal attack upon them. By good strategy Gen. Praporgescu, who was coming with reinforcements, succeeded in cleaning out the trenches at Lunci; and in a desperate four days' battle, the Olt Corps finally made its way back into Oltenia, with heavy losses.

Meanwhile the Second Army, which had actually been holding practice maneuvers at Făgărash, since the enemy had vanished in those quarters, received orders to come to the assistance of the Olt Corps, and attack vigorously whatever enemy forces they might meet. After many bloody skirmishes, they inflicted heavy losses on the enemy at Brashov, and by September 26 were holding the frontier, from Buzeu to Dâmbavicioara. The retreat of the Second Army endangered the flank of the North Army, which reached down to Făgărash; they withdrew to the heights west of the Muresh and Olt. Now if ever was the time for the Russians in the Bucovina to come to the Roumanians' assistance; and the Supreme Command felt so reluctant to doubt Russian good faith that they ordered the North Army to halt on the heights east of the Olt and await the Russians. But the latter dribbled in so slowly that the Germans were emboldened to make an attack on the North Army along its entire front;

and it was forced to retire within the Moldavian boundaries, holding open the Bistritza and Trotush passes.

The First, Second and North Armies had now been driven back out of Transylvania. Meanwhile Mackensen kept up pressure, with superior forces and equipment, in the Dobrudja; Constantza fell; and soon the last Roumanian troops had been expelled from the Dobrudja. Since the Dobrudja was prevailingly Turkish and Bulgarian when it fell to Roumania in 1878, and since the southernmost segment of it had been Bulgarian till 1913, the Dobrudja is part of the Bulgarian Irredenta. Rejoicing was widespread at Sofia, where were now to be found representatives of all the lands the Bulgarians considered theirs, from Ochrida to the mouth of the Danube, and Bulgarians from the Dobrudja again took their seats in the Sobranje, beside the Macedonians. Truly, of all the vicissitudes of the war, Bulgaria and Roumania experienced the most poignant. In 1917, the Greater Bulgaria of the Treaty of San Stefano was a reality, and Roumania had shrivelled to part of Moldavia. In 1919, Bulgaria had shrunk within narrower limits than those assigned after her defeat in the Second Balkan War, and Roumania is now governing the wide territories only once before united, by Michael the Brave in 1600.

By the end of September, the Roumanian troops were back on their Carpathian frontier—over 400 miles long, from Dorna to Vârciorova; the Danube-Dobrudja line brought up the whole to 900 miles. The Roumanians now had only half a million troops defending their line, as compared with four and a half million on the western front of 400 miles, and one and a half million on the Italian front of 375 miles; the Russian front, from Dorna to Riga, was about the length of the Roumanian, but was defended by over four million front-line troops.

The enemy's efforts to pierce the mountain line were directed against the Second Army—evidently because of the close proximity of five passes (the Bran, Strunga, Predeal, Bratocea and Buzeu) over any one of which they could soon reach Bucharest, and isolate the First from the North Army. They attacked therefore incessantly, but made only slight advances. Similar attacks were made on the North Army, all through October. But although the Germans had well-organized Alpine troops and batteries for mountain work—something the Roumanians lacked till later, when they formed their first Alpine battalions on French and Italian models—the Roumanians succeeded in holding them all along the Moldavian line. The constant hammering on the Second Army (now composed of only six exhausted divisions, the 3rd, 4th, 6th, 10th, 21st and 22nd) brought no definite results till November 17, when a general retreat of the left wing was ordered. This was caused by tremendous pressure on the First Army, further west; the Austro-Germans had concentrated on two mighty thrusts, one at Orshova on the Danube, the other near the sources of the Argesh. The First Army contained only five divisions, to guard a 300-mile front; these were the 1st, 11th, 13th, 20th and 23rd, of which only the 1st was of prime quality. Gen. Praporgescu had infused new courage and energy into them, and they were holding a line along the Olt valley and the upper Argesh; but one quiet day in late September, a stray shell found him out, and his brilliant career was ended. Nevertheless the troops held out, and even obtained a number of successes against the enemy; the most remarkable was the Battle of the Jiu (October 13-16, 1916). In the upper Jiu valley, between Petroshani and the frontier, the enemy had massed over 30 battalions of picked troops and a division of cavalry, with formidable artillery, in order to crush the 20 Roumanian battalions in their way, and enter Oltenia by the Jiu. Anticipating the attack, the Roumanians appointed Gen. Dragalina, who had won renown by his command of the 1st Division in the Cerna valley, over the whole First Army. The enemy began their attack October 9, and pressed slowly southward till Gen. Dragalina's arrival, the evening of the 11th. Reinforcements began to come in from the Roumanian divisions on the Cerna, the Danube and the Olt—themselves hard pressed by the enemy. With their help Gen. Dragalina worked out a plan of resistance; but on the 12th, in a venturesome reconnaissance, he was badly wounded by German machine-gunners, and died after a few days of suffering. He lived long enough, however, to get the first good news of the Roumanian counter-attack, which commenced the 14th, and drove the enemy in wildest confusion back over the frontier; the Roumanians even captured the cars of the German staff directing the Jiu operations. They annihilated the 11th Bavarian Division (called from its rapid movements the Flying Division), and by the 18th of October had in their hands 2000 prisoners, 42 guns and 55 machine-guns.

But the comparative quiet which prevailed for the moment on other fronts had allowed Falkenhayn to gather seven more German divisions (including two of cavalry). He concentrated immediately after the Roumanian counter-offensive a powerful army at Petroshani, composed of the 41st and 109th German Divisions, a remodeled 11th Bavarian Division, the 144th Austrian Alpine Brigade, and the 6th and 7th German Cavalry Divisions—in all, over 60,000 picked troops, with 250 cannon, among them some 8-inch guns and unnumbered machine-guns. This was named the Kuehne Army, from its commander; and Falkenhayn himself came to Petroshani to map out its campaign. Opposite the Kuehne Army the Roumanians had part of the First Army—26,000 much worn troops, with some 125 guns, none over 4-inch, and less than a hundred machine-guns. Kuehne attacked with overwhelming forces on October 28; early in November he bored his way down the Jiu into Oltenia; and on November 4 his cavalry corps and armored automobiles worked down into the plain. The Cerna and Danube troops further west, in immediate danger of being cut off, began a rapid retreat to rejoin the main body; but they were needed along the Danube to hinder Mackensen's advance, and were halted for that purpose; after fighting heroically, the survivors surrendered at Isbiceni on the Olt the very day (November 23) of the fall of Bucharest.

The First Army was now (November 5) in full retreat across Oltenia, resisting wherever a rise of ground gave cover. By the 9th they were on the Olt, and their line reached Argesh, where they touched the Second Army. They had about 55,000 men. They faced not merely the oncoming Kuehne Army, but the Army of Krafft von Delmensingen, composed of the German 10th Mountain Brigade and 216th Division, an Austrian Alpine corps and their 2nd Mountain Brigade. These two armies had over 120,000 men, with the best of equipment.

The Roumanian Second Army now extended along the Carpathian frontier, from Argesh to the sources of the Putna. They had about 75,000 men. Opposite were the Army of Gen. Morgen, containing the 8th Austrian Mountain Brigade, 12th Bavarian Division, 76th German Division and one Landsturm regiment; and Falkenhayn's left wing, composed of the Hungarian 51st Division, 187th German Division, 87th German Ersatz-division, and the 22nd Bavarian Regiment. These totalled nearly 100,000 men.

The North Army continued the frontier line from the upper Putna to north of the Trotush Pass. Its three divisions numbered about 50,000 men. It was faced by the 1st Austrian Cavalry Division, 71st Austrian Division, 30th Hungarian Division, half of the Austrian 61st Division, one Bavarian and one Austrian Landsturm regiment—altogether some 80,000 men. The Russian Ninth Army extended south from the Bucovina to the North Army. Opposite them lay the Austrian First Army, of 15 divisions, under Gen. von Arz.

The Cerna and Danube detachments on the extreme southwest were pursued by the Szivo Group, consisting of the 145th Austrian Brigade, a brigade of German cyclists, and two Bulgarian militia regiments. The 18th Roumanian Division ran from Olt to the Oltenitza, with a division of recruits as reserve north of the Oltenitza. Russian troops continued the line to Harshova and there were other Russian troops in the Dobrudja, on the Topalu-Tasaul line. Desperate efforts were made to reconstitute the 21st, 9th, 19th, 11th, 23rd and 10th Divisions, a brigade of the 5th and a cavalry brigade; but in the poverty of resources, little could be done. The Germans had further an entire army (of Gen. Koch) in the district south of Zimnicea, of 5 divisions—the 217th German, 1st and 2nd Bulgarian, 26th Turkish and the 5th German Cavalry, under von Goltz. In the Dobrudja, from Turtucaia to Boascic-Tasaul, was a Bulgaro-Turk Army, under the command of the Bulgarian Gen. Tosheff.

This was the situation when a bold maneuver of the Germans precipitated the decisive battle, called the Battle of Argesh or of Bucharest. On the night of the 9th of November Gen. Koch threw a bridge of boats across the Danube at Zimnicea, and by the 13th his five divisions stood north of the river, with only a few miles and a handful of soldiers between them and the metropolis. Bitter fighting in the mountains had drawn the last Roumanian reserves up to the relief of the weary troops on the Olt frontier. Immediately the Roumanian General Staff adopted a brilliant plan which might even yet have succeeded, had it not been for a fatal mischance.

The Roumanian First Army took over the forces defending the Danube, and all the reserves available, and was given the task of holding up the three separate enemy attacks in this region—Gen. Koch's, the drive through Oltenia and the push down from Argesh. If possible, they were to deal Koch a blow throwing his entire army into the Danube. This enemy army contained about 80,000 men, plus two cavalry divisions; the Roumanian forces along the Danube totalled some 30,000. Mackensen had now taken complete control, of Falkenhayn's divisions as well. His plan was that Koch's Army should at once advance on Bucharest and try to draw together all the Roumanian forces, while the Army of Krafft von Delmensingen and the left wing of Kuehne's Army, attacking from Argesh and Slatina, should engage the Roumanian First Army in the center, and Schmetow's cavalry and Kuehne's right wing, south of Slatina and Roshiori de Vede, should strike its left, to brush it away from Bucharest and drive it north up behind the Second Army. At the same time, Morgen's Army with all other available forces was to attack the Second Army and keep it immobile. This simple and admirable plan, backed by forces two or three time those of the Roumanians, now greatly harassed by the German cavalry wasting the plain in every direction, had one weakness, which the Roumanians immediately pounced upon. It left Koch's army isolated, with a wide gap between his left and Kuehne's right. Orders were sent the First and Second Armies to resist at every cost, while three Roumanian divisions (one of cavalry) were hurled on Koch's flank, to cut communication between him and his base at Zimnicea on the Danube. Two Russian divisions were also to engage the Bulgarian right wing, attacking from the east.

The great battle began November 16. The Roumanians in the mountains resisted heroically, and I am assured by Roumanian officers that several affluents of the Argesh and Prahova actually ran blood. The fighting was especially bitter along the Neajlov, in the identical spot where Sinan Pasha's army had been annihilated over 300 years before. In the Danube plains the maneuver against Koch's army began auspiciously; on the 19th brigades of the 9th and 19th Divisions surprised the enemy, and captured 5000 men, with 20 cannon and 50 machine-guns. But on the evening of the 18th the Germans had captured two Roumanian staff officers and found upon them a copy of the plan of battle. Falkenhayn at once detached the 11th Bavarian Division, part of the 109th German Division, and most of Schmetow's cavalry from Kuehne's Army, to dash south and fall upon the Roumanians. They arrived just as the Roumanians were completing Koch's disaster, and not merely extricated him but forced the Roumanians back toward the capital.

The game was now evidently lost; and orders were given the exhausted Roumanians along the entire Wallachian front to retire upon Bucharest. This was an operation of great difficulty; the water-courses run north and south, and the movement was to be eastward, over the rough outliers of the Carpathians. Connection had to be kept up between the various detachments, so that the enemy should not pierce through and isolate one of the larger units. This was accomplished. The First Army, now of four divisions and about 35,000 men, retreated slowly before the diabolical pressure of the seven divisions of Krafft's and half of Kuehne's armies, maintaining connection with the left wing of the Second

Army, and foiling the enemy's efforts to turn their own left. Their rear engagements with the Germans at Piteshti, Gaeshti and Titu were actually battles. The Second Army meanwhile was falling back from Câmpulung, mainly down the Dâmbovitza valley. Large Russian forces were finally on their way; but the Roumanian line was clearly too thin to hold in Wallachia, and with heavy hearts the General Staff ordered the evacuation of Bucharest, and withdrawal to the Sereth in Moldavia, there to build up a combined Russo-Roumanian Army which should drive out the enemy.

This maneuver was carried out in the midst of the most unparalleled destruction, in order that the enemy might gain as little as possible. Enormous stocks of grain went up in smoke; the oil wells were systematically wrecked by a most competent English engineer. The only exception was the property of the Roumanian Star Co. at Câmpina in the Prahova valley; the Roumanians used this to the last in their retreat, and it could only be superficially mutilated, as told on p. 22. As it was a German-owned concern, the Germans at once put it in order, and it was of great service to them.

As in all Allied countries, propaganda had spread stories of German atrocities, and the population of Bucharest firmly believed that the oncoming German soldiers would cut off their children's hands, gouge out their eyes, etc.; hundreds of families of the poorer and more ignorant classes began plodding eastward along the cluttered highways, and many a poor youngster succumbed along the road to cold and hunger. Beside them trudged the exhausted soldiers, while German aëroplanes and dirigibles hovered overhead, dropping their death-dealing bombs without let or hindrance. Thus the Second Army made its way eastward, to the north of the Ploeshti—Buzeu—Râmnic highway; then came the First

Army, reaching to the middle of the sodden steppes of the Baragan; still further south plodded the remnants of the Danube detachments, flanked by the bewildered Russians, who had arrived just in time to share the tragic retreat, and help blow up the bridges as the last troops or the last train passed over them. The sky was overcast with the smoke-clouds from burning store-houses, oil-tanks and grain-elevators; the severest winter of many years had already set in; and flocks of scavenging crows settled down upon the carcasses and corpses scattered through the slush and snow, rising when disturbed only to wheel slowly back to their ghoulish task.

CHAPTER XV

OF all the proud army of over 600,000 men with which the Roumanians began their campaign in mid-August, only 200,-000 reached the banks of the Sereth in December. About 100,000 were prisoners; some 150,000 had fallen, or were lying wounded in the abandoned territory; another 150,000 were sick or wounded in Moldavian hospitals, or wandering from place to place, trying to rejoin their vanished regiments.

Aided by a French mission of 500 officers, under General Berthelot, one of Joffre's aides at the Marne, and by smaller British and Russian delegations, the General Staff undertook, in a truly Siberian winter, the rebuilding of the Roumanian Army. Modern encampments arose from the Moldavian plain; new equipment began filtering in from Russia; aëroplanes and pilots began their work. The soldiers were organized anew, into only two armies, the First and Second; to the First were assigned three army corps, the 1st, 3rd and 5th; the Second incorporated the remains of the army covering lower Moldavia, in two corps (the 2nd and 4th). Each army corps was formed of three divisions; a division was made up of two brigades (four regiments) of infantry, a brigade of artillery, a squadron of cavalry, a battalion of pioneers and all the accessories—at last a sufficiency of machine-guns, grenades, gas-masks, helmets, not to speak of rifles! The foreign missions superintended an intensive course of training for the new units, with which were incorporated the boys of the new levy in Moldavia. During these five months, King Ferdinand passed from camp to camp, distributing decorations, and encouraging the soldiers in their reviews for the great effort to be made the next summer. Queen Marie and the Princesses Elizabeth and Marioara, in the uniforms of Red Cross nurses, went from hospital to hospital. Crown Prince Carol became a chief inspector, helping to oversee the various forms of instruction given the army, and becoming very popular—a great asset to him to-day.

Meanwhile a horrible scourge laid waste Moldavia. Late in December isolated cases of typhus appeared, and multiplied during January, 1917, reaching an appalling maximum during February and March. Lack of clothing, firewood and soap made cleanliness almost impossible. Medical supplies were pitifully meager. Some regiments actually lost half their effectives, and some towns over a third of their inhabitants. Wood for coffins gave out early, and the bodies were laid in trenches; the intense cold aided the spread of the disease. But unremitting work by the army surgeons checked the typhus in the spring, and by summer it ceased to be serious; whereas in the occupied territory, the German confiscation of soap, changes of clothing, etc., prolonged the scourge till into 1919.

In the midst of this plague occurred the most fateful event of the war—the Russian Revolution. It came, strangely enough, just in time to save Roumania. In the last few weeks of the Imperial Régime, the Russian generals in Moldavia made no secret of their renewed mastery of that country, which should go the same way as Bessarabia. When General Văitoianu once protested to the Russian General Zakharoff, at the lack of Russian aid to the Roumanians against the Germans, General Zakharoff smiled and said: "My orders are not to help the Roumanians, but to occupy Moldavia; and I have done so!"

For the moment, coöperation was maintained; but the Russian troops were naturally inferior to the Roumanian for the defense of Moldavia. The enemy made several attempts during December near Oituz, attacking Russian regiments; but Roumanian reinforcements (the Iron Division, the 15th) threw them back. The First Army was being reconstituted in the interior; the Second Army had the task of holding the frontier; but in general, for the first six months of 1917, it had no more serious task than an occasional local action.

The Entente had been preparing a powerful stroke on every front for the spring of 1917; but the Russian Revolution gave them pause. Nevertheless late in April and early in May, the French and British delivered their blow along a front of some 125 miles, penetrating deep into the German positions, and capturing 50,000 prisoners and abundant material. The Russian commander, General Korniloff, taking advantage of the comparative quiet on that front, inaugurated the only drive launched by the Russian Republic. In mid-June he attacked on the southern Galician border, on a 35-mile front, and advanced 25 miles, taking 40,000 Austro-German prisoners. With this encouragement, the Roumanian General Staff determined on an offensive in Moldavia. The First Army moved late in May from its camps to the lower Sereth, taking position between Hanul-Conachi and Iveshti. As finally constituted, the front ran as follows: Russian Ninth Army from the Bucovina to the heights above Ocna in the Trotush valley; Roumanian Second Army to Răcoasa; Russian Fourth Army to Vultureni; Roumanian First Army to Serbeshti, where the Russian Sixth Army took up the line. No dependence could be placed on the Russian Ninth Army, which was now saturated with Bolshevism; but the Fourth and Sixth it was hoped might second a Roumanian attack. By the end of June the heavy artillery was in place. The plan was to begin with a powerful bombardment, especially heavy from the Roumanian positions; then the Roumanian Second Army, under Gen. Averesco, was to strike toward Mărăshti and up the Putna, in conjunction with the right wing of the Russian Fourth Army, which was to attack above Măgura Odobeshtilor (hill 1001 m.). After an interval of one to three days, according to circumstances, the Roumanian First Army was to cross the Sereth, smash in the enemy's line, and fall on the flank of the enemy's troops already engaged up the Sereth and on the Putna. If successful, the attack would drive a wedge between the enemy troops in Moldavia and those in Transylvania, and would push those further south into a trackless waste of mountains.

As the burden would fall on the Second Army, it was given various units, and on the eve of the offensive included the Russian 8th Division, the 9th, 14th, 13th, 5th, 7th and 12th Roumanian Divisions, a brigade of frontier-guards (graniceri), the 1st and 2nd Cavalry Divisions, and a brigade of cavalry. They lay along the east bank of the Sereth from Bilieshti to Fundeni, where they crossed to the west bank, extending to Tudor Vladimirescu.

The bombardment began at 11 A. M. July 9th, 1917, and continued two days and nights. It demoralized the enemy; and although they had the advantage of position up on the hills, the Roumanians reached all their objectives, including the village and heights of Mărăshti, which have given the name to the battle. They began their charge at 4 A. M. July 11th, and within four hours had over 1000 prisoners and 20 cannon at Mărăshti alone. On the 12th further progress was made; the enemy appeared demoralized, and an Austrian order which fell into the Roumanians' hands gave directions for falling back to the other side of the mountains to reform and restore the units. The Roumanian victorious advance continued four days more; but its effect was neutralized by the Russian procedure. Their 8th Corps of the Fourth Army, after two days' good fighting, announced on the evening of the 12th that they would go no further, since they had orders from "the Revolution" to cease fighting. The 40th Corps of the Ninth Army on the 12th abandoned the position of Măgura Cashinului which they were holding (elevation 1167 m.) although in no danger from the enemy, who had retired before the Roumanian 8th Division. One could not adopt the summary methods of the Allies in Macedonia, who promptly disarmed the Russian troops when they became independent and set them to road-repairing like prisoners of war! The Roumanians had to extend their thin line to fill the gaps left by the Russians, and could of course go no further forward. So on the 16th the offensive rested, after an advance of about 12 miles uphill, on a 25-mile front, and with a booty of 50 cannon, 80 machine-guns, 80 carloads of munitions and 4000 prisoners; but the greatest benefit had been the discovery that the dreaded Germans would run, just like the rest.

The First Army made a still hotter artillery preparation for its advance, lasting from the 10th to the 13th of July; this was due to the greater strength of the German artillery on this front. At last all was ready when late on the 12th the Roumanians received word from the Russians that Kerensky was stopping every offensive on the entire front; therefore, they could not participate! For the third time during the war, the lack of promised Russian aid proved fatal. Obviously the newly won positions could not be held without Russian support; and with tears in their eyes the Roumanians obeyed the order of their staff to retire across the Sereth!

Meanwhile portentous events were taking place further north. The Germans had countered to Korniloff's victorious offensive in northwestern Bucovina by a powerful drive north of Tarnopol. Breaking the Russian front, they out-flanked it, producing a rout which speedily sucked in the Russian units from north and south. Orders were sent the best divisions of the Russian Fourth Army to proceed to the Bucovina. The Roumanian First Army, in the Putna region, was now stretched still thinner. Mackensen, who had come to take charge of the operations, saw his chance to repeat the Tarnopol success, and concentrated over 14 divisions (ten of them German) and several hundred cannon (with some 12-inch guns) opposite the left wing of the now greatly weakened Russian Fourth Army, which held the front from the Sereth to Răcoasa. He reckoned confidently on occupying Jassy, seat of the Roumanian government, on August 15th, the anniversary of the declaration of war, and the posts of administration for Moldavia were already as-signed, just as they had been by Conrad von Hoetzendorff for Lombardy and Venetia in 1916. His plan seems to have been to pierce the Russian Fourth Army at Focshani and continue with the Sereth covering his right, while a second blow two or three days later should crumple up the left wing of the Russian Ninth Army and the right of the Roumanian Second Army, and then to proceed down the Slănic and Trotush valleys.

By July 23rd, 1917, the Austro-German offensive in Bu-covina reached the Roumanian frontier near Suceava. There was danger not merely of a drive through the disorganized Russian forces down the Roumanian boundary, but still more of an attack curving southward to the Pruth. The Rou-manian General Staff issued orders for the troops of the

First Army east of the Sereth below Tecuci, to cross and replace the units of the Russian Fourth Army which were leaving; all dependable units of that army, together with the Sixth and Ninth Russian armies, were hurried up to the Bucovina, to stop the enemy's advance. The Roumanian Second Army now regained its 7th and 12th Divisions from the First Army, and extended its front north of the Oituz highway to the Doftana, to replace the 40th Russian Corps, who announced they were going home. Bolshevist and Austro-German propagandists were sapping the morale of all the Russian elements. The Roumanians throughout merely laughed at them.

Mackensen launched his first blow the night of the 23rd of July, against the 34th Russian Division, on the left of the Fourth Army. After a terrific bombardment, with waves of gas, the 216th German, 12th Bavarian and 89th German Divisions attacked at 4:30 A. M. the 24th, supported by the Sereth on their right and the railway to their left. The whole battlefield of Mărăsheshti, by the way, lies along the main line from Bucharest to Jassy, and I have twice had the privilege of listening to the story of the battle illustrated from the car window.

This first attack was successful; the Russians fled in confusion; there were no Russian troops available, and the nearest Roumanian troops, of the First Army, were across the river, south of Tecuci. Nevertheless by a forced night march, the Roumanian 5th Division stemmed the German onset. They were ordered to take the town of Strǎjescu and advance to Ciushlea. The Russian Command assured the Roumanians that Strǎjescu was still in Russian possession, and the Roumanians were approaching the town when met by a withering fire. The retreating Russians had failed even to send word of their disaster to headquarters! The Roumanians had to retire upon Doaga, but unity of front was none the less achieved.

Mackensen opened a deadly fire the evening of the 24th upon the newcomers, who were interfering with his plans, and followed it up with three attacks that night and the 25th, in the hope of annihilating the three regiments before reinforcements could arrive from the further side of the river. They held; but the Germans found a Russian division, the 71st, at Bisigheshti; they fled at the Germans' approach, and a broad gap opened between the 71st and the 13th Russian Divisions, next on their right. That threatened to turn the Roumanian 5th Division; they retreated *en échelon,* and formed a new line at an angle to the old. Under galling fire, the Roumanian 9th Division replaced the Russian 71st Division. Late on the 27th they were attacked by the 76th German Reserves and the 89th Ersatz; the Russians beside them gave way, but the Roumanians succeeded in stopping the German drive. The evening of the 29th the Germans repeated these tactics, and put to flight the Russians to the right of the Roumanian 9th Division; the Roumanian 13th Division had to take their places; attacked on the 30th, they managed to hold their new positions.

Mackensen saw more thorough measures were necessary; quiet reigned till late August 1st, when he began an infernal bombardment, directed particularly at the remnants of the 5th Division, holding the bridge-head at Cosmeshti. Overwhelming infantry forces followed up the attack, annihilated the sadly decimated 9th and 32nd Regiments, and cut connection between the 5th and 9th Divisions. The 14th Division arrived to support the 5th, just in time for another blow, late on the 2nd. The enemy was so superior in numbers that the Roumanian command decided to blow up the bridges at

Cosmeshti. By this time only 5000 men remained of the 18,-000 with which the 5th Division entered the fight, and less than one-third of their officers.

Mackensen continued searching out the few Russians still remaining in the line, and with his attack on the 5th Division on August 1, he combined a furious bombardment of the Russians who held Chicera (heights 334 and 283). They ran away without waiting for the infantry attack; the Roumanian 10th Division, which happened to be nearest, was rushed up, and after a series of attacks and repulses, succeeded in holding hill 334. The Germans attacked again the night of the 2nd, and isolated the 10th Roumanian Chasseur Regiment on hill 334, destroying all communication; but they managed to beat the Germans off, and Mackensen saw he must change his tactics.

The situation of the Roumanian First Army, during the first week of August, 1917, was as follows: On their left were troops of the Russian Sixth Army. From Suraia to near Cosmeshtii din deal, along the east bank of the Sereth, was a corps of dismounted cavalry, with some infantry behind them. Then came the 14th, 9th, 13th and 10th Roumanian Divisions, up to Mânăstioara; the Russian 8th Army Corps; and then the left of the Second Army, at Voloscani. Behind lay as reserves the 15th Division, as yet untouched, and the 5th, under reconstruction.

By August 6th, Mackensen had rearranged his forces, and struck powerfully against the 14th, 9th, 13th and 10th Divisions with a much larger army, composed of the 216th, 76th, 115th, 79th German Divisions, an Alpine corps, the 12th Bavarian Division, the 301st and 13th Austrian Divisions, a Bulgarian brigade and some units of the 212th German Division. Before the last remaining units of the Russian Fourth Army (between the First and Second Roumanian

Armies) he set the 62nd and 217th German Divisions, with orders to strike at a propitious moment. He began his attack with a bombardment from about 700 cannon, among them some 305's, on the front between Cosmeshti and Mânăstioara. The town of Mărăsheshti became the center of the fight; the Roumanians finally occupied it permanently. The fighting seethed all day long; the bravery of the Roumanians, seconded by able handling of reserves at critical moments, finally drove the Germans back; and the great victory of Mărăsheshti was won. The 10th, 13th and 9th Divisions alone took 1000 prisoners; but the cost was terrible. The 9th Division came in with only 4000 of the 18,000 with whom they had started.

But Mackensen still had one hope, and ordered an attack on the two Russian divisions still left of their Fourth Army, west of the Roumanian 10th Division. They fled as soon as the Germans hove in sight. But by this time the Roumanian High Command was used to replacing Russians; and the gap between the First and Second Armies was promptly filled by the last available Roumanian reserves. Now the 3rd Roumanian Division, on the left of the Second Army, touched the 10th Division, of the First Army, and there were no Russians left in the front line. On the 20th of August, the 2nd and 11th Divisions came in. The First Army now lay along the east bank of the Sereth; the cavalry corps extended from Suraia to Cosmeshti; then came the 14th, 15th, 10th, 2nd and 11th Divisions; in reserve were the 13th, 5th, 9th and 4th.

Meanwhile a drama almost as gripping had been played along the Second Army front. There the Germans had attacked in dense masses July 26. At that time the left wing was held by the 7th Division, recently given back by the First Army; they replaced the 40th Russian Corps, now too communistic to fight. Their right went along the brook Sărei (Doftana) to Slănic and Herăstrău, a mile west of Grozeshti; there the 6th Division continued to Măgura Cashinului; then the 8th Division ran to the Turbure brook. The 12th Division followed, and on the Lepsha hill joined the 1st; this crossed the Putna. Last came the 3rd Division, which connected with the 8th Russian Corps at Ireshti. They had no reserves. The 40th Russian Corps lay behind the 7th, to be sure, but were now permeated with pacifism, and filled with Austrian spies. The Roumanians noted frequent exchange of light signals, and found telephone lines from the Russian to the Austrian trenches.

Mackensen's plan was to attack along the Trotush, with the idea of obtaining Târg-Trotushului and Târg-Ocna, both full of Bolshevist Russian soldiers; incidentally he would capture the last Roumanian oil-wells and salt mines. He would also cut the Russian Ninth Army's supply communication, and turn the right wing of the Roumanian Second Army. His bombardment, specially directed at the 7th Division, began the 25th, and lasted till 6 P. M. July 26th, when his infantry attacked the 6th and 7th Divisions with far superior forces. He had opposite the Second Army the 225th German Division, 70th Hungarian, 15th Brigade of Bavarian Reserves, a battalion of Württemberg Jägers, the 7th Austrian Cavalry Division, 117th German Division, 8th Austrian Cavalry Division, 37th and 71st Hungarian Divisions, 1st Austrian Cavalry Division, 218th German Division, the 217th, the 3rd Regiment of Grenadiers, 59th German Regiment, and the 62nd Austrian Division.

On July 28th, the attack on the 6th Division relaxed somewhat, but the 7th Division had to give ground, retreating towards the Trotush. On the 29th, Mackensen redoubled his pressure; railway, stations and highway along the Trotush crumbled under his shells. The Roumanians launched their last hope—a counter-attack from the last heights left them over the Trotush (hill 789) with troops hurriedly detached from the First Army—a brigade of frontier guards, a battalion of mountain Chasseurs, and a division of cavalry. The Chasseurs swooped down on the Bavarians just about to enter Târg-Ocna, and in a moment they were dashing back to the heights they had just left. This was one of the prettiest exploits of the war. The Chasseurs had left Târg-Neamtz on the 25th, had averaged 25 miles a day through rough country, and at 1:30 A. M. on the 30th had reached Brăteshti, 4½ miles north of Târg-Ocna. At 10 A. M. they received their orders to attack at 4 P. M., starting at once on a detour through the hills which brought them to the welcome waters of the upper Trotush at 3:30. They descended the stream, wading across, and promptly on time attacked the Bavarians, now coming down their last hill, with machine-guns and grenades. The attack was so unexpected that the whole enemy division was infected with panic, and fled in such disorder that the Roumanian Chasseurs pursued them three miles before enemy artillery was brought to bear. They accounted for 1500 enemy killed, wounded and captured, and themselves lost only 2 officers wounded, 2 men killed and 17 wounded! That cleared the Trotush valley and gave the Roumanian Staff time to take measures necessary to relieve the pressure on the rest of the front.

Mackensen, however, knew that time was not to be lost, and began a series of powerful local attacks. These culminated in a desperate attempt, from August 16th to 21st, to take the Deal Porcului, a mountain which dominates the whole upper Sushitza valley. There were still Russian units there, who fled in disorder at the first heavy bombardment, and even hindered the Roumanian reinforcements by cluttering up the narrow mountain paths; some Bessarabian soldiers of the Russian 14th Division did however stay, with their artillery, and joined the Roumanian 6th Brigade. The Germans attacked twelve separate times, and once succeeded in laying hands on the crest, but were soon driven back again, and finally gave up.

Mackensen was beaten. With an army prevailingly German, opposed by a force part of which was Russian and melted away as he approached, he was stopped by sheer bravery, seconded by able strategy. The great battle he inaugurated on July 23, 1917, along the west bank of the Sereth, towards Adjud, and followed up on the 25th with drives down the Doftana and Slănic valleys towards Târg-Ocna, had ended, after a month and a half of desperate fighting. The Sereth battle gradually spread westward; that about Târg-Ocna, eastward. By mid-August it was all one great action, from the Sereth to the Doftana, on a 75-mile front. Mackensen needed to find only one weak spot and the whole front was gone; Moldavia would join Wallachia, Poland, northern France and Belgium. But he never found one; and by the end of August he had to retire to a line further west, after losing some 80,000 men; the Roumanians lost 20,000. After Brussiloff's offensive of the summer of 1916, this battle of Mărăsheshti was the greatest defeat of the Germans on the whole Eastern front. Gen. Cristescu, Commander-in-Chief for the first half of the battle, his successor Gen. Eremia Grigorescu, and their collaborators had won undying laurels.

Mackensen smarted under the defeat of Mărăsheshti, and on Aug. 28 he threw the Ninth German Army against Muncel, the only point on the southern front where Russians were still in the line. Again the Russians melted away; but the Roumanian defense was successful, and the German had again to retire, losing Gen. Wenninger, Commander of the Eighteenth Corps; the Roumanians lost their heroine, Ecaterina Teodoroïu, a second lieutenant in the infantry.

CHAPTER XVI

THE ARMISTICE, AND TREATY OF BUCHAREST

ALL this bravery, all these sacrifices were neutralized by the course of events during the autumn of 1917. The Russian situation went from bad to worse; in November the Bolshevists got the upper hand in the army, ordered a general demobilization, and asked the Germans for an armistice which should usher in a general peace. Russia was the only source of military supplies for Roumania—and no more would come! Operations had ceased with the fall rains, and the approach of winter; but Roumania was now beleaguered on every side, while the Germans had every facility of supply over the Transylvanian railways. By early November the German and Russian delegates were gathering at Brest-Litovsk. Premier Bratiano told me that in this crisis he felt the Allies should share responsibility in deciding Roumania's fate. He wirelessed to Clemenceau, describing the situation and asking for directions. Orders reached him to disarm the Russians still in Moldavia. "That might seem quite an undertaking," he said smiling, "for we still had about a million of them wandering around; but luckily they had mostly disarmed themselves, and I was able to report success within a week. I then asked for further instructions." The reply throws light on the earlier phases of the Allied Russian policy: "Take your troops and go help the loyal Russian forces in the Caucasus." "Doubtless in Paris it seems only a step from Roumania to the Caucasus," remarked Bratiano; "but after all it is a 1000-kilometer step, in the dead of winter, without roads, ships or railroads, and with provisions for only two weeks; it was a counsel of perfection." There was no escape; if Roumania did not sign the armistice, the entire German forces on the eastern front would be hurled against her; she would get no help, munitions or supplies from the Allies, nothing but such extraordinary counsels as these. "It was a choice," said Bratiano, "of saving something—the nucleus of an army, which could be reconstituted in favorable circumstances, or losing our last soldier up in the Triangle of Death in Moldavia, to no avail." The decision could not be long; and after four days of discussion at Focshani, an armistice was reached on Nov. 26 (Dec. 9), 1917. It was signed by Lieut.-Gen. von Morgen for Arch-Duke Joseph and Field-Marshal Mackensen; by Gen. Keltchevsky for Gen. Stcherbatcheff, Russian Commander; and by Gen. Al. Lupescu for Gen. Prezan, Roumanian Commander.

The great advantage of the armistice was the gaining of time. For the Roumanians it was essential to prolong this uncertainty until the Western Allies could bring about some improvement which would warrant resuming hostilities. Furthermore, they had great hopes of the Ukraine. Russia was breaking up into a number of states, of which the Ukraine promised to be the largest and wealthiest in resources; and several of her public men were outspoken both against the Germans and the Bolsheviki. If the Roumanians had an Ententophile Ukraine behind them, they felt they might be able to fight on. But in a few weeks even this hope failed; the Ukraine made peace with the Central Powers January 27, 1918, earlier even than Bolshevist Russia!

Roumania had before her a watchful enemy, incomparably superior in men, guns, ammunition and other supplies. He was anxious to crush what remained of the Roumanian

Army, in order to have a clear path to the wealth of the Ukraine. Behind were Bolshevist Russia and the Austrophile Ukraine. The Allies, who had encouraged her to come in under what seemed false pretenses, were further away than ever. Within her borders were a million Russian soldiers, straggling and thieving through the countryside and preaching Bolshevism. And all Paris could do was to advise her Premier to send his troops to the Caucasus!

The Roumanian High Command immediately set Roumanian reserves behind the portions of the front still held by Russian troops; they greatly strengthened the state police (gendarmes); they divided Moldavia up into military districts, each of which was entrusted to a military unit; every infraction of the regulations of the High Command was severely punished; no Russian troops, even unarmed, might approach Jassy; none might leave the front or return into Russia without surrendering their arms. These measures saved Roumania from the demoralization of her eastern neighbors.

Some of the Russian units did actually resist. The 9th Siberian and 13th Russian Divisions attacked Galatz on January 7, 1918, and their bombardment did considerable damage; but the 4th Roumanian Division, with hand-grenades and machine-guns, finally dispersed them, and the majority surrendered to the Germans along the Sereth. Units of the Russian 26th and 84th Divisions, several thousand in number, at Pashcani, on January 13, attacked the Roumanian detachment which had been sent to parley with them, killing their major as he was talking with the Russian representatives. The Roumanians gave them a brief baptism of fire, and after disarming them, shipped them over the Dniester. On January 14th some 5000 Russians of the 18th and 40th Corps, with 16 cannon, attacked six Roumanian companies near Falticeni; the battle continued till 2 A. M. on the 15th, when reinforcements arrived and the Russians surrendered. Other skirmishes took place at Timisheshti, Botoshani, Bacău and Roman. One of the most picturesque incidents was the arrival at Jassy of two trainloads of Bolshevist troops from Odessa; they professed to be coming to suppress the bourgeois Russian Staff still coöperating with the Roumanians, but surrendered their arms meekly when confronted by Roumanian Chasseurs and Frontier-Guards in the station. It is easy to imagine the scorn of the Russians which every Roumanian officer has who lived through the winters of 1917 and 1918 in Moldavia. Two Roumanian generals told me they did not know of a case where a Russian officer whipped out his revolver and ordered his troops to obey. They came in shoals to their Roumanian officer friends, weeping and wringing their hands and lamenting their inability to restore discipline; not one made a serious effort, they said. Denikin, by the way, was one of these Russian officers who promptly gave in and these Roumanians who knew him had nothing but contempt for him.

Order was restored in Moldavia; but Bessarabia was in complete anarchy, a prey to wandering Russian bands. As we have seen, their autonomous government proved too weak, and Roumanian troops were asked to enter and take control of the situation. On January 13, 1918, they marched into Kishineff; on the first of March, after many a skirmish with the Bolshevists, they reached the Dniester. The recovery of Bessarabia was some slight compensation for the trials on the Moldavian front.

The Central Powers viewed with a hostile eye the departure of the Russian troops from the Roumanian front, and the entry of Roumanian troops into Bessarabia; and on February 17, 1918, they gave notice of the cancellation of the armistice; however, on the 21st it was renewed till March 6, to allow peace negotiations to begin. Nothing else was possible for Roumania now. The Ukraine had signed the Peace of Brest-Litovsk on January 27, 1918; Bolshevist Russia had resisted longer, as so dramatically told by Col. Raymond Robins, confirmed by Capt. Sadoul, but yielded on February 17. On April 24 (May 7), the Roumanians signed the document which is known as the Peace of Bucharest, and which is summarized below:

I. The state of war ceases; diplomatic and consular relations are resumed after ratification.

II. The entire Roumanian army is to be demobilized, and the pre-war military budget is to be reëstablished. Divisions 11–15 demobilize at Focshani; of the other 10, two may remain mobilized in Bessarabia till the Ukraine quiets down. The other 8 are to be reduced to 20,000 infantry, 3200 cavalry and 9000 artillery. No concentration of these troops shall be made before the general peace.

The excess of armament, horses, cars and munitions shall be surrendered to the occupied territory, to be guarded by the authorities of occupation. The troops in Moldavia shall be allowed 250 cartridges per rifle, 2500 per machine-gun, 150 shells per cannon. The Bessarabian divisions shall have munitions on a war footing.

The Roumanian troops demobilized are to remain in Moldavia. Demobilized officers and men may return to their homes in the occupied territory. Those on active service will need the laissez-passer of the German Kommandantur. River and sea forces, with all their equipment, are likewise to stay in Moldavia.

III. The entire Dobrudja is to be ceded: New Dobrudja, i. e., that taken in 1913, is retroceded to Bulgaria, together with a rectification of the frontier up to the Cernavoda—Constantza railway; the remainder of the Dobrudja, from this line to the Danube (Arm of St. George) is ceded to the Central Powers, *in condominio*.

The Central Powers will see that Roumania has a commercial outlet assured to the sea via Cernavoda—Constantza.

A rectification of the frontier in favor of Austria-Hungary shall take place along the Carpathians, bringing the frontier 5–10 miles further down toward the plain.

IV. Both sides waive war indemnities.

V. The Roumanian territories occupied by the military forces of the Central Powers shall be evacuated at a date to be agreed upon later. Meanwhile six divisions shall remain in occupation.

After ratification, the civil administration in the occupied territory shall be handed over to the Roumanian authorities.

The Roumanian authorities shall accede to the following provisions which the High Command of the Army of Occupation considers necessary in the interests of public security in the occupied territory:

Means of communication—railroads, mails, telegraph, telephone, etc., remain until new orders under the military administration of occupation. Civil and penal jurisdiction over the persons forming part of the Army of Occupation, as well as political rights over them remain in all their extent with the Central Powers. Their tribunals shall also try other persons and cases affecting the security of the troops of occupation.

Return into the occupied territory shall be allowed only in proportion to the extent to which the Roumanian Government supplies provisions. Even after ratification requisitions shall be made of cereals, vegetables, fodder, wool, cattle, meat, wood, petroleum and its derivates; likewise the right shall continue to take the necessary measures for securing, treating, transporting and distributing these products.

The Roumanian Government must accede to the demands of the German High Command in the execution of requisitions for the needs of the Army of Occupation.

The maintenance of the Army of Occupation, and the cost of requisitioning, shall be at the expense of the Roumanian Government.

Expenses incurred in the occupied territory by the Central Powers for public works (including industrial enterprises) shall be returned to them at evacuation.

VI. All the Contracting Powers have the right to keep war-vessels on the Danube, in their waters. Each Power represented in the Commission for the Mouths of the Danube shall keep two light war-vessels at the mouths of the Danube.

VII. All worships shall be recognized: Roman-Catholic, Uniate, Protestant, Mohammedan and Jewish; they shall have the same freedom and protection as the Orthodox.

All residents of Roumania shall become citizens without special measures, including the Jews.

VIII. Special agreements shall regulate economic relations, public and private law, exchange of prisoners and of interned civilians, the decree of amnesty, etc.

The Treaty of Peace shall enter into effect upon its ratification.

CHAPTER XVII

ROUMANIA UNDER THE GERMANS

THE Germans applied to Roumania the principles of exploitation which had now been worked out in Belgium, northern France, the Frioul and Poland. Their motto is well expressed in an order of the G. H. Q. of August 21, 1917 (No. 26,280): "The most important duty of the military administration in Roumania is the most intensive possible economic exploitation of the country to the profit of Berlin." Let us see how the Germans went to work.

The Treaty forbade war indemnities; but it was nevertheless stipulated that subjects of the Central Powers should be indemnified for war losses. There should have been Roumanian members in a Joint Commission to determine the amounts; but their appointment was continually put off, the Commission adjudged the amounts demanded, and advised raising the sums in some cases. They permitted claims based on the losses of persons who had sold stocks or property in a panic, and assigned large sums to the families of persons interned. They had an easy method of paying, by the notes of the Banca Generală Română. This bank, which had had close relations with the Deutsche Bank before the war, was made their bank of issue by the Germans. It is instructive to study their financial methods. The additional agreement, Art. V, provided:

"Roumania shall reimburse from her own funds with notes of the Roumanian National Bank, or by other means of payment, within a period of six months from the ratification of the Peace Treaty, the notes issued by the Banca Generală Română at the instance of the Administration of Occupation. These notes shall not be reissued, and thus the deposits and sums in the German Reichsbank to cover them shall be rendered available. Up to their withdrawal, the notes of the Banca Generală Română shall be recognized as legal means of payment; after the ratification of the Peace Treaty, no more such notes shall be issued."

However, while Roumania was forced to ratify the Treaty at once, the Germans postponed indefinitely the exchange of ratification, and continued the issue of the bank-notes of the Banca Generală Română. They admitted a circulation of over 2,283,000,000 francs in these notes; and when, after the war, the Roumanian Government decided to recognize them as legal tender, if brought in to be stamped, the amount was discovered to be nearly four billion francs of fiat money, at the charge of the Roumanian Government. The Central Powers had demanded a war contribution of 250 million francs on their first occupation of Wallachia, to be raised by districts; but in spite of the terrorism exercised, they raised only 25 millions in cash; so they issued departmental bonds for the missing 225 millions, taxing each department of Wallachia for its quota; then they made the Roumanian National Bank take over the entire issue, and pay for it with 180 million marks' worth of bonds belonging to the National Bank, which happened to be deposited in Berlin when the war broke out. Then the Germans made these bonds the reserve for the issue of new notes by the Banca Generală Română, their bank of issue at Bucharest; there was thus this small reserve for the four billions!

Roumania's financial condition had been enviable. The budget had shown a surplus ever since 1902. Governmental obligations at 5% were quoted above par; the 4%'s varied between 93 and par. In 1910, the Roumanian National Bank held a cash reserve of 574 million francs in gold, and 80 millions in gold bonds; its management was most conservative, as shown by its failure ever to take advantage of its full legal note-issuing capacity; in 1900, a year of financial crisis, its issue reached 94% of the legal maximum; not even during the war did it surpass its legal quota, and it continued to publish a weekly statement long after other European national banks had taken refuge in darkness.

The fate of this gold is romantic and mysterious. In the spring of 1920 the Roumanian public was much disturbed by reports that considerable sums in Roumanian gold were appearing in western Europe. It was known that the gold reserve of the National Bank had been shipped to Moscow during the German invasion; and it had been whispered about that Lenin and Trotzky had used this gold to pay their indemnity to the Germans under the Brest-Litovsk Treaty, and that the Germans were using it to pay their first obligations to France and England. The story went on to say that the Roumanian Government had protested to the French Government, and had received for a reply only a polite version of the proverb *"Pecunia non olet."* In view of all this, the Roumanian National Bank thought it wise to issue a statement in June, 1920, to the effect that the Roumanian gold-pieces in question were doubtless put into circulation by individual Roumanians who had taken refuge in neutral countries during the invasion, and that in all the gold sent to Moscow, Roumanian gold-pieces figured for only 750,000 francs. The total gold reserve of the Roumanian National Bank sent to Moscow, a little over 315 million francs, in French, English, Austrian, German, Italian and Turkish gold coin, was deposited in one of the structures of the Kremlin, guarded by a steel door which can only be opened by three keys, of which the Russian Government has only one, the other two being in the possession of the French Foreign Office. Without them, it would be necessary to blow up all this part of the Kremlin to get at the money. At the time of the battle of Mărășheshti, the Roumanian Government sent to Moscow all the gold still in its possession at Jassy. This was deposited in the Russian Government's safe deposit vaults; the Soviet financial authorities assured the Roumanians that they would watch over the deposit with the utmost solicitude, as being the property of the Roumanian people; and Krassin, on his mission to Lloyd George, assured the Roumanian commercial attaché at Copenhagen that the treasure was intact, and that the Soviet Government stood ready to return it to Roumania at any moment, as an acknowledgment of the correct attitude of Roumania in the Polish-Russian controversy. Of its subsequent fate, we are not informed.

The Roumanians were not only bequeathed the problem of the Banca Generală notes by the Germans; but their troubles with Russian rubles began during the German occupation; and at its close they were confronted with the paper crowns of the Austro-Hungarian issue in the Bucovina, Transylvania and the Banat. Speculators well understood that the final redemption of these crowns and rubles would be at a higher rate than in the surrounding territory; indeed, there was generally a high profit in smuggling them in at any time, and the Roumanian authorities were forced to inquisitorial measures to defend themselves. For instance, in May, 1920, there was discovered a package of one million and a half crowns on the locomotive of the Orient Express at the frontier station towards Hungary; and on June 22, 1920, a French aëroplane from Constantinople which had just alighted at the Pipera aërodrome at Bucharest was found to have a package containing 700,000 Kerensky rubles and 171,385 Romanoff rubles! Curiously enough, currency inconveniences did not end here; I found by experience in late 1919 that though the notes of the Banca Generală circulated in Roumania itself on a perfect equality with those of the National Bank, even in the Bucovina they were discriminated against, and in Hungary and Jugo-Slavia stood lower than those of the National Bank. The final conversion of crowns and rubles into Roumanian francs (lei) was at a rate considerably above the market—expensive to the taxpayer, but grateful to the new provinces.

Thus the financial harm done Roumania by the Germans will long bear noxious fruit. But a further study of the Treaty will make clear how thoroughly they intended to exploit her in every financial relation. By Article 24, any German employed in Roumania before the war and then dismissed on account of his nationality, should be reinstated with at least the same salary. By VI. 25 and III. 25 of the Treaty, Roumania had to pay for the support of prisoners at the rate of 2000 marks (2500 francs) per officer and 1000 marks (1250 francs) per man, to be raised to 5 and 2.50 francs daily after April 1, 1918. This resulted in a long delay in the return of the prisoners from Germany, where their labor was grateful, and where Germany was drawing in addition fifty cents a day for their maintenance! On their return, 50% of those from Bulgaria and 40% of those from Germany and Austria were found to be suffering from tuberculosis, to which all peoples of southeastern Europe are peculiarly subject. Bulgaria not having signed the Geneva Convention of 1906, exacted an additional indemnity for the repatriation of the prisoners, of a thousand cars of Bessarabian wheat. The total yearly indemnity for a prisoner had to be paid, even if he died the first day of captivity. This item of cash indemnity for prisoners amounted to some 150 million francs. Roumania had also (under Article IX) to restore or pay for all river or sea vessels and all railway material belonging to the Central Powers. The Roumanian Government was also to reimburse the Germans for their expenses in harbor and wharf improvement, the new oil pipe-line to Giurgiu, railway repairs, etc. The support of the Army of Occupation (six divisions) was set at 300 million francs in December, 1916, but progressively raised to 700 million. All these financial burdens, with the losses of territory, were reckoned at fifteen billion francs by Roumanian financial experts. And how much German indemnity did the Allies assign Roumania?

Lack of space forbids study of the very interesting banking plans of the Germans, which will be found detailed in Prof. G. D. Creanga's valuable "Les Finances Roumaines sous le Régime de l'Occupation et de la Paix Allemandes," Paris, 1919. But their economic exploitation of Roumania, so admirably described in Dr. Antipa's recent book (see Bibliography), deserves a brief exposition. The Economic Convention monopolized Roumanian production for the benefit of Germany and Austro-Hungary till 1926; all exports elsewhere were prohibited. The prices fixed in Article XII for 1918–19 were: for wheat and rye, 38 francs the quintal (220½ lbs.; apparently about $65 per ton, but the Germans had an ingenious system of exchange, by which it came to considerably less); barley, oats and Indian corn, 29. These were about one-half current market prices; the Roumanian State had fixed the price of wheat at 70 francs! The price for the years 1920 to 1926 was to be fixed by a German-Austrian-Roumanian Commission, the chairman to be appointed by the President of Switzerland. The Roumanian population was to be rationed even after general peace, and representatives of Germany and Austro-Hungary should determine the exportable surplus. The seller should pay all taxes; Roumania was to pay the farmer, and eventually collect from Germany and Austria. All oil lands were to be ceded for 90 years to a German company, to be designated by the German and Austrian governments; the Roumanian State was to receive 8% on the gross output for the first 30 years, 9% for the second, and 10% for the third. It should also share in the profits of the company, but only after the distribution of 8% dividends to the stockholders. The Roumanian Government should give this company all mining and forest rights necessary; it should validate the liquidation of all American, Belgian, Dutch, English and French holdings, which had been seized by the Erdölindustrieanlagengesellschaft. The German oil-land company (Oelländereienpachtgesellschaft) was then to turn the crude oil over to another German company, again to be designated by the German and Austrian-Hungarian governments; the Roumanian state was to cede this company all its pipe-lines and tanks. The Roumanian Government was to receive 3.60 francs per 2205 lbs. of crude oil (0.2% of the value!) and 4 francs for the same amount of derivates (about ½%). There could be no importation of oil except with the consent of this company. The Germans set freight tariffs very low (at the expense of the Roumanian State), in order to increase their commercial advantage; the Roumanian State had to make up any deficit in the railway balance—the Administration of Occupation running the railways! The laws of Roumania prohibit the owning or long-term lease of rural property by foreigners; the Peace Treaty provided that German companies might acquire both urban and rural property on 30-year leases, twice renewable—evidently with great German colonization projects in view. The agrarian law of 1917 provided for the expropriation of six and a quarter million acres of farm-land for the benefit of the peasantry; the Treaty provided that all persons owning city or farm property in 1918 should not be liable to expropriation. Furthermore, Germany did not neglect the aspect of Roumania as a reservoir of labor; the Peace Treaty allowed the Germans to recruit Roumanian laborers and send them to the German colonies or elsewhere, replacing them in Roumania with German colonists. They began this colonization in southern Bessarabia and in the Dobrudja, where there already were German villages; their idea was to make a chain of them around the Black Sea, winding up in Asia Minor. Roumania was to become a link in the greater pan-German chain; her products were put at the service of German industrialism; she must buy German and Austrian products. Roumanians were to become helots of the modern Sparta.

The Germans are admirable classical scholars. Tacitus tells us that as a result of the Roman requisitions in conquered Britain, the poor Celtic peasant had to buy back at a higher price his own property requisitioned from him, or go sell his wheat in a distant market, when the Romans had already set one at his door. See how the German system worked out in Roumania. The German authorities requisition a peasant's oxen, paying him 400 francs for the pair. They give him requisition scrip, to be paid by the Roumanian Government. He now has no oxen to plow his land. The authorities notify him that under Mackensen's ordinances 2 and 224, he must cultivate his land, under penalty of fine and imprisonment, or else have it cultivated at his expense by the military authorities. In his dilemma, they offer to sell him back his own oxen for 1500 francs. He can, of course, do no better elsewhere, so accepts the proposal; but the plowing once over, the authorities step in again and requisition the cattle a second time for 400 francs. Thus the German military authorities gain a pair of oxen and 1500 francs for nothing; the peasant is out 700 francs and his oxen; the Roumanian Government is out 800 francs. There was also an ingenious system of fines. Eggs were requisitioned, at one or two cents apiece; the hens and pullets were all listed, and a standard production of eggs postulated; if the normal number of eggs were not forthcoming, the owner was fined ten cents per missing egg. If he wanted an egg for his own use, he must pay the authorities between ten and twenty cents apiece. Eggs, milk, butter, meat, poultry and fats were destined *exclusively* to German needs. Requisitioning kept on after the signing of the Peace Treaty, which should have stopped it, and reached a maximum during the summer and autumn of 1918, when it became evident that final victory would elude the Germans, and that this was their last chance.

Perhaps the most serious feature of this evil was its consequences to public health. Roumanian children and invalids were deprived of milk, butter, eggs, chicken and other necessaries, except at prohibitive prices. The confiscation of fats made soap almost impossible to get, and typhus (which can only be fought by cleanliness) raged far longer in the occupied territory than in Moldavia. Dr. Antipa, the distinguished biologist, accepted the post of Minister of Agriculture in the ministry formed at Bucharest under the German administration, in order better to protect his country's interests. He was so outraged by what he saw of the iniquities of the German system of requisitioning that he went one day to Mackensen and said to him: "Marshal, my biological studies have made me familiar with every living organism which Nature has evolved for the purpose of preying on lesser organisms; but not one of them is as successful in sucking the juices of its victim as is your requisitioning machine in draining the life-blood of the Roumanian peasant." But to all such protests the Germans had a ready answer; it was pitiful, to be sure, but the need and destitution of their own beleaguered people were so much greater than the Roumanians'!

The Germans were incidentally responsible for some improvements, as in Belgium. Brussels was never so clean as during the German occupation; the same was true of Bucharest. The Germans were annoyed by the troops of dogs which infested Bucharest somewhat as they once did Constantinople. They sent out and rounded them all up. The dogs reappeared shortly in the form of gloves, soap and sausages (the latter sent up to Germany!); and the streets of Bucharest were the gainers. The Germans disapproved of the plum brandy, the tzuica, distilled by every orchard owner, and commandeered the plums for their marmalade factories; and the German army had a new source of jam. The German passion for order caused many a surface amelioration in Roumania. But this was far outweighed by the incidental damage of the occupation, not to speak of the systematic exploitation. Every Roumanian family has tales of wanton destruction, wilful harm done by the invaders. The beautiful new hotel at Sinaia was wrecked; the lower floor of one wing was turned into a cavalry stable; the parquet flooring was torn up to build the fires whose smoke issued from the windows, and left black smudges over the white stucco of the outer walls. A Roumanian officer friend of mine found on reoccupying his Bucharest home that the Bohemian officer who had been housed there had taken away every article of furniture he possessed; a brother of his, whose place had been occupied by Turkish officers, lost not merely all his furniture but also the floors and walls, which were dug out and burned! On the other hand, some German officers were very punctilious; this officer's sister had a luxurious home, taken possession of by a high German officer, who left everything in good condition. The Bratianos were greatly relieved, on reëntering their Bucharest villa, to find that ex-Premier Bratiano's unique collection of books of travel dealing with Roumania, now a public library, was still intact, though various other books (largely in German) had disappeared, and that Mme. Bratiano's wonderful chest full of Roumanian costumes—the second or third largest set in existence—had suffered only slight pilfering. Such cases however were exceptional; Bulgaria, Austria and Germany were full of Roumanian loot, and the Allied commission investigating in Belgium after the war reported that they had found quantities of Roumanian rugs, costumes, etc., evidently brought up by German officers. Prof. Oprescu was told by a well-informed German official that over 12,000,000 marks' worth of peasant art products were carried off by the Germans.

The Germans themselves supply us with the material for determining how much they abstracted from Roumania officially during 1917—their "Bericht der Militärverwaltung in Rumänien." Their economic staff (Wirtschaftsstab) had an organization which reached into the most remote hamlets; anti-Jewish sentiment in Roumania was inflamed by the prominence of Roumanian Jews among their subordinates; speaking Yiddish, they were very useful to the invaders. There were seventeen sections to the Wirtschaftsstab, and each section was subdivided; that on food supplies, e. g., had seven groups, designated by letters (A. Export, B. Cereals, C. Fats and Vegetable Oils, D. Eggs, E. Tobacco, F. Wine, G. Fruits). We learn from the report that during 1917 there were exported from Roumania 33 cars of silk, 160 of hemp, 1546 of wool, 63 of cloth, 143 of bagging, 439 various textiles, 1401 tanning materials, 4426 of leather, 35 various skins, 209 arms and munitions, ten tons of copper coins, 49 cars of paper—in all, some 72,000 tons of textiles, leather, metals, chemical substances and raw materials. This from a country racked with war! They shipped out 1,422,585 metric tons (of 2205 lbs.) of cereals in 1917. There was not even honor among thieves. A note of the Imperial Ministry of Marine, addressed June 17, 1918, to the Ministry of War, Section of War-Material, numbered B VII d. 16,211, after noting that Turkey only shares one-quarter in the profits on Roumanian war-booty, begs to have the price for oil and motorine for the navy's use set so low that there can be no profit, since there is no reason why Turkey should profit from the war necessities of her allies. This Wirtschaftsstab had its own budget, which for 1917–1918 was, in francs:

Revenues 1,368,255
Expenses 53,000,000

The deficit, of 51,631,745 francs, was met from the 250 million war levy. For 1918–1919, the budget was:

Revenues 1,455,220
Expenses 401,455,220

The deficit of four hundred million francs was to be covered by the forced loan of 400 millions.

Another source of income was the fines for infractions of regulations. The German-Bulgar administration of the Do-brudja raised in fines in seven communes of the district of Constantza, the sum of 1,190,000 francs. They laid an infinity of taxes, varying according to locality; the dog tax, e. g., was general in 1917, but local in 1918. There was a chimney tax; a head tax of 10 francs for every person above 16; a meat tax; a land tax, which for the district of Constantza was 4 francs per acre for holdings under 25 acres, and 16 for those above; a license tax, which for some companies was raised to a million francs; a circulation tax, of 5 cents for each time one left Focshani, e. g., after 6 P. M.; for 40 cents one got a permanent pass. It cost a franc to make a formal request to the German authorities. In some districts a pass cost four eggs. All owners of poultry had to pay a tax of two eggs per week. There was a pasturage tax, a tax for exemption from forced labor, etc., taxes for street-cleaning—all these in addition to the regular taxes of the Roumanian Government.

As a result, the spring of 1919 found Roumania without coal, wood, or wheat, with less than 20% of her stock supply of 1916, without forage, so that even cavalry officers had to stand by and watch their beloved mounts die of starvation—and this long after the war had come to an end. The Germans left only a hundred locomotives in the country (and 50 of them disabled), of the 1200 owned by the State Railways before the war. On account of the destruction of the oil-wells, the Germans had converted many of these to coal-burners, and the Roumanians had to convert them back again. Even late in 1919, Roumania still presented a graphic picture of desolation.

CHAPTER XVIII

THE BÉLA KUN CAMPAIGN

IF I have been handling controversial material hitherto, my task becomes doubly difficult as I approach Roumania's treatment at the Paris Peace Conference; the Hungarian campaign of 1919; and the present political and economic situation. Some of the most essential elements for forming a judgment in these matters are still veiled in obscurity; others are all too obvious, but lend themselves to differing interpretations.

Defeat had been a specially bitter blow to Hungary. Chief movers in the declaration of war against Serbia, the Magyars felt that the Great War was particularly *their* war; and had the Central Powers won, Magyar haughtiness would have been worse than Prussian. They had never been invaded, and their farmers and manufacturers had profited enormously. The realization of disaster was all the more poignant, and gave added force to the efforts of the Socialists and Communists finally to get the better of Magyar Junkerism. During the five months of the Károlyi régime, these discontented elements gathered strength, and came under the control of a clever Jew who called himself Béla Kun. He was in close touch with the Russian Soviets, and acted in conjunction with them (see my "Bessarabia," Chapter XXVI.) The 133 days of Béla Kun's Red Terror form one of the most interesting episodes in the aftermath of the war. We are concerned only with his aggressions on the Roumanians.

The first clash between Béla Kun's troops and the Rou-

manians occurred in April, 1919. We have seen that the
Roumanians were promised by the Allies, before they entered the war, the whole of the Banat, with the Theiss for a
western boundary. The Peace Conference was more or less
anti-Roumanian in feeling; and Béla Kun evidently was
given to understand that the territory east of the river for
a considerable distance would be Hungarian. The strange
partiality of the Peace Conference to this adventurer needs
clearing up. Dr. Dillon preserves the sinister rumors which
filled Paris on this subject; but they are clearly only part
of the explanation. At any rate, Béla Kun's troops were not
strong enough for the task of driving out the Roumanians
forcibly—the latter refused to leave till the Peace Conference
should make a formal open announcement, incorporated into
a signed treaty—and the brief campaign closed with Béla
Kun's withdrawal west of the Theiss, on April 16, 1919.

Encouraged by the attitude of the Peace Conference,
egged on by the Russian Communists, and anxious for the
popularity that extending Hungarian boundaries would give
him, Béla Kun now bent all his energies to the creation of a
powerful and well equipped army. He was much helped in
this by possession of Mackensen's material, including heavy
artillery. A preliminary campaign against the Bohemians was
successful in regaining a slice of Slovakia; and by the 20th
of July he felt strong enough to attack the Roumanians,
particularly as his spies had ascertained that they had few
troops in the Banat, and not many in Transylvania, the bulk
of their army being on the eastern front, where Béla Kun's
Russian Bolshevik allies were constantly threatening. Béla
Kun's forces would seem to have been as follows: the First
Army Corps centered at Czegléd, consisted of the 2nd Division (at Kecskemét), the 6th (at Nagy-Körös) and the 7th
(at Szolnok). The Second Corps was formed on the other

side of the Danube, and comprised the 4th Brigade and the 8th Division. The Third Corps' headquarters were at Hatvan; it was composed of the 1st Division (at Miskolcz), the 5th (at Jász-Ladány) and two brigades of Szeklers, the 2nd (at Szerencs) and the 3rd (at Sárospatak). The Fourth Army Corps included the 4th Division (at Kistelek), the 3rd (on the Czecho-Slovak frontier) and the 9th (of Red Workers, at Buda-Pesth). They had also several battalions of frontier-guards down in the south, to guard against an incursion from the Franco-Serb troops, of whom (like the Roumanians) they did not have a very high opinion. They had some 75 field batteries, and a quantity of Mackensen's heavy artillery—12- and even 16-inch guns. In general, their divisions were made up of three or four infantry regiments, each regiment with three or four battalions, and each battalion with four companies of about 130 men, plus a company of workers, and a Red Guard. Béla Kun's whole army apparently totalled at least 160 battalions (about 90,000 men), 6 squadrons, 75 batteries and 964 machine-guns. Of these, about 150 battalions with 60 batteries were on the Theiss front, opposite the Roumanians.

As we lack any detailed and authoritative description of this campaign, which is politically and strategically one of the most interesting of the war, especially in its effective use of cavalry, I induced the Roumanian High Command in Buda-Pesth to make up for me from staff reports a full analysis (with maps), and utilize it for this account.

Béla Kun had completed the arrangement of his forces in mid-July; and by the 19th his practice artillery fire and aërial reconnoissance were in full swing. The Roumanians had only two groups opposite him—the North Group, composed of the 16th Division, which was guarding the Theiss from the mouth of the Somesh (Szamos) to Abád Szalók, and the 2nd Division of Chasseurs in reserve; and the South Group—the 18th Division, along the Theiss from Abád Szalók to the mouth of the Muresh, with the 1st Division of Chasseurs in reserve. The reserves scattered through Transylvania consisted of the 1st Division, at Careia Mare (Nágy-Károly); the 2nd Division of Cavalry, in the region Uj-Féhérto—Hajdú-Hadház—Nyir-Adony—Balkány; the 6th Division, at Oradia Mare (Grosswardein, Nagy-Várad); and the 1st Division of Cavalry, in the region Sarkad—Szeghalom. The Roumanians thus had only two divisions along the river, with two more in reserve; Béla Kun attacked with six divisions and three brigades. At 3 A. M. on July 20th, 1919, he launched three of these divisions against the thin Roumanian line at Szolnok, after a heavy bombardment from the large Mackensen cannon. Secondary attacks were started at the same time in the Tokay and Poroszló sectors in the north, and in the Csongrád district in the south.

In the north, the Hungarians crossed the Theiss at 8:30 A. M. near Szabolcs, Sziget and Tisza-Dob. With far superior forces they occupied the villages of Timar, Rakamaz and Tisza-Eszlár. The troops which had crossed at Tisza-Dob and Tisza-Dada were however met with reserve forces, and driven back across the Theiss by evening of the 20th. In the south, the enemy crossed near Szolnok, Szentes and Mindszent, driving back the Roumanians, and occupying Török-Szt.-Miklós, Szentes and Hódmezö-Vasárhely. In the face of this powerful attack, the commander of the South Group, Gen. Holban, concentrated the 1st Brigade of the 1st Division of Chasseurs at Orosháza, with a battalion from the 2nd Brigade; the 6th Regiment of the 2nd Battalion was sent hurriedly to Puszta-Sz.-Tornya. The High Command in Transylvania at once determined on a clever maneuver. The

Hungarian troops in the northern sectors should be attacked and driven back across the Theiss; but in the south, the enemy should be allowed to advance up to a line west of Kis-Ujszállas, Mezötúr and Orosháza. Meanwhile the 2nd Division of Cavalry should concentrate in the region Madaras—Karczag; the 6th Division about Báránd—Udvari; and the First about Püspök-Ladány—Kaba. These three divisions should constitute the Maneuver Group, under Gen. Moshoiu, with headquarters at Debreczin. He should also receive Gen. Olteanu's 5th Brigade of Roshiori (red-coated cavalry, from "roshiu," red); and the 1st Division of Cavalry should await his orders. The 20th and 21st Divisions, further inland in Transylvania, were started westward, and reached the front July 24th.

On July 21st, the enemy continued eastward from the Theiss in the southern sectors, driving back the 91st and 92nd Roumanian Regiments with heavy losses. The Roumanians lost in these actions about 5000 killed. Another regiment of Chasseurs and a thousand dismounted cavalry were hastily dispatched to their aid. The 1st Cavalry Division also sent a brigade of Roshiori and some mounted artillery to Gyoma, to await their orders. The 1st Division of Chasseurs now touched the 18th Division on its right, and the 76th French Division on its left, in the Jugo-Slav district. Orders were sent the North Group to keep the enemy engaged while the main action should evolve around Szolnok, while the South Group should entice the enemy towards Mezötúr—Túrkeve and even east of the Bereteu (Berettyo). The 1st Chasseurs should clean up the district about the confluence of the Crish (Körös) and the Theiss, proceeding then to the main action at Szolnok. Gen. Moshoiu's Maneuver Group was to attack on the flank and rear the enemy's troops as soon as they left Szolnok; the plan was to cut the enemy to pieces between the Theiss and the Bereteu.

On July 22nd, the Hungarians succeeded in crossing the Theiss again, between Tisza-Füred and Tisza-Oers, and occupied the former town at 5:30 P. M. They maintained themselves there or in the vicinity till the 26th. In the south, the Hungarians crossed on the 22nd at Tisza-Roff and Tisza-Süly, driving back the 18th Chasseur Regiment nearly to Madaras, and defeating with heavy losses a battalion, battery and squadron belonging to the First Chasseur Division. On the 23rd they took Kis-Ujszállas, and with the help of local irregulars, the town of Mezötúr. The Roumanians retreated along the south bank of the Bereteu. Further south, advance troops of the 1st Chasseurs took Mindszent; the Hungarians now lined the entire west bank of the Theiss from the Crish to the Muresh.

In view of the dangerous situation, which there was no hope of remedying from Roumania, on account of the transportation crisis, the High Command decided to form other mobile units to aid Gen. Moshoiu's Maneuver Group. Gen. Pap was given part of the 18th Division and the 4th and 6th regiments of the 1st Division of Chasseurs, to keep concentrated in the Kis-Ujszállas—Túrkeve—Mezötúr district and immobilize the enemy south of the Bereteu. Gen. Leca was put in charge of the 1st Brigade of Chasseurs, two battalions of the 90th Infantry, and one of the 89th, together with the 4th Brigade of Roshiori, to distract the enemy's attention north of Szarvas and Oecsöd. A third group, under Col. Pirici, and composed of the 107th Regiment of infantry, two companies of the 1st Chasseurs, and a battalion from the 89th Infantry, was sent to prevent any crossing south of the point where the Crish empties into the Theiss.

Gen. Moshoiu began his maneuver on July 23rd, launching the 1st Division of infantry and the 12th Brigade of the 6th from Karczag in the direction of Hornimir, to cut the enemy's communications via Szolnok. On the 24th, his troops took Kunhegyes, and drove the main body to near Kenderes, where they offered bitter resistance. It was therefore decided to have the South Group attack on the 25th between Oecsöd and Túrkeve with all available troops, along the Bereteu and the Crish. Meanwhile the North Group was kept busy by numerous minor attacks; in the south, the 84th Infantry and 10th Chasseurs took Tisza-Füred from the enemy on the 24th.

On the 25th, the Hungarians managed to drive the 1st Division out of Fegyvernek, but were stopped a couple of miles east. That same morning the 11th Brigade took Kis-Ujszállas, and the three new mobile units started; Gen. Pap's group took Túrkeve, Gen. Leca's moved in three columns upon Szolnok, Török-Szt.-Miklós and Mezötúr, and Col. Pirici's occupied Szentes. The Roumanian combination of the hammer blow and the pincers movement was immediately successful. On July 26th, a Roumanian offensive in the north in two columns, one towards Venczellö—Balsa —Szabolcs, the other along the highway and railroad to Rakamaz, drove the Hungarians across the Theiss. By 9 P. M., the Maneuver Group also had the satisfaction of seeing its last Hungarian opponents reach the other shore of the river; Gen. Pap's and Gen. Leca's divisions met at Szolnok, where Hungarians still held the bridge-head, and sent them packing westward, also.

What was left of Béla Kun's army was now west of the Theiss. It was still a respectable force, with much heavy artillery. Sound strategy and political considerations demanded that it be captured or annihilated; Béla Kun's Russian allies were still menacing; so the Roumanian High

Command determined to follow it up and destroy it, if possible. Accordingly, the troops were concentrated along the river and regrouped, so that on the 29th of July there were six main units: Gen. Holban's group, consisting of the 2nd Chasseur Division east of Fegyvernek, and the 1st, south of that point; Gen. Moshoiu's, of the 6th Division of infantry at Török-Szt.-Miklós, and the 1st, at Szolnok; Gen. Dumitrescu's, of the 7th Division, the 2nd Cavalry Division, and a regiment of Alpinists, all at Madaras; the North Group, of the 16th Division, the 49th Brigade of the 20th, and three mountain batteries, covering the sector north of Abád-Szalók; the 18th Division, plus the 107th Regiment of infantry and the 11th Brigade of artillery, to the south of Abád-Szalók; and a reserve consisting of the 2nd Division, to be concentrated between Arad and Kunhegyes. The strategy determined on was sound, clever, and completely successful. The troops were to cross the river the night of the 29th; the main attack should be delivered in the Kis-Köre—Fegyvernek sector, where the enemy had his two main groups; and in the midst of this attack, the cavalry division should attack him from the rear, and cut his railway communication with Buda-Pesth. Gen. Holban was to cross first, followed by Gen. Moshoiu. Gen. Dumitrescu was to cross to Kis-Köre, and then cut the Miskólcz—Buda-Pesth railroad in the region of Kál, as well as attack the enemy's troops trying to prevent the main crossing at Fegyvernek—Tisza-Bó; his cavalry and Alpinists should continue the work of cutting railway communication. The North Group were to cross and immobilize the enemy in their sector, but not work west of a line five or six miles from the river.

Gen. Holban crossed during the morning of the 30th, and by night his troops held several villages west of the river. Gen. Dumitrescu crossed the following day, building a bridge at Kis-Köre, and his cavalry set out for Kál, to cut the railway, and turn the enemy's position. The 7th Division concentrated in the zone Heves—Atány—Tarna-Szt.-Miklós, to act as pivot for the cavalry maneuver, assure freedom of action to the main body of troops, and if necessary, act with them. Gen. Moshoiu's group crossed also on the 31st, at Tisza-Bó, reaching Bessenyszög after desperate resistance, and forming a line with the 2nd Chasseurs a mile east of Rékas and north of Szolnok, with the left wing resting on the Theiss. Gen. Holban's troops reached Kis-Er the 31st, and continued their advance August 1st, as did Gen. Moshoiu's; but the enemy drew heavy reinforcements from Abony and attacked in the region of Szolnok, driving some of the 18th Division back across the Theiss, and forcing others, of the 6th Division, northwest of Szolnok, to cross the Zagyva River to avoid being surrounded.

On August 2nd the Roumanian High Command became convinced, from a study of the enemy's strategy and from the reports of their intelligence department, that Béla Kun's intention was to retire at once to Buda-Pesth, leaving only troops enough to cover his retreat, and utilize the resources of the capital for a final blow. Gen. Holban was therefore set over a strategic vanguard, consisting of the 2nd Cavalry Division, 3rd and 5th Brigades of Roshiori and the 1st Chasseur Division; the cavalry to support the 5th Brigade toward Alberti and the 3rd to Nagy-Káta, covering the district between the Jász-Berény—Hatvan—Aszód railway on the north and the Kecskemét—Buda-Pesth line on the south, cutting this latter and those between Szolnok and Nagy-Káta and Szolnok and Alberti. The 1st Chasseurs were to advance into the district Tápió-Szele—Tápió-Györgye. Gen. Moshoiu's Maneuver Group was now constituted of the 2nd Chasseurs and the 1st Infantry; the former was ordered to occupy Jász-Al-Szt.-György and Jász-Ladány, while the latter advanced in the district of Roszas-Uy-Mir—hill 98 Rékas—Ujszász. The 2nd Division of infantry formed a reserve, concentrating about Bessenyszög. The right flank was protected by the 2nd Brigade of Roshiori, who were to reconnoiter toward the northeast; and by troops of the 7th Division, sent to Poroszló to help the 49th Brigade in crossing, and then deploy in the region of Jász-Mihálytelej—Jász-Apáti. The left wing was guarded by the 6th Division and the 4th Roshiori Brigade, under Gen. Olteanu; the former was to occupy the country around Abony, supported by the 4th Brigade along the line Abony—Törtel—Nagy-Körös—Kecskemét. The 49th Brigade, after crossing at Tisza-Füred, with artillery borrowed from the 16th Division, was to occupy the Eger-Lövö—Eger-Farms zone, and form the pivot for the turning maneuver of the 2nd Roshiori Brigade.

All these operations were successfully inaugurated on August 2. Gen. Moshoiu's troops met with desperate resistance between Szolnok and Abony; but at night Hungarian officers came to treat for the surrender of the 3rd, 5th and 6th Hungarian Divisions, holding the district Czegléd—Abony. Others on a similar mission from the 4th Division, at Csongrád, came to the bridge-head at Szentes. Word arrived also at headquarters that isolated units in the north had now become detached from the main Hungarian force, which were south and west of the line Czegléd—Abony—Uj-Kécske; outside this line were fragments of the 1st Hungarian Army Corps, viz., the 2nd and 7th Divisions, and the 5th Division of the 3rd Corps. Down by Kecskemét were part of the 4th Army Corps, and the 4th Division was in confusion further south along the Theiss and on the Franco-Serb line. To eliminate all these troops, the Roumanian High Command ordered on August 3rd that the

5th Roshiori should push further west to cut communication with Buda-Pesth, establishing contact with the 3rd, who were to advance from Jász-Apati toward Jász-Berény— Monor; the Alpinists should join the cavalry. Of the Maneuver Group, the 1st Division was ordered to move to Czegléd, and the 2nd Chasseurs to Tápió-Szele. On the right wing, the 7th Division was sent to Jász-Berény, protected by a cavalry regiment in the Hatvan district, and by another on its rear. Its task was to reconnoiter the Miskólcz zone and join the 16th Division, which was crossing at Tokay. The movement was to pivot around the 49th Brigade. On the left wing, the 6th Division was to proceed to Nagy-Körös and the 4th Brigade of Roshiori to Alberti, then turn south to threaten the enemy's rear, and cut the Szegedin—Buda-Pesth railway.

These operations started on the 3rd of August. Gen. Dumitrescu's troops surrounded and captured the Hungarian 1st Division. Gen. Holban's 2nd Division of cavalry reached by evening a point only nine miles east of Buda-Pesth, and his 3rd Brigade of Roshiori got to the Danube not far southeast of the capital. Gen. Moshoiu's Maneuver Group took Czegléd and reached its other objectives. Gen. Olteanu's 4th Brigade turned the enemy's position near Kecskemét, and the 6th Division received the surrender of the Hungarian 12th Brigade of infantry, with three battalions and four batteries of the 3rd Division, and their staff.

For August 4th, the High Command ordered Gen. Moshoiu to work south to the Franco-Serb line; Gen. Holban and Gen. Dumitrescu to continue west to the Danube and north to the Czecho-Slovak frontier; the cavalry division to encircle Buda-Pesth to the west. During the day, Gen. Davidoglu, of Gen. Dumitrescu's group, occupied Erlau, and Gen. Holban took Hatvan, where he found 38 badly-needed locomotives. The 2nd Cavalry Division reached the Buda-Pesth bridge-head during the morning; and at 6 P. M. the city was formally occupied by the 1st Division of Chasseurs. A detachment composed of the 4th Regiment of Chasseurs, artillery from the 23rd Regiment, and part of the 6th Regiment of Roshiori paraded through the heart of Buda-Pesth before Gen. Mărdărescu, Commander-in-Chief for Transylvania, Gen. Panaitescu, his Chief of Staff, Gen. Holban, Commander of the Strategic Advance-Guard, and a huge concourse, in whose faces could be seen the struggle between humiliation at the triumph of the despised Wallachs, and relief at the overthrow of the Red Terror.

The Allied Commissioners then governing Buda-Pesth seemed nearly as hostile to the Roumanians as were the Hungarians. Acting doubtless under orders from Paris, they had done everything possible to keep the Roumanians out of Buda-Pesth. Gen. Prezan, the Roumanian Chief of Staff, told me that they sent out two young Italian officers as delegates to him, to forbid his entry into the city. "I said to them," he continued, " 'Why, how is this? You wear the Italian uniform! You Italians and we Roumanians have fought for years side by side against the Hungarian; and now you appear to plead for him! You must be impostors, masquerading in Italian uniforms!' So I put them under technical arrest and held them for 24 hours, to give them a lesson, and then let them go." The same hostility marked their attitude to the Roumanian administration of Buda-Pesth. The Roumanians were under the clear duty, after their experience of over a thousand years with the Magyar, culminating in April and July, 1919, to put him *hors de combat,* unable to renew his offensive; but when they set about this, certainly no more vindictively or thoroughly than the Allies against the German, Paris and her representatives in Buda-Pesth discovered a deep sympathy for the downtrodden Magyar, chevalier of Eastern Europe, and a strong prejudice against the treacherous Balkan semi-savages who by a freak of war were now oppressing them. Control of the world's cables, seconded by vigorous Hungarian propaganda, carried this view broadcast, and gave the world a thoroughly distorted impression. Having had the rare good fortune to see Buda-Pesth under Roumanian control in October, 1919, I shall narrate my experiences in the following chapter.

CHAPTER XIX

THE ROUMANIANS IN BUDA-PESTH

PROBABLY no episode of the war needs, or would try, an impartial historian, more than the few months of Roumanian occupation of the Hungarian capital. I must own that I left Buda-Pesth bewildered; and I had wandered about the city alone several times, introducing myself as an American newspaper correspondent, calling on various and most interesting personages, talking with the Hungarians in German, with the Roumanians in French or German, and with Italians and French in their native tongues, so that no interpreter or official companion hampered me in trying to get at the truth. I interviewed Premier Friedrich and two of his Ministers, as well as a couple of Hungarian nobles; Director Vészi, of the great German daily the *Pester Lloyd,* who gave me over an hour of his time; Prof. Goldziher, the distinguished Semitic scholar in the University; Dr. Arnold Kiss, the Chief Rabbi; and a host of store-keepers, petty employés, etc. Of the Roumanians, I talked with Gen. Mărdărescu, a bluff old soldier of few words; Col. Diamandi, the Roumanian High Commissioner, who gave me a most painstaking and detailed account of the situation from their point of view; and a score of officers who had made the campaign. I was made welcome at Italian headquarters, and had pleasant interviews with a number of their officers. Gen. Bandholtz, the American military representative, Col. Yates, the military attaché at Bucharest, who had been for some time at Buda-Pesth, and other Americans gave me their point of view. Capt. Gardner Richardson, Prof. R. H. Lutz, of Stanford University, and other members of the American Food Commission, as well as representatives of the American Red Cross, told me their versions. I talked also with various British and French officers, German and American business men; and ever since, in Bucharest, Paris, New York, Seattle, I have been gaining new and often still more puzzling impressions. Doubtless few situations have ever combined more complex factors than did Buda-Pesth under the Roumanians. No man there at the moment could appreciate more than a few of them; no historian will ever clear them up fully. It would have been bad enough without the constant meddling of the Paris Conference; and my first experience threw vivid light on the accuracy of the information on which Paris acted.

In Paris, I had talked with a number of my friends in the American Peace Commission; and one of them, in very high position, told me on October 14, 1919, that if I got to Buda-Pesth, I should find that the Roumanians had "left only the paving-stones." I went first to Bucharest, and was impressed with the desolation I saw everywhere; meadows and pastures without cattle, cities without horses, stores with inadequate stocks; I was ready to believe that Czernin spoke the truth when he boasted that the Hungarians and Germans had taken 82% of Roumania's cattle, and all available sheep and horses. The thoroughness of the Austro-German spoliation left no sphere untouched. When I first entered my room in one of Bucharest's best hotels, I noticed that on the bed were only two sheets and a blanket—no spread or quilt, though the nights were already cold, and the hotel, from lack of coal, was chilly as the grave. I rang for the chambermaid and asked if I might not have another blanket. "Another blanket!"—and she held up her hands in holy horror. "There are no more blankets. There is only one blanket to a bed in all Bucharest. When the Germans were here, they commandeered all but one blanket; and when they left, they took that one with them for the journey, if they could." I found that even the officers in the Roumanian Army had only one blanket apiece; and Gen. Prezan, the Chief of Staff, told me that although he had a private car, it had no bedding, so that he had to take his blanket off his hotel bed when he left Bucharest on a journey, and bring it back when he returned. This throws light also on the criticism passed on the Roumanians in an American Red Cross report—that in their prison camps, although the nights were cold, their prisoners had only one blanket apiece.

Early on the morning of October 25, I crossed the Theiss River on my way from Bucharest to Buda-Pesth, and as we rolled through the Hungarian plain, I was amazed. Every farm-house had huge hay-cocks (I rode over a hundred miles through Wallachia in an automobile and saw only one), abundance of sleek cattle and handsome horses, and innumerable troops of geese and poultry. From the station in Buda-Pesth I went to the Ritz (Duna Palota), one of their best hotels, and got a beautiful room on the Danube side, with a commodious bath and *hot water* (for six weeks I was without hot water at Bucharest), for 42 crowns (at that time 63 cents; I was paying 25 lei, nearly a dollar just then, at Bucharest for a vastly inferior room; Bucharest was considered by the American Red Cross the most expensive city for an American in Europe). I looked at the bed; two heavy fine woolen blankets, a silk spread, a down quilt. I was amused at Mr. Vészi's surprise later when I told him that at Bucharest I was sleeping under one blanket, my bath-robe and my light overcoat, with a suit of clothes on top on specially cold nights; and I couldn't help imagining how the Hungarians would have howled if the Roumanians had requisitioned in Buda-Pesth as they had in Bucharest.

My surprise increased when I sat down to the abundant and excellent luncheon in the hotel dining-room, at prices (in American, French or Roumanian money) about ⅔ those I had had to pay in Bucharest. Nothing was inferior except bread, which was darker and full of corn meal. Knowing Hungary was good wheat country, I inquired and was told that the Hungarian farmers were holding their wheat for higher prices, and the Roumanians, with great difficulty, were bringing in grain from Transylvania, so as not to have the city starve on their hands.

I had occasion to do some shopping. I supposed that the Reds had cleaned out everything, and had just been told in Paris of Roumanian thoroughness; but to my still greater surprise, I found the shops attractive and well patronized, and a far greater stock and variety than in Bucharest. I wanted an umbrella, and found large and luxurious supplies in two stores near my hotel; the one I bought for about $3 did good service for years. Strong and handsome silk shirts were on sale at about $5 apiece. An American friend bought two heavy pig-skin suitcases for about $15 apiece. I found a Zeiss 8-magnifying field glass for $10 and a Voightländer 10-magnifying army service glass for $27. Currency was so scarce that when I went with the oculist who sold me these to the nearest branch bank, where he did business, and tried to change $40, it developed that they did not have $40 in "blue money" in the bank; so they credited him with the equivalent of the $40 on his account, and he gave me $3 in crowns. Béla Kun flooded Buda-Pesth with cheap photographic reprints of the Hungarian money, and made people accept them; when I was there, some issues of these were no longer current except that the much abused streetcars would take them at face! The "blue money" was the official Hungarian currency, printed off the same plates as in the old days.

Still more surprising was the fact that private individuals could get a little coal, which was also impossible in Bucharest; the Bratianos apologized one day to me for not receiving me in the parlor; they could get no coal, so had shut up all but two rooms downstairs; and he was the ex-Premier and at that moment the power behind the throne! Prof. Goldziher told me that (being an invalid) he had had to have his apartment warmed, and had been able to buy 15 centners (1½ long tons), for 980 crowns (about $15)! But at any rate they had some coal, and in Bucharest, as in Rome during much of the war, we were dependent on wood.

The usual art exhibitions were going on, and I saw a number of good landscapes and portraits by Hungarian artists. The races were on, and they ran for the Prince of Wales Cup, as of old, while I was there. The theaters and opera houses (not to speak of the cinemas) were going full tilt; for the evening of October 28 I had my choice of "Othello" at the National Theater; "The Magic Flute" at the National Opera House; "The Thief" at the Comedy; and eight other plays or light operas. When I returned to the hotel at afternoon tea time, I could hardly make my way through the crush of fashionably dressed men and women who crowded the tables or stood about waiting for a vacant one. Everywhere there was evidence of huge amounts of money, and abundance of opportunities for the spending of it.

Then I visited the markets, to get some idea of the food situation. They were crowded with peasants and buyers; I quote from the current market report of the *Pester Lloyd* (October 27): "In the Garai-Tér (a big public market) the poultry-stalls were over-supplied; buyers were present in great numbers, to be sure, and yet prices for ducks and geese fell ten to twelve crowns per kilo (2.2 lbs.)." Geese were selling at 56 crowns the kilo; a pair of large live fowls, 120-140 crowns; beef, 44-52 per kilo; butter, 120-140; eggs, 5 crowns each; dried beans, 10-12 per kilo. Unskilled labor was getting 8 crowns an hour; the professional class suffered, and people with small fixed incomes. Editor Vészi looked quizzically at his clothes and said: "This suit has lasted 3 years, and it must do for 2 years more; if I want a new one, it will cost me 3000 crowns; a new pair of shoes would take 1000 crowns." In Bucharest, these prices were still higher.

Imagine after this experience my feelings when one of Friedrich's Ministers had the superb effrontery to tell me, with tears in his voice, that the Roumanians had carried off every ox, every horse, every agricultural instrument in all of occupied Hungary, requisitioning even the seed grain, so that they would inevitably perish next year. This was precisely what they had told several American correspondents (whom they then had personally accompanied about), and had succeeded in getting into our papers and magazines; see C. J. C. Street's interesting account in his book on Czecho-Slovakia of the hoodwinking of one well-known American writer. I felt like telling him that if he expected me to believe that, he should at least have cleared a zone a kilometer wide on each side of the railway of all the evidence of farm prosperity which I had seen.

There was no difficulty in seeing through that propaganda. A representative of the American Food Commission had reported (from many miles away) that on arriving, the Roumanians had interfered with the milk supply, and caused the death of a number of children. I tried to run this down, and I found that there had been an outbreak of foot and mouth disease in July in the largest dairy farm supplying the city, which had much cut down the milk supply; but the Roumanians showed me affidavits from the heads of all the city hospitals stating that the Roumanians had not interfered in any way with their supplies. This was confirmed by the report of the Inter-Allied Commission (Capt. Will Shafroth, American Mission; Capt. Sairlebout, French Mission; Lieut. Molesworth, English Mission; Lieut. Braccio, Italian Mission), who interviewed the heads of the eight hospitals of Buda-Pesth and reported: "The Roumanian authorities have not at any moment since the occupation of Buda-Pesth by the Roumanian Army taken or requisitioned in the children's hospitals of Buda-Pesth either sanitary material or hospital supplies of any sort. Certain hospitals are now receiving much less in the way of supplies than before the arrival of the Roumanian troops. It is hard to find out the exact reason. The greater part of these medical supplies was furnished Buda-Pesth by Vienna and Berlin. Three hospitals, among them the Maternity Hospital, are receiving at this moment about a third of the quantity of milk which they received in the month of July under the Communist régime. This inadequacy is explained to us by the statements of Mr. Louis Gerlei, director of the Central Milk Co., who furnishes the hospitals with milk, as due: (1) to the lack of means of transport; (2) to the quantity of milk which arrives sour and cannot be delivered, on account of the excessive time consumed between the local creameries and his central creamery in Buda-Pesth; (3) the quantity of milk which disappears from the Jozsefvaros

station, taken by needy persons and soldiers; (4) the pro-
ducer prefers to sell his milk to individuals who pay a higher
rate than the central creamery."

My photograph of this document (which is in French)
bears no date, but it was handed in on September 28 or 29,
1919. The Inter-Allied Council or the Commission of the
Four Generals, as it was called, was much annoyed at this
report, which (however grudgingly) cut the ground from
under the American Food Commission official in Vienna who
had given currency to the wicked rumor that the Roumanians were taking milk from the Hungarian babies. It
also gave the lie to reports industriously circulated that the
Roumanians were confiscating Hungarian hospital supplies.
The Commission at once sent a note to the Roumanians
(No. 493, of September 29, signed by the President for the
day, General Graziani) expressing their conviction that the
Roumanians would immediately speed up transport, and put
competent guards at the station of Jozsefvaros. The Roumanians also were greatly disappointed in the report; they
contended that the Inter-Allied Commission had seriously
misunderstood Mr. Gerlei of the Central Creamery, and had
suppressed all reference to the ravages of foot and mouth
disease in the herds of Count Karoly Kaposztasmegyer,
which were the chief factor in the decreased milk supply.
I find the report disingenuous in saying that it was hard
to determine the reason for the falling off of medical supplies; every one in Buda-Pesth knew that toward the end
of the Béla Kun campaign, freight traffic with Vienna had
practically ceased, and with Berlin was non-existent.

The Roumanians on the other hand were very indignant
with the Allied Commission and the Hungarians because
they were not allowed to resume possession of their own
hospital supplies, carried off by the Hungarians from Rou-

mania and Odessa and still stored in Buda-Pesth. I examined several of these boxes, in one of which was the entire stock of drugs of a country druggist in southern Wallachia, with even his boxes of labels! Their effort to take this property of theirs seems to have been the origin of the story telegraphed in all directions that they were trying to ship away Hungarian hospital supplies. A member of the American Food Commission told me that the Roumanians were seen packing Hungarian Red Cross supplies into boxes with Russian labels. This would seem to be a Hungarian propaganda explanation, a little twisted (the labels were all in Roumanian on the boxes I examined, and stenciled long before), of the Roumanian story. The Roumanians were also bitter because they were not allowed to take a lot of their own historical documents temporarily deposited in the Burg, or the objects hastily brought to Buda-Pesth from Transylvanian museums by the Hungarians. General Bandholtz boasted that he had personally blocked their efforts to regain their Transylvanian museum property; but I feel sure that if the Germans had taken up to Frankfort from the Strasburg Museum the objects of most interest in early Alsatian history and art, and the French had taken them back to Strasburg on their occupation of Frankfort, public opinion and the War Department would hardly have supported an American general in Frankfort who kept the French away from the museum door; and yet the cases would be exactly alike.

I had much sympathy for General Bandholtz. Convinced from some unfortunate experiences that *all* Roumanians are liars, he went ahead on that assumption, and indeed felt very much alone, having the good American lack of confidence in all foreigners except the English. Current report in Buda-Pesth made him the victim of Hungarian deception, and in one instance, in a very amusing manner. Friedrich told me that the Roumanians had made three separate attempts to kidnap him, and that on one occasion he appealed to Bandholtz, whose office was not far away, and that Bandholtz came and kept the Roumanians off for hours. The latter confirmed this. According to report, Friedrich (who, by the way, was later accused of planning the murder of a political opponent) had got up the whole attempt himself, and hired these soldiers, in order to intensify the American General's anti-Roumanian feeling. True or false, this story gives a good idea of the atmosphere of the Hungarian capital. I brought up Friedrich's kidnaping story with a Roumanian general and he made the obvious rejoinder: "Why, what in the world could we do with Friedrich if we did kidnap him? He would be far more embarrassing to us kidnaped or murdered than up there on the Burg." And, indeed, when I asked Friedrich what motive the Roumanians had in trying to kidnap him, he shrugged his shoulders, and broke into a declamation that he was risking his life for his country every moment, and fully expected to die at the hand of a Roumanian assassin before his term expired. Hungarians told me he was much more likely to fall victim to a Hungarian revolver.

General Bandholtz was also very much worked up over Roumanian requisitions, and made every effort to stop them, as indeed he was directed to do from Paris, which viewed with alarm the subtraction by the Roumanians of so much of the common booty. The Roumanian point of view was that they had been wantonly attacked by the Hungarians; that they had appealed to Paris to stop Béla Kun; that Paris had declined to go beyond warnings, at which he laughed; and that the war which then broke out was like any other, and the precautions to be taken after it, such as

would naturally follow. No doubt the Roumanians interpreted liberally the provision of their General Staff that
they should requisition all machinery, etc., used in turning
out war supplies; but it was hard to get details of any excess. I asked Editor Vészi for instances, and all he could
bring up was an attempt to take the machinery of a print-
ing plant. Much was made of their taking telephone instru-
ments, type-writers, etc.; but those were the first things
confiscated as military necessities by the Hungarians and
the Germans when they occupied Bucharest. An attentive
study of the Treaty of Versailles will throw much light on
what is lawful and proper to take from a defeated enemy.

I found it also impossible to get at the truth in the matter
of Roumanian rightful tenure (as viewed from Paris) of
Buda-Pesth. Friedrich told me the Roumanians were holding on till the wine should all be made and the crops all
in, and that they would go then after confiscating everything they could lay their hands on. Commissioner Diamandi
told me they had three times begged Paris to be relieved,
so that they could take their army back to Roumania, where
the danger from Russia was constant; and three times Paris
had told them not to go. General Bandholtz told me he had
personally delivered an ultimatum of the Supreme Council
to the Roumanians some three weeks before, ordering them
to leave at once, and that the High Command had finally
told him that for tactical reasons it was impossible to go as
yet. The corn doubtless was that the Roumanians would
not leave without being replaced by Allied troops, who
should hold in check the new White Army, which was being organized in Western Hungary, and which they feared
would be more chauvinistic than the Red Army.

To a casual visitor there was no sign of Roumanian
occupation or interference with the normal city life of Buda-

Pesth. The new force of Hungarian Mounted Police, which Colonel Yates had been training, kept order; and the newspapers reported political meetings much as usual. That same Minister of Friedrich's told me that the Roumanians had not allowed three persons to meet together and discuss politics, just after Commissioner Diamandi had informed me that the total number of persons who had gathered in public meetings under the Roumanian administration was 150,000, and that no untoward incident had occurred!

On the constructive side, the Roumanians deserve great praise for what they did in Buda-Pesth. When they entered the city, they found it exhausted by the Red Terror. Editor Vészi told me that for all those 133 days, his wife and he had tasted neither bread, meat nor fresh vegetables. The peasants had no confidence in the Red régime, and brought little produce in. The Roumanians found no communal authority except an improvised so-called Socialist administration, which had little authority or influence. The children especially of the city were badly undernourished; and although the Roumanians had great difficulty with supplies themselves, they did their best to relieve that situation. They at once authorized the free circulation in Hungary of all agents of the Hungarian Food Administration, some 1200 in number. Orders were sent out to have grain cars take precedence even of military supplies on the railroads. The food captured from the Hungarian Army was put at the disposal of Hungarian civil authorities. Four daily Buda-Pesth food trains in each direction were put on. Over 50 tons of frozen meat, 20 of salt meat, 20 of fresh veal and ten cars of fats, which had been secretly held in the city, were distributed to the people. Orders were issued to begin at once sending 10,000 cars of potatoes from the region east of the Theiss. Fourteen canteens were opened for free distribution of food to women, children and old people. Forty communes about Buda-Pesth were exempted from all army requisitions, so that their food surplus might be shipped into the city. This was all the more necessary in that the population of Buda-Pesth was now two millions, Premier Friedrich assured me, of whom six or seven hundred thousand were fugitive Jews from Galicia and Russia.

I have the detailed report, by regiments, of the number of children fed regularly at the Roumanian soldiers' mess; in Buda-Pesth it amounts to about 4000 definitely checked up, while one or two regiments reported that they fed whoever appeared and begged for food, without keeping track. This means many scores of thousands of rations, from a scanty commissariat. General Prezan told me that the farmers' stock and produce were levied upon only in the strip between the Theiss and the so-called "Clemenceau Line" east of it, and there only 30% was commandeered. General Greenly, the British observer with the Roumanian troops, reported that the Roumanians behaved at least as well as a British army of occupation would have. Rabbi Kiss said in so many words that he thought the Hungarian people had little to complain of at the hands of the Roumanians. Of course, the Jews in Buda-Pesth were very grateful to the Roumanians for maintaining perfect order and thus preventing the savage reprisals which would otherwise have followed the Béla Kun régime (in which Jews had been so prominent) and which apparently did follow the withdrawal of the Roumanians, as indicated by the reports of the American Hungarian Jews on the violent anti-Semitism of the Horthy régime, and the petition to the Peace Conference of January, 1920, signed by over 100,000 Jews of Buda-Pesth, begging the Conference to ask the Roumanians to reoccupy the city.

ROUMANIAN HOSPITAL SUPPLIES, LOOTED DRUGS, ETC., WHICH THEY FOUND STORED
IN BUDA-PESTH BY THE HUNGARIANS

The Hungarians charged that the Roumanians commandeered all but 27 of their locomotives. I saw many more than 27 locomotives in Hungary myself; and General Prezan, Chief of Staff, told me that he took British advice to determine how many locomotives the Hungarians needed on their State Railways for ordinary commercial purposes; that the English authorities said they thought 2000 would be sufficient; and that he left them 2300. General Bandholtz' explanation of such discrepancies was that both sides were prevaricating, but that the chief trouble was lack of discipline in the Roumanian Army, so that the excellent orders given by those in authority were not carried out by their inferiors; that the infraction of such orders was even winked at, in case Hungarians were the sufferers. There may well have been isolated cases to support his thesis; but a general accusation of lack of discipline in the Roumanian Army is absurd. I heard complaints in Roumania, as in Italy, France and England, that the quality especially of the lower grades of officers had deteriorated in consequence of the length of the war and the death of so many thousand of their best young men; but the general impression I derived of Roumanian Army discipline was that it was what would be expected from officers trained mainly in Germany, then drilled by the French, and chastened by years of war experience. I think we may leave that question to Mackensen and Béla Kun!

We have seen the prejudice that existed against the Roumanians among their allies in Buda-Pesth, and the lack of foundation of the mischievous rumor that they had interfered with the Buda-Pesth milk supply. My Buda-Pesth experience gave me an opportunity also of sounding the prejudice that prevailed in Paris. I have narrated my astonishment at the condition of things in the Hungarian capital, so different from that indicated by my friend on the American Peace Commission, who had told me I should find only the paving-stones. He is a just and honorable man, highly thought of by all his associates, and by the Roumanians. He had based his impression on the reports that had come in to Paris. My own acquaintance with Italian politics had given me some idea of the worthlessness of most of the confidential reports about conditions in Italy sent in to and swallowed by the American Peace Commission—about as trustworthy as those sent in to Berlin in 1914 about conditions in Great Britain. I had just convinced myself by inspection that the reports from Buda-Pesth were equally exaggerated and partial. I wrote him a letter giving him my impressions, and enclosing the market report of October 27 from the *Pester Lloyd*. He replied to me from Paris under date of November 18: "I received your letter describing your visit to Buda-Pesth, and read it with much interest. If the Roumanians have done so little to the country, it is unfortunate that they will not permit the Inter-Allied Commission to look into this question. They have recently sent a note in which they cleverly sidestep the suggestion made that the requisition question should be examined by a joint commission on which they would be represented." (Of course the Roumanian position was that after the Allies had failed to restrain Béla Kun, had failed to help the Roumanians, and had failed to send troops to replace their troops in policing Hungary, it was a piece of pure impertinence in the Allies to propose to take a hand in the disposal of the spoils. This seemed "clever" at Paris, as well as presumptuous. Were not the Roumanians one of the small nations, whose business was to be seen but not heard, and facilitate Franco-British commercial penetration in place of German?)

The letter continues: "I don't think it is safe to judge conditions from what one sees out of a railroad carriage as they tell me even in Poland and Austria, where we know the conditions are desperate, everything looks normal from a car window. I think you would be really interested in learning the real situation by getting the figures from our Army people. You will find that the Roumanians helped themselves rather liberally to cattle and foodstuffs. On that one point, all the Allied representatives seem to agree.

"When I make these suggestions, I am really doing it so the Roumanians will know what the truth is, as I am informed that they are kept more or less in ignorance of the truth and are undoubtedly ignorant of the position taken by the Allies in their case.

"In this connection, for my own satisfaction, I would like to know the truth of the stories in regard to the treatment of the prisoners by the Roumanians. A commission composed of an American officer, an Italian, and a Red Cross official, made an investigation and their report was rather savage.

"I am not at all unsympathetic with the Roumanians or their point of view, but it is perfectly hopeless for them to think that they can try to row in the boat with other powers and set their own stroke, particularly as there happens to be some one near the bow of the boat. The American officers we have there are very high-class men and I cannot believe that they, not to mention all the other officers, have it entirely wrong, particularly when what they have said has been borne out by Hoover's people and the railroad people. The Roumanians are charming and clever people and tell a very convincing story, unless one happens to be on the other side of the fence and has had some experience with them."

This is a good example of the state of mind induced at Paris in an honorable man who is exasperated at the waywardness of these Roumanians, and has exaggerated reports at his elbow. He does not even mention the market report, from which I quote on page 209, but dismisses that as a thing seen from a car window. The best-known Hoover report at Paris on things Roumanian—the one I heard on all sides there—was the one from Vienna about Roumanian interference with the milk supply which I have shown to be baseless. I was able to send my friend immediately a Red Cross report just made out in Bucharest on the treatment of the prisoners. It criticized shortage of beds, bed-linen, blankets, drugs and screens (all things unobtainable even for army officers at the moment in Bucharest), and gave some particular instances of neglect, but pronounced the food palatable and sufficient in quantity. I saw many groups of prisoners in Roumania, and they gave no impression of being ill-treated. Undoubtedly they suffered from the frightful dearth of food and materials which afflicted Roumania during the terrible winter after the close of the war, when transportation was almost entirely crippled.

In fine, the Roumanians occupied Bucharest and most of Hungary, for fourteen or fifteen critical weeks, after a disastrous Communistic experiment. Their occupation was marked by no serious disorders, at a time when to keep order was in itself an achievement; by improvement of the public health (deaths in Buda-Pesth in August, 1919, 1420, as compared with 1553 in July, and 1764 in August, 1918); by non-interference in Hungarian politics and in the intrigues directed from Paris (Mr. Vészi said he complained only of the stupidity and bad judgment of some of the Roumanian censors, but that he thought, considering the circumstances, that the censorship itself was not unreasonable); by a protecting attitude towards the Jews; and by commandeering which (whether one agree with General Greenly or General Bandholtz) was infinitely mild compared with the stripping of Roumania by the Hungarians and their allies.

CHAPTER XX

THE PEACE CONFERENCE AND ROUMANIA

It had rankled in the minds of Roumanian statesmen that at the Peace Conference of Berlin in 1878, they had been relegated to an inferior status, and had not even been listened to until after decisions had been made which affected them vitally. They were also nettled because the western world regarded them (with more or less reason, too, until the land reforms of our day) as a government of great landowners, reactionary and anti-Semitic in internal matters, and imperialistic and unscrupulous in foreign affairs. Consequently, when they entered the war, they stipulated in the treaty that at the Peace Conference afterwards, they should be treated as equals. Much of the friction at Paris might have been avoided if this stipulation had been remembered by the "Big Four." It is still impossible to get at the truth of the relations between Roumania and the Conference; but it is clear that the mistakes made by the "Big Four" in dealing with the Roumanian situation were among their most serious ones, and resulted in enormous loss of prestige, especially in Eastern Europe.

Those who knew the inner gossip of the Conference affirm that Clemenceau and his *alter ego,* Mandel, were anti-Roumanian from the start; that Lloyd George was ignorant of the facts necessary for an opinion; and that President Wilson and General Bliss, while equally ignorant of the Roumanian situation, formed anti-Roumanian prejudices deeper than their anti-Italian ones. Mr. Wilson's idea of handling the Roumanian situation was analogous to his procedure with Italy. There, the American influence at Paris was thrown openly against the Orlando Ministry, in the hope of electing another that would be easier to deal with. In the case of Roumania, a similar program was outlined, to eliminate the obnoxious Bratiano and bring into power a more pliant ministry. Immense pressure is also alleged to have been brought to bear on the American delegation, to secure immediate civic equality (or even special privileges, as it developed) for the Jews in Roumania. Furthermore, the enthusiastic group of American college professors who advised the American delegation, hardly one of whom knew Roumania even from casual travel, and no one of whom had ever resided there, were determined to settle the Roumanian problem strictly in accordance with the dictates of historians and geographers, no one of whom knew that region from long residence. I cannot resist telling an anecdote related by my late friend, Count Macchi di Cellere, Italian Ambassador to the United States. He told me, in September, 1919, that when he went to Europe on the *George Washington* with President Wilson's party, he thought it unbecoming an ambassador to discuss the problems shortly to be attacked by the Peace Conference. One day, however, he was drawn into an argument over one of the Adriatic problems with one of the historical experts accompanying our Peace Commission—gentlemen whom a facetious member of the Columbia Faculty dubbed the "experteers." Count Macchi di Cellere made some observation which this expert construed as a reflection on his knowledge of the elements of this particular problem. "Sir," said he, "I would have you know that for the past six months I have done nothing but study Adriatic problems." "Professor," replied the

Ambassador, "the blood in my veins has been struggling with those problems for the past three thousand years."

Roumania's case, therefore, was handicapped by numerous factors; a personal prejudice of Clemenceau's against Bratiano, communicated to other delegates; a general feeling that Roumania was a backward Balkan country, where the peasants and the Jews were exploited by a political gang of wealthy land-owners and concessionaires; a remarkable sympathy with Hungary, and some on the part of the Americans with Bulgaria; and a determination to cancel the secret treaty and lay out new boundaries without reference to strategic considerations (useless, in view of the League of Nations) or historic claims, or even commercial ties, but with regard to ethnology and linguistics.

Friction between the Conference and Roumania was due chiefly to two episodes; the Béla Kun attack on Roumania and her occupation of Buda-Pesth, and Roumania's refusal to sign the Minorities Treaty. In a separate chapter I discuss the Béla Kun campaign; and my own observations in Buda-Pesth and Transylvania threw lurid light, to me, on the whole Magyar-Roumanian situation. It remains here to summarize the activity of the Conference during this period, and to point out why the Roumanians resisted—a resistance which Take Jonesco counted against Bratiano as a political blunder of the first magnitude, but which was continued by his own ministry in August-September, 1920, in the Roumanian refusal to accept the division of the German reparation payments among the Allies.

At the outset, Roumania's representatives discovered that the Great Powers had no intention of honoring the treaty pledge that Roumania was to be treated as on an equality (presumably with Italy, which had come into the war with a similar treaty). Their initial mistake was in giving Roumania only two representatives, whereas Belgium and Jugo-Slavia were assigned three, although Roumania is a much larger state, and had a smaller proportion of former enemy subjects than Jugo-Slavia. Mr. Bratiano was certainly one of the foremost statesmen of our generation; nevertheless he and the other Roumanians at the Conference were systematically neglected. They were not given copies of the Treaty of Versailles till after mere correspondents had obtained them, and were not allowed to see the Treaty of St. Germain till summoned to write their names on the dotted line. As the Great Powers had discovered that Czecho-Slovakia, Poland, Roumania, Jugo-Slavia and Greece had made in the spring of 1919 a tentative agreement to act in concert and thus avoid being crushed by the French-British-American combination, they assigned consecutive hours to the representatives of these states for the signing, so that there would be no chance for a meeting and a collective protest.

Such despotic methods, worse even than those of the Treaty of Berlin, could only be tolerated if inspired by full knowledge of conditions. Unfortunately, this was lacking. Only that knowledge could give a criterion for action; and the whole Béla Kun episode, as well as the final back-down of the Supreme Council on the obnoxious provisions of the Minorities Treaty, shows how poorly informed or how misguided were the leaders of the Conference. Charges that financial concessions, particularly in connection with petroleum, were demanded of the Roumanians as the price for what they considered their rights, were repeated to me in some detail but are almost impossible to verify. There can, however, be no doubt that all manner of financial pressure was brought to bear on Roumania to induce her to sign the treaty, just as with Italy in the Adriatic controversy.

Peculiarly striking was the attitude of the Conference toward the Jewish question in Roumania. Some American Roumanian Jews, who treasured resentment against the Roumanian Government for the discrimination of which they had been the victims years before, are said to have brought up the question in the spring of 1919, and enlisted, it is said, very powerful financial interests on their side. Bratiano's government had, however, already drafted legislation giving both Jews and peasants the civil rights they had lacked in the past; and the Roumanian delegates felt that under these circumstances it would be graceful and symbolic for them to propose universal religious tolerance, as a tangible fruit of the Paris Conference. The famous Article 21 of the original Covenant of the League of Nations, which the Roumanians had hoped would solve their problems, with those of all the others, ran: "The High Contracting Parties agree in declaring that no obstacle shall interfere with the free exercise of every belief, religion or opinion whose practice is not incompatible with public order and morals, and that in their respective jurisdictions no one shall be disturbed in his life, liberty or pursuit of happiness by reason of his adherence to such a belief, religion or opinion." They supposed that in proposing this they were merely seconding the desires of the American Delegation; but when Clemenceau sent them to see Colonel House, he admitted that an embarrassing situation had arisen, and advised them to see President Wilson, who told them that unfortunately nothing could be done for the moment. Roumania's generous desires, embodied in the Roumanian law of June, 1919, were too advanced for the Conference. The British Constitution forbade a Roman Catholic to become sovereign or Chief Justice. The French Republic and the Kingdom of Italy were not on cordial terms with the Vatican. Every one knows that a Catholic, a Jew or a Mohammedan could hardly be elected President of the United States, even if not specifically excluded. But what definitely killed Roumania's enlightened proposal was a clever move on the part of the Japanese delegates. They saw an opportunity to secure a pronouncement for equality of races, as a corollary of the decree of religious tolerance; and the American representatives, who had no hesitation in condemning Roumanian discrimination against the Jews, were suddenly confronted with the moral obligation to urge the repeal of the "grandfather clauses" of the Southern States, and of the anti-Japanese legislation of the Pacific Slope. The Conference could of course through the League abolish war; but racial discrimination in the United States was beyond its jurisdiction; and American opposition forced the Roumanians to withdraw their proposal.

Roumania's attitude, backed up as it was by the new law giving Jews the vote, did not, however, satisfy the Conference. They insisted that Roumania should sign the special Minorities Treaty, together with Poland, Czecho-Slovakia and Jugo-Slavia. Powerful financial groups which desired to take advantage of the economic clauses of the treaty, aided the movement, as did the idealists of the west. Poland and Czecho-Slovakia signed without much ado, and their representatives made no bones of their feeling that their signatures had been secured under duress. Jugo-Slavia and Roumania held out for months, and Roumania was able to secure essential changes in the document. I stress this fact because a false impression has arisen, due to the publication of the treaty *as finally signed*. To understand the Roumanian attitude, one must study the treaty as it was set before them. Here it is; my copy is headed 6ᵉ Epreuve (6th proof), 8 août 1919. Whatever may have been the case with the Treaty of Versailles, this treaty was clearly first drafted in French, for the English is translation English, with occasional errors. My copy has French and English on opposite pages; I transcribe the English:

"DRAFT OF A TREATY
Between
THE UNITED STATES OF AMERICA, GREAT BRIT-AIN, FRANCE, ITALY, AND JAPAN, Described as the Principal Allied and Associated Powers,

On the one hand;

And ROUMANIA,

On the other hand;

Whereas under Treaties to which the principal Allied and Associated Powers are parties large accessions of territory are being and will be made to the Kingdom of Roumania, and

Whereas in the Treaty of Berlin the independence of the Kingdom of Roumania was only recognized subject to certain conditions, and

Whereas the principal Allied and Associated Powers now desire to recognize unconditionally the independence of the Kingdom of Roumania as regards both its former and its new territories, and

Whereas Roumania is desires (*sic*) of its own free will to give full guarantees of liberty and justice to all inhabitants both of the old Kingdom of Roumania and of the territory added thereto, to whatever race or religion they may belong.

For this purpose the following Representatives of the High Contracting Parties:

THE PRESIDENT OF THE UNITED STATES OF AMERICA, HIS MAJESTY THE KING OF THE UNITED KINGDOM OF GREAT BRITAIN AND IRE-LAND AND OF THE BRITISH DOMINIONS BEYOND THE SEAS, EMPEROR OF INDIA, THE PRESIDENT OF THE FRENCH REPUBLIC, HIS MAJESTY THE

KING OF ITALY, H. M. THE EMPEROR OF JAPAN, HIS MAJESTY THE KING OF ROUMANIA.

After having exchanged their full powers, found in good and due form, have agreed as follows:

The Allied and Associated Powers, signatories to the Treaty of Berlin, of the 13th July 1878, taking into consideration the obligations contracted under the present Treaty by the Roumanian Government, recognise that Roumania is definitely discharged from the conditions attached to the recognition of its independance (*sic*) by Article 44 of the said Treaty of Berlin."

This preamble was one of the chief stumbling-blocks in the treaty. Roumania having been a sovereign state in Europe for a generation, why in the world should the Treaty of Berlin be exhumed—particularly as neither Europe nor America considers that a model treaty? Evidently it was only an ingenious legal pretext for justifying the minorities clauses of the new treaty. Roumania promised to give the Jews full civil rights in the Treaty of Berlin, and never did; ergo, we have a legal hold on Roumania, for that was one of the conditions of her independence, and she has never fulfilled it. Roumanian opposition finally deleted this preamble.

"CHAPTER I

ARTICLE 1

Roumania undertakes that the stipulations contained in Articles 2 to 8 of this chapter shall be recognized as fundamental laws, and that no laws, regulation or official action shall conflict or interfere with these stipulations, nor shall any law, regulation or official action prevail over them.

Article 2

Roumania undertakes to assure full and complete protection of life and liberty to all inhabitants of Roumania without distinction of birth, nationality, language, race or religion.

All inhabitants of Roumania shall be entitled to the free exercise, whether public or private, of any creed, religion or belief, whose practices are not inconsistent with public order and public morals (Fr. les bonnes mœurs).

Article 3

Roumania admits and declares to be Roumanian nationals *ipso facto* and without the requirement of any formality, all persons habitually resident at the date of the coming into force of the present Treaty within the whole territory of Roumania, including the extensions made by the Treaties of Peace with Austria, Hungary, and Bulgaria, or any other extensions which may hereafter be made, who are not at that date nationals of any other foreign state except Anstrias (*sic*), Hungary and Bulgaria.

Nevertheless, Austrian, Hungarian and Bulgarian nationals who are over eighteen years of age will be entitled under the conditions contained in the said Treaties to opt (*sic*) for any other nationality which may be open to them. Option by a husband will cover his wife and option by parents will cover their children under eighteen years of age.

Persons who have exercised the above right to opt must, except where it is otherwise provided in the Treaty of Peace with Austria, Hungary and Bulgaria, transfer within the succeeding twelve months, their place of residence to the State for wich (*sic*) they have opted. They will be entitled to retain their immovable property in Roumanian territory. They may carry with them their movable property of every description. No export duties may be imposed upon them in connection with the removal of such property.

Article 4

Roumania admits and declares to be Roumanian nationals *ipso facto* and without the requirement of any formality persons of Austrian, Hungarian or Bulgarian nationality who were born in the territory ceded to Roumania by the treaties of Peace with Austria, Hungary and Bulgaria of parents habitually resident there, even if at the date of the coming into force of the present Treaty they are not themselves habitually resident there.

Nevertheless, within two years after the coming into force of the present Treaty, these persons may make a declaration before the competent Roumanian authorities in the country in which they are resident, stating that they abandon Roumanian nationality, and they will then cease to be considered as Roumanian nationals. In this connection a declaration by a husband will cover his wife, and a declaration by parents will cover their children under eighteen years of age.

Article 5

Roumania undertakes to put no hindrance in the way of the exercise of the right which the persons concerned have, under the Treaties concluded or to be concluded by the Allied and Associated Powers with Austria, Hungary or Bulgaria, to choose whether or not they will acquire Roumanian nationality.

Article 6

All persons born in Roumanian territory who are not born nationals of another State shall *ipso facto* become Roumanian nationals.

Article 7

All Roumanian nationals shall be equal before the law and shall enjoy the same civil and political rights without distinction as to race, language or religion.

Differences of religion, creed or confession shall not prejudice any Roumanian national in matters relating to the enjoyment of civil or political rights, as for instance admission to public employments, functions and honors, or the exercice (*sic*) of professions and industries.

No restrictions shall be imposed on the free use by any Roumanian national of any language in private intercourse, in commerce, in religion, in the press or in publications of any kind, or at public meetings.

Notwithstanding any establishment by the Roumanian Government of an official language, adequate facilities shall be given to Roumanian nationals of non-Roumanian speech for the use of their language, either orally or in writing, before the courts.

ARTICLE 8

Roumanian nationals who belong to racial, religious or linguistic minorities shall enjoy the same treatment and security in law and in fact as the other Roumanian nationals. In particular they shall have an equal right to establish, manage and control at their own expense charitable, religious and social institutions, schools and other educational establishments, with the right to use their own language and to exercise their religion freely therein.

ARTICLE 9

Roumania will provide in the public educational system in towns and districts in which a considerable proportion of Roumanian nationals of other than Roumanian speech are resident adequate facilities for ensuring that in the primary schools the instruction shall be given to the children of such Roumanian nationals through the medium of their own language. This provision shall not prevent the Roumanian Government from making the teaching of the Roumanian language obligatory in the said schools.

In towns and districts where there is a considerable proportion of Roumanian nationals belonging to racial, religious or linguistic minorities, these minorities shall be assured an equitable share in the enjoyment and application of the sums which may be provided out of public funds under the State, municipal or other budget, for educational, religious or charitable purposes.

ARTICLE 10

Educational Committees appointed locally by the Jewish communities of Roumania, will, subject to the general control of the State, provide for the distribution of the proportional share of public funds allocated to Jewish schools in accordance with Article 9, and for the organization and management of these schools.

The provisions of Article 9 concerning the use of languages in schools shall apply to these schools.

ARTICLE 11

Jews shall not be compelled to perform any act which constitutes a violation of their Sabbath nor shall they be placed under any disability by reason of their refusal to attend courts of law or to perform any legal business on their Sabbath. This provision however shall not exempt Jews from such obligations as shall be imposed upon all other Roumanian citizens for the necessary purposes of military service, national defense or the preservation of public order.

Roumania declares her intention to refrain from ordering or permitting elections, whether general or local, to be held on a Saturday, nor will registration for electoral or other purposes be compelled to be performed on a Saturday.

ARTICLE 12

Roumania agrees of (*sic*) accord to the communities of the Saxons and Czecklers (*sic*) in Transylvania local autonomy in regard of scholastic and religious matters, under the control of the Roumanian State.

ARTICLE 13

Roumania agrees that the stipulations in the foregoing Articles, so far as they affect persons belonging to racial, religious or linguistic minorities, constitute obligations of international concern and shall be placed under the guarantee of the League of Nations. They shall not be modified without the assent of a majority of the Council of the League of Nations. The United States, the British Empire, France, Italy and Japan hereby agree not to withhold their assent from any modification in these Articles which is in due form assented to by a majority of the Council of the League of Nations.

Roumania agrees that any Member of the Council of the League of Nations shall have the right to bring to the attention of the Council any infraction, or any danger of infraction, of any of these obligations, and that the Council may thereupon take such action and give such direction as it may deem proper and effective in the circumstances.

Roumania further agrees that any difference of opinion as to questions of law or fact arising out of these Articles between the Roumanian Government and any one of the Principal Allied and Associated Powers or any other Power, a Member of the Council of the League of Nations, shall be held to be a dispute of an international character under Article 14 of the Covenant of the League of Nations. The Roumanian Government hereby consents that any such dispute shall, if the other party thereto demands, be referred to the Permanent Court of International Justice. The decision of the Permanent Court shall be final and shall have the same force and effect as an award under Article 13 of the Covenant."

The Roumanian feeling was that (however admirable these provisions might appear theoretically) this chapter intermeddled in the internal affairs of a friendly state. What

would have been our reply in the United States if Allies to
whom we owed huge sums of money should insist that we
incorporate into our fundamental law provisions that, e. g.,
Pennsylvania Dutch, New England French Canadians, and
New Mexico Spaniards must always have primary schools
in their own vernacular at public expense; that we must
never prohibit the use of German or Russian in publications
or meetings; that Jewish schools should not merely be maintained at public expense but that their control should be
taken out of the local school superintendent's hands and
lodged in those of a local Jewish committee; that we must
promise never to hold elections or even registration on
Saturday; that our law courts might never summon a Jew
to testify on Saturday; or that any German or Russian who
thought that his rights were *likely to be* infringed could
complain to any member of the Council of the League of
Nations, and we should have to stand trial? What should
we have done if informed that we could have no more credit,
could not even have the supplies in our Allies' harbors already bought and paid for, unless we swallowed all this just
as it stood? But let us pursue the Treaty further:

"CHAPTER II

ARTICLE 14

Roumania undertakes to make no Treaty, Convention or
arrangement and to take no other action which will prevent
her from joining in any general Convention for the equitable
treatment of the commerce of other States that may be concluded under the auspices of the League of Nations within
five years from the coming into force of the present Treaty.

Roumania also undertakes to extend to all the Allied and

Associated Powers any favors or privileges in Customs matters, which it may grant during the same period of five years to any State with which since August 1914 the Allied and Associated Powers have been at war or to any State which in virtue of Article 6 of Part X of the Treaty of Austria has special Customs arrangements with such States.

ARTICLE 15

Pending the conclusion of the general convention referred to above, Roumania undertakes to treat on the same footing as national vessels or vessels of the most favored nation the vessels of all the Allied and Associated Powers which accord similar treatment to Roumanian vessels. As an exception from this provision, the right of Roumania or of any other Allied or Associated Power to confine her maritime coasting trade to national vessels is expressly reserved.

ARTICLE 16

Pending the conclusion under the auspices of the League of Nations of a general convention to secure and maintain freedom of communications and of transit, Roumania undertakes to accord freedom of transit to persons, goods, vessels, carriages, wagons and mails in transit to or from any Allied or Associated State over Roumanian territory, including territorial waters, and to treat them at least as favorably as the persons, goods, vessels, carriages, wagons and mails respectively of Roumanian or of any other more favored nationality, origin, importation or ownership, as regards facilities, charges, restrictions, and all other matters.

All charges imposed in Roumania on such traffic in transit shall be reasonable having regard to the conditions of the traffic. Goods in transit shall be exempt from all customs or other duties.

Tariffs for transit across Roumania and tariffs between Roumania and any Allied or Associated Power involving through tickets or waybills shall be established at the request of the Allied or Associated Power concerned.

Freedom of transit will extend to postal, telegraphic and telephonic services.

Provided that no Allied or Associated Power can claim the benefit of these provisions on behalf of any part of its territory in which reciprocal treatment is not accorded in respect of the same subject matter.

If within a period of five years from the coming into force of this Treaty no general convention as aforesaid shall have been concluded under the auspices of the League of Nations, Roumania shall be at liberty at any time thereafter to give twelve months notice to the Secretary General of the League of Nations to terminate the obligations of the present Article.

ARTICLE 17

Pending the conclusion of a general Convention on the international Régime of Waterways, Roumania undertakes to apply to such portions of the River System of the Pruth as may lie within, or form the boundary of, her territory, the régime set out in the first paragraph of Article 332 and in Articles 333–338 of the Treaty of Peace with Germany.

ARTICLE 18

All rights and privileges accorded by the foregoing articles to the Allied and Associated Powers shall be accorded equally to all States members of the League of Nations.

THE PRESENT TREATY, of which the French and English texts are both authentic, shall be ratified. It shall come into force at the same time as the Treaty of Peace with Austaia (*sic*).

The deposit of ratifications shall be made at Paris.

Powers of which the seat of the Government is outside Europe will be entitled merely to inform the Government of the French Republic through their diplomatic representative at Paris that their ratification has been given; in that case they must transmit the instrument of ratification as soon as possible.

A procès-verbal of the deposit of ratifications will be drawn up.

The French Government will transmit to all the signatory Powers a certified copy of the procès-verbal of the deposit of ratifications.

IN FAITH WHEREOF the above-named Plenipotentiaries have signed the present Treaty.

Done at Versailles, in a single copy which will remain deposited in the archives of the French Republic, and of which authenticated copies will be transmitted to each of the Signatory Powers."

Here again one must ask: how would the United States have regarded a demand that we set "reasonable" charges for freight in transit, outsiders to be the judges, and otherwise surrender our rate-making power to an international commission?

It will now be clear why the Roumanian delegation at Paris fought so steadfastly against signing the treaty in the form in which it was set before them. The Eighth Plenary Session of the Peace Conference, on May 31, 1919, was devoted to objections to this treaty. I use a copy of the official French minutes. Bratiano handed in a written memorandum; when he rose to speak, Clemenceau remarked that this memorandum had been in his hands only three minutes; whereupon Bratiano rejoined that the treaty itself had been in his less than 24 hours! Annex A of this memorandum deals with the Bucovina; Annex B repeated what Bratiano had previously written to Berthelot, that Roumania had now assured complete equality of rights and liberties, political and religious, to all her citizens, without distinction of race or confession. "She considers as a Roumanian citizen every person born in Roumania and not a foreign subject, as well as every inhabitant of the territories recently united with Roumania who was a subject of the governments formerly in possession of those territories, except as they may declare their preference for another citizenship." Roumania, the annex states, had favored the guarantees proposed for all the countries included in the League of Nations, but objected strongly to any discrimination, and pointed out the danger that certain minorities, unduly favored by outside help, would become a superclass of citizens, depending not on their own government, but on some external force. Roumania "cannot subscribe to stipulations limiting her rights as a sovereign state . . . or brook a special régime, to which other sovereign states are not subject. That is why she declares herself ready to insert in the treaty draft . . . 'Roumania grants to all the minorities, linguistic, racial or religious, dwelling within her new boundaries, rights equal to those belonging to the other citizens.' "

Annex C took the same position with regard to the sections of the treaty which, Roumania thought, infringed her independence in the matter of freight rates, etc. Roumania was willing to accept all regulations of these matters which the League of Nations might establish for *all* countries. In Annex D Roumania stated her willingness to sign the Treaty with Austria, with reserves as indicated, but warned the Conference not to assume that she would acquiesce in similar fashion in the treaties with the other enemy states.

In his comment on Bratiano's objections, Clemenceau remarked: "As regards minority rights, I am very happy to know that Mr. Bratiano thinks precisely as do we all. The question is to know whether, by reason of the historic past of certain peoples, it may be necessary to give, I won't say supplementary guarantees, but guarantees of a more complete order, which may be recognized as necessary. That is a question on which we shall have to take sides. I beg Mr. Bratiano and all those who may have observations of the same nature to present, to be fully assured that there is no thought of humiliating anybody, of treading on the sovereign rights of any nation whatsoever, but that, to tell the truth, the history of the whole world, with respect to minorities, is not altogether the same. There are in this regard distinctions so necessary that we wish to humiliate no one in proposing a right of control at the hands of foreign governments, as Mr. Bratiano phrases it in his text, but by the League of Nations, of which we are accepting the control over ourselves under the conditions which have been indicated by Mr. Bratiano. So there can be no question here of humiliating any one, or of treading on any one's sovereignty."

Bratiano soon took exception to various statements of Clemenceau's, noting particularly that Clemenceau's allusion to the League of Nations as the controlling agent was not borne out by Bratiano's draft, which mentioned the principal Allied and Associated Powers as the agent—"the dispositions which these powers judge necessary to protect in Roumania the interests, etc." "So," he continued, "as I was just saying, it is the Great Powers who intervene to assure minority rights within the Kingdom of Roumania. It is against that principle that I have proposed a modification, because Roumania was an independent country before the war, and I do not think that her attitude during the war can in any way have justified a surrender of this political independence."

"It is not my business," said Clemenceau, "to judge Roumania's attitude. I admit that Mr. Bratiano's remark with regard to protection by the Governments instead of by the League of Nations, conforms with the text under discussion. Granting that, my observations remain, and I do not think that it is humiliating for Roumania to receive friendly counsels given by the United States, Great Britain, Italy, France. I simply told him that historical traditions have perpetuated themselves in certain countries, that rectifications based on these traditions have long been demanded, even in other treaties of which Mr. Bratiano is not without knowledge, and that they could not be secured. Under these conditions, the text of which he complains, and of which I think the other Slav (!) states will not complain, is rather an encouragement and a support. We should like to see our friendly activity interpreted in the sense I have sketched and not that which he has chosen to give it—wrongly, I feel."

In reply, Bratiano observed that one of the prime purposes of the Conference had been to establish equal rights for states large and small, and to make rulings which should serve as principles and precedents. "Among these rulings I call your attention to one tending to establish to-day different classes, as regards state sovereignty. In the name of Roumania, I cannot admit this principle. It is not a question of friendly counsels here, but of a contractual agreement. The Roumanian Government will always be disposed to accept the counsels of its great friends. But counsels inscribed in treaties, under the form of precise engagements of one government to another, no longer have this purely friendly character. History provides us with precedents in this matter. Thus, the Russians intervened in the policy of Turkey, to protect the Christians, and the result for Turkey was inevitably her dissolution. In appearance, the action was sympathetic, but it had no logic unless it had as final purpose the independence of the Christian peoples. With any other end in view, it is not possible to admit such action, either in the interest of the states involved, or the minorities. . . . We wish, with you, to build a new world to take the place of the old one. This new world should be so established that the states may find in their citizens devoted sons, and a life of brotherly agreement. If the minorities know that the liberties they enjoy are guaranteed them not by the solicitude of the state to which they belong, but by the protection of some foreign government, whatever it may be, the base of the state will be undermined. . . . It is in the name, gentlemen, not only of the independence of the Roumanian state, but in the name of two great principles which this Conference represents, that I have formulated these observations. One of these deals with peace, order and fraternity between the various peoples of one and the same state, the other looks to the equality of all states, large and small, with reference to their rights of home legislation. That is why I ask, in the name of Roumania, that conditions be not imposed on her which she cannot accept."

After a promise by Clemenceau that Bratiano's observations would be submitted to a new examination by the Heads of Governments, Paderewski for Poland, Kramarsch for Czecho-Slovakia and Trumbitch for Jugo-Slavia, were heard; then President Wilson took the floor. He would deeply regret, he said, a breaking-up of the session with the fixed idea in anyone's mind that the Great Powers were bent on imposing their will on the Lesser Powers in a spirit of authority and pride. "We wish," he said, "to ensure world peace, and to force all factors that might disturb and endanger the future, to disappear. One of the essential conditions for this is an equitable distribution of territory according to the affinities and desires of the inhabitants. Having secured that, the Allied and Associated Powers will guarantee the maintenance of the terms (as just as possible) which we shall have reached. It is they who will undertake the engagement and the burden, it must be on them that the responsibility will chiefly fall, just as it is they who in the nature of things have made the most considerable effort during the war, and we must not forget that it is force which is the final guarantee of public peace. Under these conditions is it unfair that, speaking not as dictators but as counselors and friends, they should say to you: We cannot guarantee your boundaries if we do not believe that they satisfy certain principles of right? . . . The same reasoning applies to the minorities question. It is with the same solicitude that the statute regarding minorities was mentioned. If you wish the principal Allied and Associated Powers to guarantee the very existence of governments, is it unfair that they should require satisfaction with regard to the conditions which they consider indispensable for the avoidance of future causes of war? We ask our friends of Serbia and Roumania to believe that we have no intention this afternoon of dealing any blow to long-established and universally recognized governments; but to the territories that these long-established governments are to recover, the present Peace Treaty will add much. It is impossible, for instance, on the one hand to treat the Kingdom of the Serbs, Croats and Slovenes as a unit, in consequence of the events which we have witnessed, and on the other to treat as a state apart in certain respects, the Kingdom of Serbia. If these states are formally established, thanks to the treaty which we are making together, those who in the last analysis will guarantee its execution have the right to see to it that the conditions on which these states are to be definitively established, shall be such as to ensure public peace. Our desire in this is not to intervene in such a way as to annoy these states in any respect, but to help them and to help the common cause. We hope that you will not hesitate to accept our point of view, for we see no other way to regulate this question.

"How could the Government of the United States, if it believed that the regulations agreed upon contained unstable and dangerous elements, present itself before Congress, before the American people, and claim that it had helped in ensuring world peace? If the world should again find itself disturbed, if the conditions which we all consider fundamental should again be called in question, the guarantee given you means that the United States will send their army and their fleet to this side of the ocean. Is it surprising that under these conditions, they wish to act so that the regulation of the various problems may seem to them entirely satisfactory? I would say in particular to Mr. Bratiano that we have not the faintest desire to tread on the sovereignty of his country, that we wish to do nothing that may displease him. Roumania will issue from this war great and powerful, with increases of territory due to common effort and to the strength of our arms. We have then the right to insist on certain conditions which to our mind will make this success final. I beg my friend Mr. Bratiano, my friend Mr. Kramarsch, my friend Mr. Trumbitch, to believe that if, in the section just discussed, we made mention only of the Great Powers, it was not because they wish to impose their conditions, but simply because they wish to assure themselves that they can guarantee with all their available strength the sum total of the advantages which this treaty confers on you as it does on us. The point is, we must work together, and this coöperation can only be based on harmony. To leave the solution of these questions to further negotiations, as has been suggested, would mean that when this Conference has finished its labors, separate groups would decide among themselves what ought in reality to form part of the general basis for world peace. That seems impossible. I hope that we shall arrive—that is our purpose—at a cordial and voluntary coöperation on the only possible basis. That basis must be so expressed: it is where force resides (du côté de la force) that the maintenance of peace will be ensured; it is where force resides that the supreme guarantee of this peace will rest. You must not err in the meaning we ascribe to the word 'force.' The United States have never had any aggressive intentions, and you know the motive of their intervention in the affairs of the Old World. We are pursuing a common goal; all we wish is to help you reach that goal, in concert with us; our only wish is to associate ourselves with you, and we wish to do nothing that may be opposed to your real interests."

"President Wilson's lofty personality," replied Bratiano, "gives all his words and counsels a specially authoritative character. I would permit myself, in the name of the great principles which the President himself has proclaimed, to call his friendly attention to the fear that certain applications of principles established with best of intentions, may work out to results diametrically opposed to the ends sought. As I was just saying, there should issue from the labors of this Conference a result beyond all discussion. It has accomplished a great work of justice. It has established not merely guarantees against the enemy, but also the equality of all states, great and small. If principles such as it is to-day desired to insert in the Treaty with Austria had been put into the Statute of the Society of Nations, we should not have opposed it. President Wilson will please recall that the Roumanian Delegation voted to have these principles established once for all and for everybody. To act as is planned in the present treaty is to establish different grades of sovereignty. With all the sentiments of friendship and deep admiration which I hold toward the Italian people, I cannot imagine why, under identical conditions, countries like Roumania or Serbia should be treated differently from Italy. On the other hand, as I had the honor to explain, it is desired to establish a fraternal relation between peoples forced by their geographic position to constitute themselves into one state. It would be a capital error to make these relations of friendship depend on a third party, no matter who that might be. We must not lose sight of the fact that while there are at the head of the present Great Powers men actuated by the noblest of principles, it may easily happen that political changes may cause these same states to be represented by other men, or that new interests may arise which may turn certain governments away from their previous attitude, and may lead them on to activities not conceived after these high principles, but in favor of certain special interests.

"It is certain that the Great Powers, by their sacrifices, assured the victory of the great cause of all; but I shall allow myself to add to the words the President has pronounced (for which I thank him in the name of all the smaller states) when he affirms that the solicitude of all the great political factors has been gained for us, and that he wishes to guarantee the security of all—I shall add, I say, that the responsibility of each state remains none the less complete, whatever its size, as regards its own independence and security. Thus, at this moment, Roumania is obliged to ensure with her own troops the defense not alone of her boundaries, but also of a cause interesting all Central Europe. So, while the Great Powers have a more considerable rôle, by virtue of their size, the responsibility and the rôle of the independent states, no matter what their size, remain complete.

"I beg the representatives of the Great Powers and especially President Wilson not to restrict by dangerous application, great principles which are dear to us all. No effort is needed to secure recognition of the rights of minorities; not a state at this moment represented here is not convinced of the need of respecting and developing these liberties. So allow these states to develop under the only conditions permitting the peaceful consolidation of the general political status we are to establish to-day.

"Animated by sentiments both of respect and of gratitude toward the Great Powers for the services which they have rendered, I beg them urgently to examine with all the interest attaching to such great principles, the proposals and statements made by the Roumanian Government; for it is necessary that these proposals be admitted, otherwise Roumania would no longer preserve in her entirety the independence which she enjoyed in the past, for the regulation of questions of a domestic character."

Since the raising of these fundamental questions threatened to delay again the presentation of this treaty to the Austrian delegates, Venizelos suggested that these clauses be detached from the main Treaty with Austria, since they did not interest Austria directly, and that the five heads of Great Powers, with the heads of Powers with Limited Interests, should meet and endeavor to come to an agreement. That ushered in months of fighting.

I was distressed that the American representatives insisted upon their signing, with as much force as the others. One American diplomat asked me to use what influence I might have to make them see they must sign at once. "But,"

I protested, "I have been reading the treaty over and I think many of their objections are valid." "Oh, yes," he replied, "I know there are various things there that are a little strong, but they've got to understand they must sign, and then we'll be reasonable in the enforcement. They must be made to realize they can't keep on 'gumming the game' like this."

But the steam-roller met a snag. No Roumanian public man could be found to sign such a document. Finally the Peace Conference had to admit defeat, withdrawing practically all the obnoxious clauses, as will be seen by comparing my draft with the signed treaty. All the fierce opposition roused in Roumania against the Conference and the League of Nations, which this treaty visualized as a continuation of Conference methods, all the economic and financial pressure which sorely hampered Roumania's recovery, was thrown away, and Roumania preserved her independence.

The Roumanians scored a similar victory in the matter of Béla Kun. As a result of the "ignorance of the question, misinformation and divergence of purposes" (the characterization of a judicious Roumanian diplomat, who absolves the Conference of any sinister motive), Paris vacillated, while Roumanian policy, based on self-defense against Hungary, was fairly consistent. Hungary, under Béla Kun, had broken the armistice conditions; and in the spring of 1919, the Roumanian Staff learned that he was planning a campaign against Roumania. This campaign was diverted to Czecho-Slovakia, to be sure; but Béla Kun paid slight attention to the fulminations of the Peace Conference against him, and went on with his preparations against Roumania, which culminated in the campaign of late July, an account of which is given in Chapter XVIII. This campaign, after initial successes, collapsed completely before the clever strategy of the Roumanians; Kun had to flee, and a new transitional socialist government, under Peidll, was formed at Buda-Pesth. This seemed on the face of it to be an acceptance by the Hungarians of Clemenceau's ultimatum of July 26th, which told the Hungarian people that they must expel Kun or face a blockade. But the Roumanian High Command felt no confidence in Hungarian promises, and decided that the only sensible policy was to disarm the Hungarians and make it impossible for them to start a new campaign. A breach at once occurred with Paris. On August 2nd the Supreme Council sent a message to the Roumanian Government requesting that their army cease its advance upon Buda-Pesth immediately. Military exigency, thought the Roumanian Chief of Staff, necessitated the disregard of this "request," and the occupation of Buda-Pesth followed.

On August 5 the Supreme Council sent instructions to the Inter-Allied Council in Buda-Pesth to direct the Roumanians to leave as soon as they had disarmed the Red Guard. Gen. Bandholtz was sent from Paris to be the American representative on the Inter-Allied Commission in Buda-Pesth. On the 6th, the situation was further complicated by the overthrow of the Peidll Government, and the brief installation of the Archduke Joseph as Governor; his Premier, Friedrich, became at once dictator of the Hungarian state, and lasted several months. He was one of the most unscrupulous of Hungarian politicians, and was accused of inspiring the murder, or attempted murder, of several of his opponents, including Károlyi. He at once brought all his arts into play in prejudicing the Inter-Allied Council against the Roumanians, and in misinforming credulous Paris. Hungarian methods were amply shown in the mutilation of the text of the Roumanian ultimatum to Hungary; as received at Paris, it lacked the restriction of live-stock requisition—the Roumanians asked 30% of that existing in the district east of the Theiss only—and gave the world the impression that the Roumanians were demanding 30% of the live-stock of all Hungary! No wonder that the Supreme Council thought the Roumanian terms excessive, and refused to recognize the ultimatum.

In this and similar ways, whatever anti-Roumanian feeling existed at Paris and abroad, was skillfully inflamed. Perhaps the most successful stroke, from the Hungarian standpoint, was the unfortunate credulity of a Food Administration officer (outside of Hungary) who lent his authority to the lying rumor that the Roumanians had interfered with the milk supply of Buda-Pesth hospitals, and had thus caused the death of a number of babies (see p. 210). This "savagery" made a deep impression all over the world, and the painstaking refutation of the story by the Roumanians has received very little publicity. In propaganda, a clever lie, perpetrated at the right moment, is infinitely effective.

But it is high time to leave this overheated atmosphere, charged with prejudice and passion, and return to the Roumanian people themselves. In the succeeding chapters we shall see what they have contributed to culture, in their vigorous and harmonious language, their fascinating literature and their piquant art and architecture.

CHAPTER XXI

ROUMANIAN ART AND ARCHITECTURE

THE Roumanians are the only Romance people who belong to the Greek Orthodox Church; their language is Roman, but their civilization sprang from Constantinople. Of the other branches of the Latin race, only the Portuguese and the Spaniards, the Venetians and the Sicilians show strong Oriental influence in their art; and with them, painting and the lesser arts soon cast off the Eastern tradition. In Roumania, Greek artistic supremacy gave way to that of Christian Byzantium, and Western influence was late and slight. To understand Roumanian art and architecture, one must know Persia and Turkey, Armenia and Georgia, to appreciate much that strikes us as strange and exotic.

The beginnings of art in Roumania are very ancient. The Ægean civilization embraced Roumania; inland at Cucuteni, near Jassy, are found painted potsherds and terra-cotta figurines of the "owl's head" type, identical in style with those of Asia Minor. Geometric vases occur also; and it is clear that the Thracians who lived in these plains north of the Danube were affected by the civilization of the Greek islands. The Black Sea coast was colonized by Greeks; and the Archæological Museum of Bucharest is full of fragments of statues and monuments from Histria and from Tomi—Constantza of to-day, first known to the western world as the remote place of exile for the poet Ovid.

Long before Ovid's day, the Romans had come to know and respect the Dacians—that branch of the Thracians who lived in what is now Roumania, north of the Danube. They were too proud and strong to come under the Roman yoke as easily as had the Macedonians and the Greeks. It was reserved for Trajan to vanquish their famous king Decebalus, and bring Dacia into the Roman Empire. We are fortunate in having a record of this campaign from the best period of Roman art; the marble reliefs on Trajan's Column at Rome show us Dacian soldiers and cavaliers in their struggles with the Romans, and reveal the astounding fact that Dacian dress has changed but little in the past 1800 years; the Roumanian peasant still wears his shirt outside, and his trousers are still tight and clinging!

Roumanian archæologists try to find Trajan's inspiration in the huge monument, down in the Dobrudja, called by its Turkish name Adam-Klissi (Church of the Man). This is much like Hadrian's Tomb in Rome, and was decorated with large carved reliefs, representing Roman soldiers and barbarians. I examined the reliefs in the King Charles Park at Bucharest; they are crude and rough in execution, and it seems to me impossible that they should be as early as Trajan; I should assign them to the latest period of Roman occupation. They doubtless represent some victory over invading Sarmatians, just before the final evacuation of Dacia by the Romans.

In the third century, Dacia passed out of Roman hands; its first new masters were the Goths. We can get some idea of their civilization from the gold ornaments which have come to light in a dozen different sites of Greater Roumania; one or two of these are comparable to the Visigothic gold treasure from near Toledo, now in the Musée de Cluny, or the trophies preserved at Monza. In 1797, at Shimleul Silvaniei (Hung. Szilágy-Somlyó), in northwestern Transylvania, two Roumanian small boys unearthed a treasure of fourteen golden Imperial medallions, from Maximilian to Valentinian (290–374 A. D.); a magnificent double gold necklace; a silver brooch; golden garnet earrings; bracelets ending in snake's heads with garnet eyes; a garnet torque and garnet rings; and a gold seal decorated with garnets and pearls. The necklace terminates in a topaz globe, on which stand two golden lions; along its sides are attached over 50 ornaments and tiny models of farm and household objects, like scissors, hammers, a plowshare, etc.; the most striking is perhaps a tiny boat, with a naked man at the tiller. In 1799 a peasant at Nagy-Szent-Miklós (Sân-Nicolaul-Mare), in the Torontal (Banat), dug up a golden treasure of 23 objects for the table—cups, goblets, a drinking-horn, etc.—known as the Attila Treasure; but it is Gothic, not Hunnish. Most interesting of all is the Pietroasa Treasure. This was found in 1837 in a heap of stone blocks on a Moldavian hill-top, the ruins of a Gothic temple and castle. As one of the largest pieces and four of the smaller were in the form of birds (eagles), the peasants who found the treasure called it "The Hen with the Golden Chickens," and the name stuck; there is a curious resemblance to the "Gallina cum VII pullicinis"—the Hen with the Seven Chickens—which the Gothic Queen Theodelind gave to the Monza Cathedral in the year 595. There are altogether thirteen pieces—bracelets (one of which has a runic inscription), a large circular platter on a round support, two round pateras, two open-work baskets, one 8-sided and one 12-sided, a high narrow pitcher, several large brooches, etc. The most interesting piece is the patera, which is decorated with the likenesses, in raised relief, of the gods of Walhalla —Odin, Thor, Freya, Tyr, Baldur and their companions. The runic inscription seems to read "Gutani ocwi hailag," of which the first and last words must mean "sacred to

Gutan (Odin)." The conventionalized eagles of the brooches, and the leopards which form the handles of the graceful baskets, rouse the admiration of all who feel the charm of that strange early mediæval art which we call Merovingian.

After the Goths, darkness descends on Dacia; Huns, Slavs and other semi-savage tribes pour down into its plains, and art ceases to exist, except as shepherds and peasants transmit traditional textile designs in their spinning and weaving. Roumanian archæologists find the first dawn of a new era in the ruins of a tiny fortified Byzantine church, Sân-Nicoară, near Argesh, which was the first capital of Wallachia. Sân-Nicoară seems to date from the late 900's— a period during which almost all churches must still have been of wood. The earliest church to come down to us is perhaps a later church of St. Nicholas at Argesh, built beside the ruins of the smaller one. This, of the thirteenth century, was erected by some prince of the Bessarab family (who gave their name to Bessarabia); his body, in a red silk jacket decorated with fleurs-de-lis, with pearls and gold buttons, was recently brought to light. This church is a handsome bit of thoroughly Byzantine architecture, decorated with remarkable frescoes.

Roumanian church painting was (according to the canons of the Oriental Church) regulated by the manual elaborated by the monks of Mt. Athos. Eighteenth and nineteenth century frescoes in Roumanian churches are still laid out under regulations first drawn up by Panselinus of Saloniki, in the twelfth century; his rules govern the painting of the icons—the religious images—in every Roumanian church and home. Panselinus' rule was the latest manual at the time when the Wallachian and Moldavian Principalities were founded; his precepts became an integral part of Roumanian Orthodox Christianity, in its struggles against Mohammedanism to the south and against Roman Catholicism and Protestantism to the west. The traditional art of the icon seems as much a part of his religion to the average Roumanian as do the exact words of the King James version to the average English or American Protestant. His stiff unreal icon symbolizes the centuries of battle which kept the faith unchanged through all the attacks of enemies.

It was a simple style which Panselinus embalmed. The backgrounds are uniform, whether plain gilt or architectonic. The figures are outlined in the same plane and in easy attitudes; they tend to lengthen out, like El Greco's, under ascetic influences. The whole composition is governed by the law of frontality; whether the figures look toward us or are in profile, their bodies are seen from in front. Mountains become stairs; perspective is rudimentary; trees are bushy stalks. Costumes are ancient—the tunic and mantle thrown over the shoulder. The whole icon breathes forth an antique perfume; for correctness in drawing and color it substitutes the conventional charm of a mediæval manuscript.

Church painting, then, offers little distinctive in Roumania; the frescoes and icons differ but slightly from those across the Serbian border. In Moldavia, there is visible certain Russian (and still more Polish) influence. But characteristically Roumanian are the huge fortified monasteries which arise in scores under the great voyevodes of the fifteenth and sixteenth centuries. All available resources of art and architecture were lavished upon them and their churches; we know over forty churches built by Stephen the Great alone (1457–1504). These monasteries had fortified walls; within, they provided the cells, refectory, offices and private chapels needed by the monks, and handsome apartments for the Prince and for guests. In the center rises the church, of simple but distinguished architecture, and well proportioned towers and cupolas. It has an outside porch (pronaos) with a colonnade, which is open in Wallachia, closed in Moldavia; the balustrade of this pronaos and of the stair-case leading up to it shows much variety of style during the centuries. Elaborate frescoes adorn the outer walls.

One of the first of these monasteries is that founded by Radu (Ralph) the Great, the wealthy and pious Prince of Wallachia at the beginning of the sixteenth century. Among his vineyards on the hillside over the Ialomitza River, near the city of Târgovishte, his architects erected a white marble church in the center of a monastery group called the Deal (hill). Over the porch rise two high towers, with one still higher over the rear; delicate and playful arabesques run over the façade, the windows and even the bases of the towers. Up in Moldavia, Stephen the Great had just been building a series of solid brick or stone monasteries, decorated outside with enameled terra-cotta plaques, and already showing Gothic influence from neighboring Poland, but in the windows alone; Gothic arches of the nave do not come in till the reign of Basil the Wolf, in the seventeenth century. To commemorate his victory over the Tartars, Stephen founded the monastery of Putna in the Bucovina, which is his own last resting place. He had found only four monasteries in Moldavia: Neamtz, which was built on a spur of the Carpathians about 1390 and became the center of Church Slavonic lore; Bistritza, founded a few years later under Alexander the Good; Pobrata, apparently a more ancient foundation; and Moldovitza, whose charter, also of Alexander the Good, dates from October 31, 1402. Stephen renewed, enlarged or beautified all these; but Putna

COUNTRY CHURCH NEAR ARAD

MONASTERY CHURCH, SUCEVITZA

was his special foster-child. It was begun in the summer of 1466; and we have a donation to Pobrata, signed by Stephen from Putna in 1471. Putna has been much worked over since Stephen's day; but the church preserves many features of that time, including the slender steeple over the center of the nave, and the sturdy bell-tower, standing, like an Italian campanile, apart from the church, in the center of the enclosing wall. Tower, steeple, arches, friezes are decorated with round enameled plaques, in various colors, which show upon them coats of arms, dragons, and other strange animals; Gothic touches, doubtless due to Transylvanian architects, appear in the windows and doors. Stephen lavished all manner of adornment upon Putna; to-day, we have in this and other of his foundations, an occasional cross, and a few richly woven tapestries. These tapestries, which were hung over the monuments of princes and wealthy boyars, preserve interesting likenesses of the deceased, and throw much light on the history of costume. Especially interesting was the discovery at Câmpulung in 1920, in the royal tombs dating from 1266 to 1344, of the purple silk pseudo-imperial mantle of Vladislav Bessarab, together with his pearl-encrusted crown, which was taken as the model for that used at King Ferdinand's coronation at Alba-Julia.

Stephen's foundations of Putna, Humor and Voronetz are all in the Bucovina. The most famous Moldavian church dates from Basil the Wolf (1624–1653)—the Three Hierarchs of Jassy. This also has a row of enameled plaques running about it; but its chief external decoration, even on the two eight-sided towers, is arcade after arcade of niches and stalactite work, carved in the stone. These lines of niches, filled with paintings of saints, are characteristic of Moldavian churches. The Three Hierarchs fortunately still possesses most of its treasures of jewels, tapestries, etc.

In Wallachia, the earliest monasteries—Voditza, Cotmeana and Tismana—arose under Byzantine architectural influence, transmitted by the Serbs; they seem to have been the first church designers in Wallachia (except for the very early Sân-Nicoară). The abbey of Cofia, though dating from the beginnings of Roumanian architecture (about 1400), is one of the finest examples. The most celebrated monastery and church are undoubtedly those of the first capital, Argesh. Built under Neagoe Voda (Bessarab IV, 1512–1521), they form a complex of great architectural interest; unfortunately the church had to be dismantled and restored in recent years. It is crowned with two large eight-sided towers, one with rectangular windows, the other with rounded ones; over the entrance are two lower towers, in which the rounded narrow windows are set askew, slanting on each tower in the direction of the other. Arcades of pilasters run about the church, enclosing sculptured medallions; and carved arabesques, with beautiful intertwining patterns, meet the eye everywhere, even on the towers. The lavish use of blue and gilt, combined with these strange helicoid towers, gives an exotic effect. This church guards the mortal remains of the Roumanian ruling house.

The seventeenth and eighteenth centuries saw a great increase in foreign influence—a Gothic stream coming from the north and northwest, a Venetian and Genoese current from overseas. Wealthy and devout princes built monasteries and palaces fascinating in their reminiscences of the Golden Horn on the one hand, of the Grand Canal on the other. The epoch of Sherban Cantacuzene (1678–1688) and Constantine Brancovan (1688–1714) in Wallachia vies (on a smaller scale) with the contemporary period of Louis XIV. The monastery of Hurez and the palaces of Mogoshoaia and Potlogi are *chefs d'œuvre* of Roumanian architecture and art, and models followed by the architects of to-day. Bucharest has charming examples of the eighteenth century development of this distinctly Roumanian style, in the Stavrapoleos church, and the suburban monasteries of Văcăreshti and Cotroceni (of which to-day only the church is standing).

The monastery of Hurez lies in a lonely wooded valley of western Wallachia, on the edge of a forest from which it derives its name (hurez—horned owl). The church has the usual pridvor (vestibule) with columns, a small pronaos and broad naos (nave), and an altar under arched walls. The lines are harmonious, and the frescoes are well preserved, and most interesting. Particularly characteristic of the period is the lavishness of the sculptural decoration, to be seen, for instance, in the carvings of the balustrade and the varied ornamentation of the columns. There is a curious analogy between this flowering forth of Roumanian architecture and the contemporary developments under Churriguera in Spain and Bernini in Italy, all characterized by florid exuberance, protesting against the jejune classicism which had been fashionable.

The nineteenth century witnessed a struggle between western architectural influences, brought in by architects who had studied in Paris, or by French and Viennese masters, favored by wealthy Roumanians who wished to give a western *cachet* to their homes; and other architects, who have tried with remarkable success to adapt the traditional Byzantine style to modern requirements. They have adorned Bucharest and other Roumanian cities with charming residences and even banks and government buildings in a style both dignified and original. P. Antonesco and N. Michaësco are perhaps the best known of the representatives of this movement in architecture, which has produced something genuinely Roumanian. The Bucharest Exposition of 1906, some of the buildings of which are preserved in the King Charles Park, had some admirable examples. Other well-known masters of this style are Burcus, Mincu, Maimarolu, Budeshti, P. Smarandesco, George Cantacuzene, etc. The imposing home of the Roumanian School of Architecture is one of the handsomest recent additions to Bucharest.

Painting is the art in which modern Roumania perhaps finds its most congenial expression. Two generations ago, Theodore Aman (whose name is preserved in the Aman Art Museum of Bucharest) won renown by his historical canvases. The greatest figure in Roumanian painting was N. Grigorescu; trained at Barbizon, he is nevertheless purely Roumanian in feeling and conception. Among Grigorescu's contemporaries Andrescu and Luchian were the most famous. Of the present generation, perhaps the best known are Simonidi, who lives in Paris; Verona, who was for many years President of the "Tinerimea Artistică" (Young Artists), and has Grigorescu's fondness for light and color, with astounding facility; Vermont, famous for his large canvases, like the "Jesus appearing to his Disciples" in Dr. C. Angelescu's collection; Strâmbu, a most conscientious and painstaking artist; Aricescu, whose specialty is the dreamy Danube landscape; Steriade, a keen and brilliant analyst; Petrashcu, a master of contrast and color; Iser, whose work shows vigorous design and relief; Stoïca, painter of war scenes as well as of portraits; S. Popescu, specialist in powerful Moroccan landscapes; S. Dumitrescu, admirable for his technique; Stoïnescu, a bold experimenter in color harmonies; Bunescu, fond of winter scenes; and many others. There are several successful women painters, like Mme. Storck, Mme. Rodica Maniu and Mme. Ion Pillat.

Roumanian painters, like Roumanian writers, remain

true to their native soil and to the delicate artistic sense shown even by humble peasants. Brought up among the charming products of peasant art, trained to keen observation, they have not been receptive to Cubist and Modernist tendencies. No one can visit an exhibition of Roumanian paintings without admiring their inborn color sense, their gift for composition, and their sharpness of vision. Henri Focillon well said: "Roumanian art rests upon a sensitiveness, a fineness, and an accuracy of presentation, an integrity of emphasis, which are admirable when one considers that all of German, Magyar and Slav Europe surrounds, without penetrating, the culture and the art of our friends."

The first, and probably the greatest, of modern Roumanian sculptors, was John Georgescu; he died young, but had already done remarkable work. N. Pavelescu-Dimo, Balacescu, Cristescu were important also in that generation. Today, the best-known Roumanian sculptors are J. Matzacanu, Severin, Jalea and Brancush, whose work is more cosmopolitan than specifically Roumanian.

CHAPTER XXII

THE ROUMANIAN PEASANT ARTS

ALL of Eastern Europe—Bohemia, the Ukraine, Serbia, Greece—offers a special charm in the preservation among the peasants of an ancient artistic instinct which has almost disappeared in the manufacturing peoples of the west. We have seen how the Roumanian peasant has clung through centuries of invasion and oppression to his language, his nationality, his attachment to the soil; he has been equally tenacious of the household arts which flourished before Trajan ever passed the Iron Gates. Only recently did they begin to fade before German textiles, Austrian chinaware, aniline dyes; and the efforts of patriotic Roumanians,— Queen Marie, Princess Elise Shtirbey (Mme. John Bratiano) and her associates in the society "Albina," Prof. A. Tzigara-Samurcash, head of the splendid Ethnographic Museum of Bucharest, and many others—are causing a distinct revival, and preserving a fascinating record. I have seen in Bucharest an album of over 60 hand-colored plates which perpetuate the most beautiful designs of Roumanian embroidery and which, if means could only be found for its publication, would be a stimulus to artistic production in any textile center.

The key-note of the Roumanian peasant's household is self-sufficiency. I have visited a peasant's establishment at Braza-de-jos, near Câmpina, where father and sons had built a neat house, a substantial barn and several sheds, in one of which was the inevitable still, connected with the tank in which bushels of plums were fermenting for the "tzuica"; and they had adorned the porch, the windows, etc., with their own carvings. The mother and daughters had spun and woven every article of clothing, every rug, every curtain. That is the typical country home throughout Roumania. They often make their own furniture and pottery, and take pride in their artistic qualities. The men's work overlaps the women's; the "caciula"—the high fur cap of Eastern Europe—and the leather sandals (the "opinci") are his handiwork, and he tans the skins for them; he is often competent to embroider the gay vest and trousers, his holiday attire. The women, on the other hand, grow and treat the hemp, as well as do other farm work; and of course it falls to them to spin and card the wool.

It is the national costume that first rouses the visitor's admiration. One notices resemblances in patterns and colors to those of one or other Balkan people—the "fota" (tunic), brightly embroidered with tapestry designs, and probably of Albanian origin, is used by all the South Slavs, especially the Serbs and Macedonians—but a special Roumanian character is given by greater harmony and refinement of the coloring, a more conscious regularity of the pattern, an instinctive avoidance of the crude and glaring. The purest tradition in costume has been kept in the remote Carpathian glens; the shepherd of the mountain pastures is here also the most typical Roumanian. His "opinci" (leather sandals) appear on Trajan's Column and the Adam-Klissi monument; his "gluga," a sheepskin hood coming down to the breast, is equally ancient. He wears either the "caciula," the high lambskin cap, or a "pălărie," a pointed broad-brimmed felt hat, much like that of the Balkan shepherd. The sheepskin vest, "pieptar," worn with the wool inside, is often so richly embroidered in colored silk that the skin disappears from view; the shirt is also lavishly embroidered, particularly about the shoulders and on the lower hem; it is caught about the waist by a belt, and is not tucked in, but worn outside, coming to a little above the knee. This is the style shown on Trajan's Column! Men's night-gowns, as well as women's, are richly embroidered. Over his shirt and vest the shepherd throws a black sheepskin jacket (cojoc) and a long cloak, also with the wool inside. His white woolen trousers are tight and never pressed. Thus attired, he demonstrates how much our taste in clothing has saddened and degenerated; and he revives a vanished age with absolute fidelity.

Still more handsome and striking are the women's costumes. Queen Marie deserves great credit for the wholeheartedness with which she has thrown herself into the movement in favor of the native costume, as opposed to Paris fashions; when King Ferdinand and she made their triumphal progress through Transylvania, Bessarabia, the Banat, everywhere she wore the local costume, which was always becoming. Her example and that of many aristocratic Roumanian ladies are encouraging the peasant girls to keep up the fine old tradition of a distinctive dress. In one Sunday automobile drive in 1927 out of Bucharest, I have seen over a thousand women in costume.

Over their undergarment, the "cămasha," which comes down to the ankles, the Roumanian peasant women wear the "fota," or rather, generally two "fote"; the longer one, the "opreg," comes behind, and the "shortz" or "făstac," in front. They are lavishly embroidered; the patterns vary in different regions, and an expert can assign a given "fota" to its district. The "fota," in one piece ("vâlnic" or "zăvelca") is much less common. The belt (brâu) is sometimes embroidered with gold, sometimes broad with a long

COLONNADE, MOGOSHOAIA

TYPICAL CITY RESIDENCE, MODERN ROUMANIAN STYLE

TRANSYLVANIAN GIRL AT THE LOOM

ROUMANIAN RUG PATTERN

PEASANT EARTHENWARE

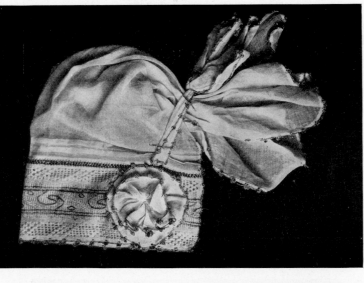

EMBROIDERED BABY'S BONNET, HOME-
MADE, CLOTH AND ALL, PRAHOVA
VALLEY

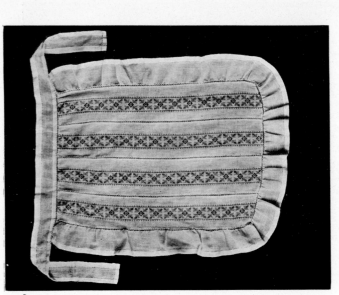

EMBROIDERED APRON MADE OF COTTON
CLOTH WOVEN ON THE LOOM, PRAHOVA
VALLEY

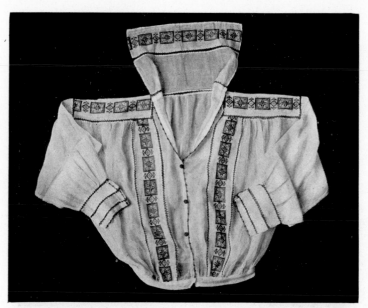

EMBROIDERED WAISTS, ALL HOME-MADE,
PRAHOVA VALLEY

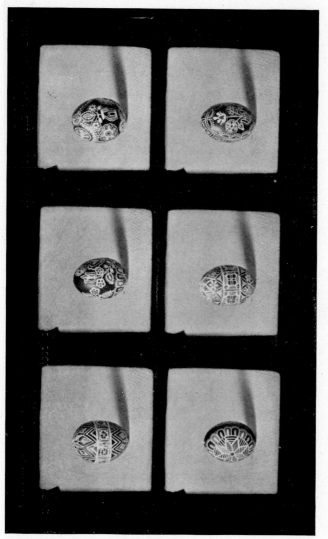

PAINTED EASTER EGGS

(COURTESY OF CLEVELAND MUSEUM OF FINE ARTS)

WEALTHY PEASANT GIRL (DISTRICT OF MUSCEL) IN RICHLY EMBROIDERED COSTUME

From "LA ROUMANIE EN IMAGES"

ROUMANIAN COSTUME FROM NEAR DANUBE

COLLECTION OF MME. JOHN BRATIANO

fringe. An afternoon in the Ethnographic Museum at Bucharest, or beside the well-filled chest of some wealthy amateur, is a series of delightful surprises, and of growing admiration for the taste and skill of these illiterate peasant women. Alas, that such survivals of the old qualitative civilization seem likely to disappear before cheap and vulgar standard production of our quantitative age!

Not merely does the "fota" vary greatly according to the region; so does the head-dress, and the style of arranging the hair. The finest head-dress was the "testema," made of linen or batiste, but now rarely seen. Married women wear a long white transparent veil, the "marama," wound about the head and then waving free. In many mountain districts, especially in the Banat, the married women wear the "conciu"—a petite diadem of wood or metal, from which hangs a long embroidered cloth. Towels are simply and charmingly embroidered. They take special pride in the home-made rugs or runners ("scoartze, laicere") which deck the walls as well as cover the floor. Never have I seen neater and cleaner homes, more tastefully decorated, than these peasant homes in the sub-Carpathian valleys, with their pleasant porches, overhung with vines and gay with geraniums and other flowers; when I entered their portals, the immaculate floors and walls brought back to me the feeling I had as a small boy when I used to pass a threshold of a New England "best room."

The colors of these costumes are brilliant and yet harmonious. The effect is often heightened by the necklaces of silver and even gold coins. Whoever has seen the "hora," the traditional folk-dance, under the brilliant Roumanian sun, with the eddying lines of bright-clad women and white-trousered men, gracefully carrying out the immemorial figures and steps, has had a glimpse of the old Thracian civilization, neighbor and kinsman of that of the Greeks.

Space forbids any detailed account of the lesser arts; but I must not omit some description of the famous painted Easter eggs, of which the Cleveland Art Museum contains such excellent examples. Here again, the Roumanians follow a custom still prevalent all over Eastern Europe, and do so with special taste and skill. The usage evidently goes back of Christian days, for the old church formula for blessing Easter eggs expressly states that it is for the purpose of driving out of them any unclean spirit. The people have several traditions to explain the usage; S. F. Marian, the folk-lorist, devotes a whole chapter to them in his valuable "Serbările la Români" (Roumanian Festivals). According to the commonest, while Jesus was being tortured on the cross, the Virgin offered a great basketful of eggs to the persecuting Jews to try and buy them off; unsuccessful, she laid the basket beside the cross, and the blood from Jesus' wounds ran over them, staining some of them completely red. When Jesus saw this, he said to his disciples standing by: "From this day forth, in memory of my crucifixion, ye shall stain eggs red and ring-streaked, as I myself have to-day." After his resurrection, Mary, the mother of Jesus, was the first to prepare the red eggs and Easter buns, and to every one she met, she said: "Christ is risen," and gave him an egg and a bun. And since that time, Christians have always done this.

If one compares Roumanian Easter eggs with those of Poland, Moravia and Bohemia, one finds simpler themes and softer coloring, on the whole. In those countries, there is apt to be in each village an old woman who colors the eggs for a number of families; in Roumania, in general, each housewife still prides herself on preparing her own eggs. She washes them in sour milk, and warms them by the fire, where a cupful of wax is melting. The instrument she uses is a sort of wooden pencil with a tiny metal tube at the end. With this, she picks up the melted wax and carefully draws lines or rows of points on the egg, varying the design on each. If the eggs are merely to be dyed red, they are left some time in the dye and then put in boiling water, which takes off the wax, and leaves the white background in its place, so that we now have a red egg with a white pattern. If another color is to be used, the wax is left on after the egg comes out of the first dye, and additional wax is put on over the red, to hold whatever pattern is to appear in red; then the egg is laid in the new dye, black, for instance. When the black has thoroughly overlaid the egg, boiling water takes off all the wax, and we have a black egg with a red and white pattern. By postponing the boiling water and drawing more patterns in wax we can get, e. g., a green egg with designs in red, black and white. The favorite backgrounds are red, yellow and black; green and blue are less common. Aniline dyes are replacing the traditional vegetable colors, from herbs, galls, etc., collected by the peasants; and the ancient designs are disappearing, for they take too much time and trouble. They were borrowed from leaf-outlines or flower-petals, the eagle's wing or the snail's shell, or were conventionalized into labyrinths, stars and other figures; there are also all manner of geometric patterns. Some of these are so graceful that through the efforts of Mme. John Bratiano, Mme. Marie Panaitescu and others, they have been perpetuated as models for embroidery, rugs, etc.

This brief survey of the domestic arts gives some idea of the independent character and self-sufficiency of the Roumanian peasant. These qualities show out also in his dwellings. Our modern city civilization is foreign to him; even

Bucharest is prevailingly a city of detached houses, and is said to cover as much ground as Paris, though with only a fifth as many inhabitants. Every Roumanian wants his fruit and shade trees, his flower-bed and vegetable garden beside even his city house, with the result that Bucharest is even more than Washington the city of magnificent distances. Foreign observers have always noticed this. An Austrian commission sent down in 1720 to report on Oltenia, which Austria had just annexed, remarks: "The peasant does not dwell in villages down here as he does in Germany and elsewhere, but one sees now here, now there, three, four or five more or less poorly-constructed houses" and they note that he follows his own judgment in choosing a site. Even to-day, the traveler through Oltenia or the Carpathian valleys sees one tiny settlement after another up on the hillside or at the mouth of a side valley—six or eight modest wooden houses, with granaries or barns beside them, and generally surrounded by a fence or hedge. The villages in the plain are different—a long row of dwellings bordering the highway, and clustering about a square, where one sees the church and school, the general store and the café. In the mountains, the houses are built of wood and shingled, and the peasants vie with one another in the wood-carving which adorns not merely the porch and railing but even the barn-yard gate. In the plain, the better houses are built of brick, with tiled roofs; the poorer classes live in what much resemble the adobe dwellings of the Spanish and Portuguese tropics and like them are gayly colored, often with elaborate decorative designs against the background of clear color. The typical mud hut is built as in Turkey; at the four corners strong piles are rammed down, to support the beams for the roof, and these piles are then connected by straight lines of sticks, held in place with branches and brush. Then a mixture of dirt, cut straw and manure is built up around this frame-work to form the walls; they dry under the sun outside and with the fire inside. The roof is thatched with bundles of reeds in the lowlands, straw and grass on the steppe. The more ambitious surround their house with a porch; vines and flowers, combined with the gay outer painting or kalsomining, make them very attractive in summer.

The primitive peasant-house is simplicity itself. The door is generally to the left on a long side of the rectangle; one enters the "tinda," a combination of store-room and vestibule; various chests to one's left contain provisions, tools, costumes, linen and what not; the hearth (vatra) is in the further corner at the right; it is an open fire-place in front, but that is only part of what becomes a tiled stove, which is built through the back wall, so that it warms the living-room also. This latter, the "odaia," is entered from the vestibule by a low door; there is a narrow window (fereastra) in the front wall, to which corresponds the "ocnitza" on the other side, a tiny opening, generally stopped with paper instead of glass. Opposite is a long broad bench the whole width of the room, covered with mats and rugs; this forms the bed for the women and children. In summer, the men are apt to sleep out on the porch or the threshing-floor; in winter, on the floor by the stove. One can imagine the hygienic conditions of the unventilated "odaia," which is rarely over 13 or 14 feet square, and can understand why consumption is such a scourge all over the Black Sea region, where the same type of building prevails. Lambs, chickens, a cow or horse as joint tenants do not improve matters.

The first step toward a more elaborate house is to add a second "odaia" to the "tinda," on the further side. Under the overhanging eaves is generally a shed, sheltering the cart, plow, etc. It is easy to add a second story, or additional rooms. Every farmer is his own architect and builder, and it must be a very ancient form of building which prevails. One type seems to have come in with the Tartars, or to have been preserved through their influence. This kind, the "bordeu," has the floor (nothing but the ground!) about ten feet below the surface, and only the roof projects above; light comes in from windows at the gables. Xenophon found such houses in his march through Armenia, and the Tartars of Transcaucasia and Turkestan still prefer them. In Roumania, it is only the gypsies and the bitterly poor who resort to them.

CHAPTER XXIII

THE ROUMANIAN PEASANT

THE Roumanians were a pastoral people, and are now mainly agricultural. The change must have taken place on a large scale after quasi-independence under the Turks had given the country a certain stability. This was after the introduction of Indian corn from the New World, and this grain has become the national food, even more than in Italy.

The Roumanian peasant is therefore agricultural in his origin, his education and his ambitions. We have already seen that he possesses remarkable artistic talent, and that he is unusually resistant to extremes of weather and to bad sanitary conditions. Nevertheless they take their toll. Infant mortality is high. Before the war, the coefficient of mortality in the Kingdom was 25.3, and one-half of these were children under 5. That was exceeded only by Russia (31.4 in 1910). Natural selection works rudely, but those that survive can go through fire and water. The Austrian Army General Orders praise the "Zähigkeit, Genügsamkeit und Ausdauer" (toughness, contented nature and endurance) of the Roumanian Transylvanian regiments; and Gen. Diaz told me that after the crack Tyrolese and Hungarian corps, no troops were more dreaded on the Italian mountain front than these Transylvanians; they had, he said, a diabolical cleverness in finding and exploiting the best positions.

The Roumanians have been a prolific people. Their coefficient of natality (39.9) was surpassed only by the Russians (47) and Bulgarians (40.3) and the increase of population (excess of births over deaths) was 14, one of the largest in the world. Agriculturally speaking, Roumania is still a pioneer country; density of population is less than 175 per square mile. A large family is therefore a great asset to the farmer. On a typical small farm, every member is actively at work, from the little toddler who drives the geese down to the pond and his sister who helps mother about the house, to the aged grandmother who still spins and weaves, and the patriarch who closes the shed door after the oxen. This abundance of willing patient labor is Roumania's safeguard for these trying years of reconstruction—a safeguard formed by how many years and centuries of such reconstruction in the past!

Prof. Eugene Pittard, of the University of Geneva, who has made the most exhaustive anthropological study of Roumania, comes to the conclusion that the pure Roumanian type is that which prevails in southern Transylvania and the Carpathian valleys of Roumania proper. They have very short heads (cephalic index of 250 skulls which he studied was 82.34), straight nose, and dark eyes and hair. Blonds are very rare, except in northern Moldavia and Bessarabia—much rarer than among the Serbs and Bulgarians. These mountaineers are considerably taller than the plain-dwellers. They are a handsome race, and Bucharest boasts the most beautiful women in Europe.

The Roumanian peasant is a keen observer; the botanist Hacquet, who studied the flora of Moldavia late in the eighteenth century, stated that he had never seen a people with a more exact knowledge of plants and of their medicinal qualities—for which, indeed, the ancient Thracians were famous. Dr. Antipa says that many of the Thracian names of plants, transmitted to us by Dioscorides, are still in use

ELDERLY ROUMANIAN PEASANT WOMAN IN COSTUME

WEDDING PROCESSION : BEST MEN

ROUMANIAN PEASANTS (NEAR FĂGĂRASH)

among the Roumanian peasants, who have their own folk medicine, astronomy, meteorology, etc., all investigated by Roumanian scholars. Their folk-lore is remarkably rich, and they are constantly quoting pithy proverbs which testify to the quality on which they most pride themselves, their "bun simtz" (common sense). They preserve many immemorial customs. The coin for Charon is still buried with every corpse; the funeral cake which Virgil mentions is still baked; and every dying Roumanian tries to meet his end with a candle in his hand. I called one afternoon on Mme. Bratiano, and found her agitated over the collapse of a servant, who had just learned that his mother had died so suddenly that they did not have time to light a candle and put it in her hand; she said she thought that affected him more than the death itself.

On the moral side, the Roumanian peasant stands high. Crime is rare and due generally to drunkenness, jealousy or vendetta. There are fewer homicides with robbery as the motive than in any other European nation. Drinking was recognized as an evil by the government some years ago, when it took the retail liquor traffic out of the hands of the saloon-keepers, who were mainly Jews, and established government dispensaries. In the cold winters, the peasants are tempted to drink too much "tzuica" (plum brandy), and their lavish hospitality helps; they have the habit of "treating," as we do—or did. There is a strong prohibition movement; its national conventions are attended by hundreds of enthusiastic delegates. But in general the Roumanian, especially the city dweller, is like the Italian, a wine drinker, and a moderate one. He is good-natured, gentle and witty; with strangers he is reserved at first, and on his dignity. In this and several other respects the Roumanian, in the mass, struck me as more like the Spaniard than the Italian; and

I was interested in 1919 in the impressions of the Italian Minister, Martin-Franklin, who was a newcomer like myself. "Whenever I walk around Bucharest," he said, "I feel that I might be in any city of Central or Southern Italy—only that I do not notice any singing, whistling or loud talking, such as I should surely hear in Naples or Palermo." I felt that three-quarters of the clean-shaven boys I met on the street in Roumanian cities might be Americans, and I was tempted to address them in English; and Foreign Minister Mishu bore a close resemblance to my own father, who was a very dark type, and of purely British descent. I was three times mistaken for the head of the Roumanian Secret Service, and when we finally met, we acknowledged the resemblance (as Pres. Wilson did with a double of his), "with mutual chagrin."

Alas! modern city civilization is a strong deteriorating influence. The peasant boys and girls flock to the movies off the farm, just as here. Bucharest being the largest city between Constantinople and Buda-Pesth, gathers from a wide area all the forces that pander to extravagance and dissipation. An education that makes for strength of character is the only way to fight this tendency; and even in the West we cannot be proud of results along those lines. Probably the reputation which Bucharest enjoys for looseness of morals among its upper classes is much exaggerated; but I did hear various stories which reminded me of Munich, Paris or Chicago. I can only say that I was received on most cordial and friendly terms in dozens of Roumanian homes, of all classes of society, and that I found people just as correct and socially decorous as in any American city, and with the generous hospitality of our South and West. As for the peasants I met, they seemed to me a self-respecting upstanding body of men and women. Every Roumanian complains of the extent of corruption in politics; but it is certainly no worse than in various of our states and cities. We have, however, progressed further along the path of civil service reform than have the Roumanians. American business men with whom I have talked think well of Roumanian commercial morality, once one becomes accustomed to the commission or "rake-off" system which prevails all over that part of the world. They abide by their contracts, they said. A distinguished American business man, recently in Roumania, where he took extensive contracts and was reported to by subordinates who had been there a long time, characterized business as "safe" and the people as "reliable." Of course the long business depression has been a terrific strain.

We must grant the Roumanians a decided political gift. When only an aggregation of shepherds and peasant farmers, they managed somehow to maintain their nationality and self-consciousness in the midst of enemies and under almost constant oppression; they evolved a system of village councils which lasted into the nineteenth century, and traditional usages which have become a body of law; we find references to the *jus Valachicum*—the Wallach law-code—from the thirteenth century on. From those early groups of shepherds they passed to the first "knezats" and "voyevodats" under energetic chieftains; then arose the Principalities, the Kingdom of Roumania, and now, Greater Roumania, whose chief task is to direct and improve these national characteristics we have enumerated. With peace and education, the Roumanian will speedily become a potent factor in European progress. Of his intellectual gifts there is no doubt; one of the most brilliant of living physicists is G. Constantinescu, whose work has revolutionized the transmission of power for short distances. He has proved the compressibility of water; and his studies of vibratory force are epoch-making. In the political sphere, the elder Bratiano and Kogălniceanu were on a plane with their best western contemporaries; and the Roumanian politicians of to-day compare well with those of the countries round about them, and even some further off. With improved agriculture, the Roumanian peasant will be able to send his children more regularly to school, and the stigma of illiteracy will gradually disappear. As it is to-day, half of the adult population of the former kingdom can neither read nor write and in Bessarabia the proportion is still higher. An American school like Robert College would be welcomed.

CHAPTER XXIV

ROUMANIAN presents much analogy to English. Our language is a Teutonic tongue, in which the nouns have dropped all declension signs except the genitive and the plural; the Teutonic vocabulary is outnumbered by words from French and other non-related languages; there is some remnant of the primitive Celtic of Britain; nevertheless in ordinary intercourse three-quarters of the words are pure Anglo-Saxon. In the same way, Roumanian is a Romance language like Italian, Spanish, Portuguese and French, in which the Latin nouns have lost their declension except again the genitive (and dative) form, and the vocative (all the others having lost even these), and the plural; Slav, Hungarian, Turkish and other foreign words outnumber those coming from Latin; there is a certain number of words (like vatră, hearth; copil, child; buze, lips), occurring generally also in Albanian and Bulgarian, which doubtless are derived from the primitive Thracian; however in everyday speech over three-quarters of all the words are of Latin stock. This survival of Latin out here in the East is most remarkable, for the Romans held Dacia only five or six generations; then all connection with the western Latin world was cut; the country was flooded with Slavs, who for centuries dominated in church and government, and with Huns and Turks; and the language was never written for over a thousand years. Consequently, a page of Roumanian seems very strange, even to one familiar with Italian

277

or Portuguese, the languages cultivated Roumanians find easiest to understand. This strangeness is partly due to the alphabet. Up to a couple of generations ago, Roumanian was written in the Cyrillic letters still used for Bulgarian— approximately the same as in Russian; and the orthography is still a little uncertain. In general, Roumanian is written like Italian; the simple vowels have much the same values, and c and g before e and i are soft as in Italian, like ch in church and ge in George. They have a sound like that of u in "but" or final a in "Canada," found also in Bulgarian and Albanian, which is written ă; and a difficult vowel (found also in the Slav languages) something like German ü or French u, but without any puckering of the lips, which is expressed by â or î; pâine, the word for bread, sounds much like pweeneh. The consonant sounds are much the same as in English; they write t with a cedilla for tz, s with cedilla for sh. All letters are pronounced, except final i, which is a faint y sound; as in Italian, ce and ci are often just a device for the sound ch (Bercovici = Bercovitch).

How deeply the language was affected in fundamentals by Slav infiltration is shown by the pronouns mine and tine, me and thee, and the numerals. Un, doi, trei, patru, cinci (cheench), shase, sheapte, opt, noua, zece are plainly Latin (patru with p for qu, like apa for aqua); but the 'teens are made as in Slav—one on ten, two on ten, etc., unsprezece, doisprezece, etc.; the tens are on the Slav model, two-tens, three-tens, etc., douăzeci, treizeci; and 100 is the Slav word, suta.

Phonetically, the Latin words show much wear and tear, sometimes more even than French. Caballus, horse, comes out cal, as in Lombard; dies, zi. C and t were softened more than in Italian or Spanish; acel, that, as contrasted with quello, aquel; tzinere, hold, beside tenere, tener. Roumanian is like Roman and Neapolitan in rhotacizing—înger for angel, biserica for basilica; indeed, the general impression which the language first makes, especially in intonation, is that of a South Italian dialect. The very name of the language—românesc—is precisely what the peasant of Frascati or Rocca di Papa calls his dialect. Roumanian friends tell me that they succeeded in understanding Neapolitan after a few days, when Milanese and even Tuscan baffled them. It will easily be seen that a cultivated Roumanian, who knows Latin, will have little difficulty with Italian, or even Spanish, Portuguese or French; conversely, the large proportion of Slav, Hungarian, Turkish and other strange words in the Roumanian vocabulary makes it very perplexing to the Italian.

Perhaps the simplest way to give an idea of the surface peculiarities of Roumanian is to explain a short poem. I find Eminesco's "Somnoroase Păsărele" greatly appreciated in my lectures, and it illustrates to perfection the melody of the language and the rhythmic mastery of the great poet.

Somnoroase păsărele
Pe la cuiburi se adună,
Se ascund in rămurele—
    Noapte bună!

The sleepy birdlets
At their nests gather,
Hide themselves in the branchlets—
    Good night!

Doar izvoarele suspină,
Pe când codrul negru tace
Dorm shi florile 'n grădină—
    Dormi în pace!

Only the springs sigh,
While the black forest keeps silence,
The flowers also sleep in the garden—
    Sleep in peace!

Trece lebăda pe ape
Intre trestii să se culce—
Fie-tzi îngerii aproape,
    Somnul dulce!

The swan passes over the
    waters
Among the reeds that she
    may go to rest—
May angels be near thee,
        Sweet be thy sleep!

Peste-a noptzii feerie
Se ridică mândra lună.
Totu-i vis shi armonie
    Noapte bună!

Over the fairyland of the
    night
Rises the haughty moon.
All is dream and harmony
        Good night!

Explanation

Eminesco:-scu is from a common late Latin adjective ending, -iscus, meaning "belonging to, of," and related to our -ish. Ionescu is like Jones—of John.

Line 1: pasere, from the Latin passer, sparrow, is the ordinary word for "bird" in Roumanian, as in Spanish (pajaro); plural, păseri (final i only heard as a faint y), with the vowel a weakened to ă. Our form here is a diminutive, păsărea, plural păsăre. When the article, which is postpositive in Roumanian as in Bulgarian and Albanian, is added (le, fem. plur.), the form becomes păsărele. The adjective somnoros becomes somnoroase in the fem. pl.

Line 2: pe la is a double preposition, like "from beyond"; pe (Lat. per) means through, on or to; it is also used before names of living things to express the accusative: am văzut pe Domnul A., I saw Mr. A., just as in Spanish one would say: vi á Sr. A. La (Lat. illāc) is the usual preposition "to." Cui-buri (final i nearly silent) is the plural of cuib (from a Vulgar Latin cubium), nest. These plurals in -uri (from the Latin neuter plurals in -ora), are common in Roumanian, as they are in Sicilian dialect (nnomura, cugnomura for Tuscan nomi, cognomi). Se adună is reflexive 3rd person plural present indicative of aduna; in Roumanian, as in all Central and South Italian dialects, the infinitive loses the final -re (Roman voyu magnà, I want to eat); but when the infinitive is used as a noun, the -re is preserved; adunare means assembling, gathering. Roumanian makes great use of these verbal nouns in -re. Se adună is the same in the singular and plural.

Line 3: Se ascund is a parallel form from a 3rd conjugation verb, ascunde (Latin ascondere). In the third conjugation, the corresponding singular form has -e; se ascunde. Rămurele is the plural of the diminutive of rămură, fem., plus the article, as in păsărele.

Line 4: Noapte shows the curious change from Latin -ct- to -pt- which is characteristic of Roumanian; piept (pectus), fapt (factus), opt (octo) are examples. The vowel is softened by the following -e; e and i often produce a kind of umlaut in the preceding syllable in Roumanian. Bună is the feminine of bun, Lat. bonus. Why this phrase is reversed, no one seems to know; "Good morning" and "good evening" are "bună dimineatză" and "bună seară," the last sounding like dialect Italian, as does "la revedere," the Roumanian "au revoir," and "adio," "adieu."

Line 5: Doar they derive from the Latin de hora. Izvoarele is the feminine plural of the masculine noun izvor, Slav word for "spring." Italian has several such masculine nouns, like "braccio," with the plural "braccia," really a Latin neuter, but counting as feminine. In Roumanian, there are many more. Suspină shows a change of Latin r (suspiro) to n; compare the reverse in fereastră (fenestra), window.

Line 6: Pe când is a combination, pe being the preposition of 1. 2 and când the Latin quando. Codru is a primitive Thracian (?) word; being a masculine ending in a vowel, the definite article, when added, takes the form -l. Tace is a 2nd conjugation verb, from the Latin.

Line 7: Dorm is a 4th conjugation verb, from Latin dormio; the singular is doarme. Shi, the word for "and," they derive from sic, as in Italian dialects. Florile is plural of floare,

fem. (Lat. flos). 'n (în) is the Latin preposition. Grădină is
the Vulgar Latin word already adopted in Roman days from
the Teutonic "garden."

Line 8: Dormi is the imperative form, sing.; the plural is
dormitzi. Pace is the Latin word.

Line 9: Trece is a third conjugation verb, present singular,
from trece (Lat. traicere); the past participle, trecut (ending
-ut as in Italian dialect), is "past." The title of one of the
most interesting Roumanian histories, Vlahutza's "Din Trecutul Nostru" (din = Lat. de in) = "From Our Past." Le-
bǎda is Slav. The fact that the final a is long shows that it is
"the swan;" *"a* swan" would be lebǎdǎ. Such words sound
almost as if the accent were on the last syllable. Roumanian
has a weaker accent than Italian, and in that regard gives
somewhat the impression of Spanish. Ape is the plural of apǎ,
water, for Latin aqua; cf. patru, 4, from quattuor.

Line 10: Intre = Lat. inter. Trestii is fem. pl. (-ii shows
that the i is pronounced) of trestie, reed, a Slav (?) word. Sǎ
is the sign of the subjunctive, Roumanian using a special par-
ticle. Se culcǎ corresponds to the French verb se coucher,
from the Latin collocare.

Line 11: Fie is subjunctive of the verb "to be," for which
the Lat. fio is utilized. Tzi is second personal pronoun singular, in the dative. Ingerii is the plural (with article, shown by
doubled i) of înger, masc., "angel," with the rhotacizing tendency already referred to. Aproape is the combination of Latin
ad and prope.

Line 12: Somnul is somn, masc., "sleep," with the article.
Dulce is Latin.

Line 13: Peste is the combination of Latin per and extra.
A noptzii is the genitive of a feminine noun, noapte, with the
article. Noptzii alone would be the dative. Feminines ending
in -a have the genitive-dative in -e, as in Vulgar Latin; mamǎ,
mother, genitive mame. The corresponding plural form (with
article) ends in -lor, both masculine and feminine. This comes
from the Latin illorum (Italian loro, French leur). The mas-

culine singular genitive, of a noun with postfixed article, ends in -lui; fratele, the brother, genitive a fratelui. This is the same lui as in Italian. Feerie is a French importation, of which current Roumanian is almost as full as the Bucharest shop-windows. Not all Roumanians have outgrown the feeling that their vernacular, with the fresh bloom of its peasant origin, needs plentiful powdering with French. Another school, of which the great story-teller Creanga and the late poet and journalist Vlahutza were examples, believed in enriching the language directly from the peasants—an admirable enterprise, but very hard on the student with an ordinary dictionary.

Line 14: Se ridică, reflexive, like se adună, 1.2, derived from Vulgar Latin adrectico. Mândra is feminine of mândru, from late Latin mundulus. Luna is Latin.

Line 15: Tot is the Latin totus, Fr. tout. The -u used to be written, under Cyrillic influence, but now rarely is; -i is the connective form of the verb "is," the full form of which is este. Vis comes from Latin; armonie (probably through French) from Greek.

This must suffice to show some of the peculiarities of the language, and its genuinely Latin character, however overlaid with Slav and other embroidery. It is fresh and virile, and smacks of the open Macedonian mountains and the Carpathian glens. Forms like facù and avù may seem rough beside the more polished Italian fece, ebbe, or French fit and eut, but they are forceful and melodious. There is a strong movement in higher circles to avoid words not of Latin origin; one of my Roumanian officer friends told me that his father, a famous doctor, would not allow even the servants to use the Slav words "vreme" (time) and "ceas" (hour, o'clock), but insisted on "timp" and "oră." Sometimes one agrees with them; abondentza is certainly more harmonious than belshug (abundance); nevertheless in gen-

eral the attempt is unnatural, and the vernacular must prevail. Modern Greek shows what confusion results when the
theorists have too much to say. Roumanian is in far healthier
condition.

CHAPTER XXV

WE have seen that Roumanian literature did not begin till Reformation days, and that its first written monuments are religious propaganda. Much earlier, at least in origin, must be the popular traditional literature. I have already given examples of popular poetry. Besides the haiduc (brigand) ballads, with their Robin Hood flavor, there are the doine (elegies and love-poems), hore (dance-songs), and snatches of epics and historical ballads. They are so simple that with a good dictionary one can get great enjoyment from such a collection as the "Poezii Populare din Toate Tzinuturile Româneshti"—Popular Poems from all the Roumanian Territories—published by the Bucharest firm of Socec.

The best Roumanian poets—Alecsandri, Eminesco and Coshbuc—have drunk in their inspiration from these wild free sources, as well as from the world's book of poesy. I hope the examples of their work I have given are enough to show that they must be included in the number of the world's best singers. Vlahutza is generally agreed to rank next them. The Roumanian Academy gives poetry prizes, and one was recently won by a nephew of J. J. C. Bratiano, John Pillat, one of whose poems I have also found much appreciated in my lectures. Under another form, it shows the same rhythmic melody of the language:

ROMANTZA

Tzi-am dat un trandafir,   I gave you a rose, playing
     jucând   You threw it into the sea,

L'ai aruncat în mare,
Shi valurile mi l'au luat
In larga înserare.
S'a dus—shi nimeni nu mai
shtie
De-un trandafir ce moare.

And the waves took it away
from me
Into the broad gloaming.
It has gone—and no one
knows any more
Of a rose that is dying.

Tzi-am dat shi inima 'ntr-o
zi,
O zi de sărbătoare.
Râzând ai luat-o, te-ai jucat
Cu ea cu nepăsare.
Te-ai dus—shi nimeni nu mai
shtie
De inima ce moare.

I gave you also my heart one
day,
A holiday.
Laughing you took it, you
played
With it with indifference.
You have gone—and no one
knows any more
Of the heart that is dying.

We have seen that Roumanian prose literature arose from
Protestant propaganda in Transylvania in the 15th century.
It developed during the late 16th and the 17th century
under strong Slav influence; one has only to compare Coresi's
Psalter with the Church Slavonic original to see how the
language has been forced into unnatural forms, quite different from the simple and direct style of the first Roumanian
letter (1524) which has come down. Still, some of these
early translations are vigorous in style, and they have had
great effect on the language. Greek influence became predominant in the 18th century, especially in Wallachia, where
books translated from the Greek abound—Heliodorus, e. g.,
Homer, and theological works. In Transylvania, there was
much Latin and later German influence; their great historians Maior and Shincai show their Latin training. About
1830 begins the modern period, in which French literature
(and to a less degree Italian, Russian and German) have
been the dominant external factors.

The language of Coresi's Psalter (1577) has been of extraordinary influence; one can judge of its character by the following specimen (Psalm 100): 1. Strigatzi domnului tot pământul. 2. Lucratzi domnului în veselie; întratzi într'însul în bucurie. 3. Să shtitzi că domnul elu e zeul nostru; el feace noi e nu noi; e noi oamenii lui shi oi păscuite lui. 4. Intratzi în usha lui în ispovedire, în curtzile lui în cântări; ispoveditzi-vă lui shi lăudatzi numele lui. 5. Că dulce e domnul în veac meserearea lui, shi până la neam shi neam deadevârul lui.

Along with the versions of the Bible, we find controversial literature and homilies from the very start; Coresi published two collections of the latter, both based on Church Slavonic. With our modern prejudice against sermons, we are apt to underrate their literary importance; those of St. John Chrysostom, published in Roumanian translation by Greceano in 1699, are a valuable monument. The liturgy obstinately preserved Church Slavonic in Transylvania till the end of the 17th century and even later; funeral rites and prayers were the first to be read in Roumanian, and since they were to be "understanded of the people," they were in popular style.

This Protestant movement in Transylvania gave rise to Orthodox reaction in Moldavia and Wallachia; and to fight the Protestants, they had to adopt the national tongue. Leader in this was the Moldavian archbishop Varlaam, whose "Cartea româneasca de învătzătura" (Roumanian Schoolbook), published in 1643 at Jassy, is the most outstanding of this epoch. Law collections, commentaries on the Gospels and on dogma were printed. In 1649, even a complete Herodotus was brought out.

A great author of this epoch is the Metropolitan Dositheus (Dosoftei), who in 1673 published a Psalter in verse, then one in prose, Bible translations and a huge compilation, "Vietzile Sfîntilor" ("Lives of the Saints"). About 1650, Neagoe Voda wrote a forceful and engaging "Book of Instructions" to his son Theodosius.

The most important work of the 17th century, however, is the complete Roumanian Bible of 1688, in a beautiful and noble style. This is the basis of all later editions. Like the New Testament of Alba-Julia of 1648, like Varlaam's "Schoolbook," this Bible in its preface emphasizes that it is written "pentru toata lumea româneasca,"—"for the whole Roumanian world," of Wallachia, Moldavia and Transylvania,—which proves once more that the spirit of national unity among the Roumanians of the three Principalities was already strong in the 17th century.

These works were the foundations of the powerful Church Literature developed in the 18th century especially by Archbishop Antim (Anthymus) Ivireanu and by the Greceanu brothers (the just-mentioned "Chrysostom's Homilies").

Belles lettres begin with translations of Greek romances, in the second half of the 18th century; the story of Hierotocrytes and Arethusa has many lyric interludes, and these poems had considerable influence. The earliest artificial poetry (as contrasted with popular verse) is the amusing Ode of Halicz of 1674, in Roumanian hexameters; all the words are of Latin origin.

Of far greater interest is the popular literature. Our earliest prose stories are 18th century versions of various of the Alexander legends, of the Thousand and One Nights, of Æsop's Fables, of the Physiologus, etc. Calendars and astrologies of the same period are full of valuable references to popular beliefs. We even have cookbooks going back to 1749! In poetry there is a large number of ballads, the most famous being that of the Monastery of Argesh, with the same theme as the Greek poem of the Bridge of Arta. Proverbs, riddles, witty stories and anecdotes close the series of monuments of the popular literature. It must be studied in close connection with that of the Serbs and Greeks.

Roumanian histories begin with chronicles kept in the monasteries, enumerating princes and the years they ruled, to which later were added certain events of their reigns. The oldest annals of this kind are the "Analele Putnene" and "Analele Bistritzene," of the Putna and Bistritza Convents. They were written in Church Slavonic during the first decades of the 16th century. But very soon, annals of this kind were enlarged and translated into Roumanian. The first Roumanian historian is Gregory Ureche, at the beginning of the 17th century. His chronicle records events from the foundation of Moldavia (A.D. 1350) to the end of the 16th century. It was continued by Miron Costin about 50 years later; he wrote the lives of the Moldavian Princes down to 1680. Costin, who studied at Polish universities, was a poet both in Roumanian and Polish, and his "Viatza Lumii" (Life of the World) is one of the first Roumanian poems. He wrote also a history of the colonization of Dacia.

Costin's chronicle was continued by the Moldavian Boyar, John Neculce, from 1680 to the Moldavian battles of Peter the Great against the Turks. Neculce also added many legends about the early Moldavian princes. One of the most prominent characters in Roumanian, and indeed in European, letters, is the Moldavian prince, Demetrius Cantemir. He wrote the early history of the Roumanian race in his "Chronicul Vechimei Româno-Moldo-Vlahilor." He also wrote in Latin the "History of the Ottoman Empire," long a standard work, and the "Description of Moldavia." Among his Roumanian works is the life of his father, Prince Constantine Cantemir, and the so-called "Quarrel between the Brancovan and the Cantacuzene families." In Wallachia the best-known chroniclers are Stoica Ludescu, Radu (Ralph) Popescu, Radu Grecianu and Constantine Capitanu Filipescu (an ancestor of Nicholas Filipescu, the distinguished Roumanian Ententophile during the World War), all of the end of the 17th century. More important is their contemporary, Constantine Cantacuzene Stolnicul, who about 1700 wrote not only the history of his own Wallachia, but also that of Moldavia, Transylvania and even of the Macedonian Roumanians. He also wrote a history of the origin of the Roumanians beginning with Rome itself.

All these chroniclers have a strong consciousness of their Latin origin, and of the unity of the three Roumanian principalities. Ureche, Costin, Cantemir, Constantin Stolnicul endeavored to prove that the inhabitants of Moldavia, Transylvania and Wallachia are one and the same race, descended from Trajan's Roman colony. On the basis of this work of the chroniclers rose about 1800 the great Transylvanian trio, Micu, Shincai and Maior, who laid the foundations of modern Roumanian historical writing.

Samuel Micu (Clain, Klein), George Shincai and Peter Maior were educated in Roman Catholic seminaries of Rome and Vienna. They created the modern Roumanian spirit of Latin unity, which they strove to attain through their historical and philological works, thus starting a new epoch in Roumanian history. Micu's great work is the "History of the Roumanians," picturing the life of the race from its origin to his days. Shincai developed his great "Roumanian Chronicle" in the same spirit, analyzing year by year the progress of his nation in all three Roumanian countries. Maior wrote the "History of the Roumanian Church." Their activity is important also in Roumanian philology and re-

ligious literature. In philology they began the Latinist movement, which later became exaggerated, and they first discarded Cyrillic letters and reintroduced Latin characters.

In close relation with them worked John Budai Deleanu,
an excellent philologist, who wrote a good humorous epic,
the so-called "Tziganiada," describing in a dignified Homeric
style the amusing adventures of a Gypsy tribe.

Under the Phanariotes, French literature and western
ideals came rushing in. About 1815, a boyar wrote a biting
satirical comedy against the Phanariote régime—Iordache
Golescul's "Condition of Roumania"; and in the 'twenties
Alexander Beldiman told in rhyme the downfall of the
Greeks. With the new political life, a host of writers arose.
Some like the Moldavian George Asachi (died in 1869) and
the Wallachian John Eliade Rădulescu (died 1872) distinguished themselves both in prose and verse; they founded in
1829 the first Roumanian journals: *Curierul Românesc*
at Bucharest, and *Albina Românească* at Jassy; and the
philharmonic and dramatic societies which they established
(1833 in Bucharest, 1836 in Jassy) have been the chief
encouragement to the Roumanian stage. Among other pioneers in Roumanian poetry should be mentioned John
Văcărescu (died 1863), Paris Momuleanu (died 1837),
Constantine Conachi (died 1869), Basil Cârlova (died
1831), Gregory Alexandrescu (died 1885), Demetrius
Bolintineanu (died 1872), the Bessarabian fable-writer
Alexander Donici (died 1866), Constantine Negruzzi (died
1868) and the first great Roumanian poet, Basil Alecsandri,
bard of the Roumanian Renaissance and the Union, who
had the satisfaction of singing of Roumanian independence,
and of the Iron Crown of Roumania's first king. Nicholas
Bălcescu (died 1852) and the great statesman Michael
Kogălniceanu are the leaders in the writing of history; the

latter, in conjunction with Augustus T. Laurian (died 1881), founded in 1845 the first Roumanian historical review. Laurian brought out several important historical works, both in French and Roumanian.

Under these writers, the language takes final literary form. French Romanticism had affected them powerfully; but they had the good sense to keep close to the people and the past. Alecsandri drew constantly on popular ballads; Kogălniceanu was the first scientific editor of the chronicles, in 1857; Bolintineanu brought out historic poems based on popular sources; Odobescu collected traditions and enriched the language with many a picturesque archaism. The well-known critic Titus Maioresco edited a magazine, the *Convorbiri Literare* (Literary Conversations), which had an enormous influence for moderation and purity of language, combating every form of exaggeration.

This was the environment which developed the rare talents of the poets Eminesco and Coshbuc. Of different origin and temperament, they represent two characteristic aspects of the Roumanian spirit, portrayed in faultless language. Their influence has been profound; every Roumanian writer knows his Alecsandri, Eminesco and Coshbuc by heart. Eminesco's pessimistic views, expressed as they were in simpler style, have found more imitators than Coshbuc's infinitely original optimism. Still, Coshbuc's influence is to be seen in the movement for literary regeneration and a return to the language of the people which was preached at the turn of the century in the columns of the magazine *Semănătorul*, edited by Nicholas Iorga, the most outstanding figure in contemporary Roumanian letters. Iorga is a man of the highest learning and culture and an impassioned antiquarian and historical writer, whose energy and literary productiveness baffle comprehension, and yet leave him time for ceaseless political activity both in and out of the Roumanian Chamber. In his capacity as university professor, lecturer in the Roumanian Academy and editor of this review, he has trained a large number of the younger generation. One meets his pupils in every sphere in Roumania. Michael Sadoveanu, Emil Gârleanu and Sandu Aldea may be mentioned as prominent members of the so-called Nationalist Group led by Iorga; they all published their first works in the *Semănătorul*. Of recent years, Iorga found it necessary to discontinue his magazine, and the daily which has taken its place —*Neamul Românesc*—has become mainly a political sheet, while his other publication—*Floarea Darurilor*—is devoted to the translation and diffusion of foreign literary masterpieces. In 1931, Iorga's 60th birthday, coming while he was Prime Minister, was a great national testimonial of admiration. He is known as a lecturer as far afield as Portugal, England and the United States.

In Transylvania, similar work was done by the magazine *Luceafărul*, originally published in Bucharest, but then transferred to Sibiu (Hermannstadt). The younger generation of Transylvanian writers found hospitality in its columns, particularly Octavian Goga, Roumania's distinguished poet-politician, and I. Agârbiceanu, the leading Transylvanian novelist and short-story writer.

About the time that the *Semănătorul* ceased publication, a new magazine, *Viatza Românească* (Roumanian Life) began appearing at Jassy. Founded by C. Stere and Dr. I. Cantacuzene, the latter of whom gave place later to G. Ibrăileanu, it set out to represent every side of Roumanian life in all the Roumanian territories, with the special aim of raising the intellectual level. It published stories and articles based on the peasant's life and interests, and studies analyzing his needs and aspirations. Its editors called themselves "Poporanisti" (Populists), to be sure; but the chief influence of *Viatza Românească* was literary, not political, and very valuable.

Another literary movement was headed by Ovid Densusianu, Professor of Romance Philology at Bucharest. Champion of the French Symbolists, he for several years published the *Viatza Nouă* (New Life), in which appeared the work of a talented group, comprising, besides Densusianu himself ("Ervin"), D. Caracostea, Stamatiade, Sperantia and others. The *Revista Celorlaltzi* also embodied this movement for some time under I. Minulescu, the most original, eccentric and talented poet among the Roumanian Symbolists.

Another magazine of wide influence in the development of recent Roumanian literature was the *Convorbiri Critice* (Conversations on Criticism), in which Michael Dragomirescu, pupil of the veteran critic Titus Maioresco, raised the banner of "Art for art's sake," and introduced several talented writers. There were other literary magazines in Roumania during this period; one of them, the *Flacăra* (Flame), edited by Constantine I. Banu, developed several young writers of talent.

It must be confessed that the last few years before the war, Roumanian literature had largely lost its fervor. The younger generation of writers seemed to be seeking a sign, testing and then discarding one outside influence after another, and lacking any outstanding literary figure like Eminesco or Coshbuc—but of how many other countries could not the same be said! The war stopped literary production altogether, as can well be imagined; the only publication with any literary flavor during the Jassy government was the daily *România*, in which Sadoveanu, Goga and occasionally Queen Marie, published articles, stories or sketches inspired by the war.

In Chapter XXVI, I sketch the post-war literary revival; it remains here to give some connected account of the leading exponents of Roumanian literature at the turn of the century. In poetry, the chief names are those of Coshbuc (died 1918), Vlahutza (died 1919), Stephen O. Iosif (died 1913), D. Anghel, Cerna, Goga, D. Nanu, Cincinnatus Pavelescu, John Minulescu, Michael Codreanu and Cornelius Moldovanu. Of these Coshbuc and Vlahutza had perhaps done their best work many years before; the most genuinely characteristic of this period are Goga, Cerna, Iosif and Anghel. Goga is the poet of the Transylvanian peasant, Roumanian serf of Magyar task-master; his pictures of suffering under the Hungarian yoke, in "Poezii," his first volume, made a tremendous sensation, and earned him active persecution from the Hungarian Government. His later poems left this field for wider social reforms, or are philosophical or purely descriptive. In recent years, his journalistic and political activities have crowded out his poetic inspiration.

P. Cerna is one of the most remarkable talents in modern Roumanian literature. Had death not carried him off too early, he might have ranked with Coshbuc and Eminesco. His one volume of "Poezii," most of which had come out in the *Convorbiri Literare,* makes him the leading light of philosophic poetry in Roumania.

Iosif has been most successful in voicing the aspirations and the delicate nuances of the Roumanian spirit. His "Patriarchale" and "Credintze" (Beliefs) are among the most original and sincere productions of the literature. He is also well-known as a brilliant translator, his versions of Heine being universal favorites. With Anghel ("A. Mirea"), he published two volumes under the title "Caleidoscopul," unique for their fanciful originality. Anghel was formed under the influence of the French Parnassus school, and is known for his "Fantezii," masterpieces of imaginative creation. Codreanu is a sonnet-writer; his poems, originally published in *Viatza Românească*, have been issued as a separate volume. We have already spoken of Minulescu's original productions; his best-known volume is "Romantze pentru mai târziu" (Romances for Later). Other talented poets of the same generation are Donar Munteanu, Alexander Stamatiade, Alexander Gherghel and A. Popovici-Bănătzeanu.

Of the older poets who survived into this period, Coshbuc published almost nothing, and Vlahutza's energy was consumed in other directions. Made a permanent invalid by the war, he nevertheless founded in 1919, with the short-story writer Brătescu-Voineshti, the Bucharest daily *Dacia*, which carried the black-margined notice of his death beside the account of the opening of Greater Roumania's first Parliament (Nov. 21, 1919). Duilius Zamfirescu was also mute, or nearly so; Macedonschi succeeded in revising a considerable body of early work—his "Imnuri sacre" (Hymns), some of which, like "Levki" and "Noaptea de Decembrie" have won a permanent place in the literature.

Since the war John Pillat, nephew of Bratiano, favorably known for his volumes "Visuri Păgâne" (Pagan Dreams) and "Eternitătzi de o Clipă" (Eternities of a Moment), (from which I have taken the poem on page 285), has brought out another collection, "Grădina între Ziduri" (The Walled Garden), and "Florica," a publication beautiful in every sense. John Pavelescu is the sonnet-writer of to-day; Alfred Moshoiu is producing charming verse, underlaid with deep melancholy; Horia Furtuna is a skillful master of the language. To show the activity of Roumania's literary men: once when I was in Bucharest, Pillat was running for Parliament up in Bessarabia, and one day after he returned, he took me around to Police Headquarters and introduced me to Furtuna, who was a high official there!

Of the lesser modern poets, Theodore Sperantia is a talented writer in the style of the French Symbolists; his father's Roumanian Grammar is a widely used school-book. Gregorian is a powerful imaginative descriptive poet. Basil Stoïca, the Transylvanian diplomat, has written a graphic story of his country's sufferings. His poems, "In Fumul Uzinelor" (In Factory Smoke), deal with the life of the Roumanian workers in American steel-mills. Others who deserve mention, at least, are Hélène Văcăresco, whose knowledge of French and English has made her an invaluable intermediary, since her translations of her fellow-poets have been our chief source of information; Marcellus Romanescu, Nichifor Crainic, Demosthenes Botez, Helena Farago, G. Tutoveanu, V. Demetrius, Hildebrand Frollo, Dinu Rămura (Hertz), V. Stoïcescu, Mircea Rădulescu, Oreste, etc.

The elder generation of novelists and story-writers,— Caragiale, Delavrancea, Basarabescu, Duilius Zamfirescu, N. Gane, etc.—produced little or nothing during this period. Perhaps the leading writer is Michael Sadoveanu. In his short stories, one sees the influence of de Maupassant, while his exciting historical novels remind one of Sienkiewicz and the Russians. His best stories are found in "Povestiri," "Duduia Margareta," "Insemnările lui Niculae Manea," "Haia Sanis," and "Floare Ofilita"; I can recommend his "Neamul Shoimăreshtilor" as an engrossing picture of the old days of warfare between the Pole, the Moldavian and the Turk. Sandu Aldea has written many vivid stories of peasant life, such as "Pe drumul Baraganului" and "Două Neamuri." Em. Gârleanu had already made a reputation as a brilliant story-writer when a premature death carried him off; his "Bătrânii," "Cea Dintâi Durere," "Schitze din Ras-boiu," "O Noapte de Maiu" give evidence of original talent. Agârbiceanu is the leading Transylvanian story-writer; his "Dela Tzara," "Fefeleaga," etc., are full of local color. Doubtless the most outstanding figure in this genre is I. Brătescu-Voineshti. His "In Lumea Dreptatzei" and his "Scrisorile" published during the period of Roumanian neu-trality in the Jassy *Viatza Românească* are collections of masterpieces of close observation and a deep sense of the tragedy of life. His style, which is highly praised by Rou-manian critics, and which is certainly keen and dramatic, is so full of Slav words (which the poets also are apt to prefer) that I have always found him rather difficult read-ing.

Roumanians have a natural gift for the short story and the novel, and one could make an impressive list of the best-known story-writers. Alexander Cazaban has special-ized in hunting tales; N. Dunăreanu describes the life of the Dobrudjans of the Danube delta, just as M. Chiritzescu devotes himself to the peasants of the Wallachian plain, and I. Vissarion, in stories like "Nevestele lui Mosh Dorogan" and "Privighetoarea Neagră," sketches in brilliant local color the peasants of Argesh and Muscel. Victor Eftimiu, the poet, has written most interesting stories about his own home country down in Macedonia; his best-known novel is "Năluca." John Adam has brought out several volumes of stories and novels dealing with the Dobrudja; V. Caraivan, T. Pamfil Rădulescu-Codin, I. Dragoslav describe Rou-manian peasant life in one or other region, or have given literary form to folk-tales and ballads, along the lines laid down by Creanga. Lucy Byng's recent "Roumanian Stories" (Lane, 1921) present in admirable translation, a good selection from the stories and sketches of several of the authors whom I have mentioned above.

No recent writer for the stage has reached the level of Caragiale. His "Scrisoara Pierdută (Lost Letter), with its cutting satire on the politics and social life of fifty years ago, has not yet lost timeliness. His drama "Năpasta" is a powerful study of Roumanian peasant problems. "Manasse," by Ronetti-Roman, is a fine production. One of the best Roumanian historical plays is "Vlaïcu Voda," by Al. Davila. After Caragiale ceased writing, there was an appreciable gap, bridged by adaptation and translations. Then Dela-vrancea, one of Roumania's best writers, brought out a trilogy —"Apus de Soare" (1909), "Viforul" (1910), "Luceafărul" (1910), dealing with Moldavian history, which made a great sensation, and are still being played to crowded houses. Haralamb Lecca, who has been prolific in both prose and verse, had distinguished success at the National Theater with his plays, "Ca Jucătorii de Cărtzi," "Câinii" and others. In recent years Victor Eftimiu, just mentioned as a poet and story-writer, and now Director of the National Theater, has written several charming phantasies in verse, like "Inshira-te Mărgărite" and "Cocoshul Negru," the former of which is constantly running in Bucharest. Anghel and Iosif also collaborated for the stage, and their three-act light opera "Cometa" had considerable success. They worked together also on the opera libretto "Legenda Funigeelor," an adaptation of Wagner's "Flying Dutchman." Other well-known writers for the stage are: Alexander G. Florescu, author of the prose drama "Sanda"; H. Pandelea, best known for "Ultimul Vlastar"; Dinu Rămura (A. Hertz), with "Floare de Nalba" and "Paianjenul"; and Alfred Moshoiu, author of "Dansul Ielelor."

In the days before freedom of the press, the fable had much vogue as a method of conveying criticism of conditions; and even in recent years it was employed by Caragiale in "Convorbiri Critice," by Anghel and Iosif ("A. Mirea") in the "Caleidoscopul," and George Ranetti, who brought out a thin volume of witty fables. The epigram, which is also a characteristically Roumanian development, has had brilliant exponents in R. Rosetti, A. C. Cuza and the brothers Cincinnatus and John Pavelescu.

Roumania produced two important literary critics during the 19th century, Titus Maioresco and Dobrogeanu Gherea. Hilarion Chendi brought out several volumes of "Foiletoane" (Feuilletons), "Preludi," etc., marked by taste and discrimination; Eugene Lovinescu, better known as story-writer and dramatist; Simeon Mehedintzi, whose excellent critiques were published in *Convorbiri Literare*. Recently another school of critics has arisen in Roumania, who endeavor to penetrate beyond style and form, and judge of an author's success in the expression of his ideas. C. Stere, Garabet Ibrăileanu, Isabella Sadoveanu and H. Sanielevici are the leading exponents, and have published stimulating critical studies, particularly in *Viatza Românească*.

In scientific history, Roumania is best known by the works of Alexander Xenopol (whose Roumanian history, in French and in German, is generally reputed the best); John Bogdan; the Bucovinan Demetrius Onciul whose convenient summary "Din Istoria României" I have found clear and helpful; Nicholas I. Iorga, whose enormous productivity I have outlined earlier; Constantine Giurescu, and John Sârbu. History as a literary genre is represented by various of Iorga's works—"Istoria lui Shtefan cel Mare," "Sate shi Mănăstirii din România" and "Drumuri shi Orashe"—and by Vlahutza's little volume "Din Trecutul Nostru" (Out of Our Past), one of the most graphic and charming series of historic episodes I have ever read in any language. George Bratiano (see Chapter XXVII) has distinguished himself in mediæval history.

Archæological studies were well represented in the elder generation by Odobescu, Tocilescu and Teohari Antonescu; after their death, Iorga became preëminent in this field also, particularly as regards ancient and mediæval art. The best-known modern writers are George Murnu, A. Tzigara-Samurcash, Director of the National Ethnographic Museum, A. Baltazar and especially the historian Alexander Lepadatu, who published in the admirable Bulletin of the Commission on Historic Monuments—volumes as superbly printed and illustrated as anything in the West—a valuable series of studies on Roumanian architecture. The field of Byzantine studies is represented by O. Tafrali.

The best-known Roumanian writer on philosophical subjects was Basil Conta. His successors were Rădulescu-Motru, author of an extensive study on "Puterea Sufletească" (Spiritual Force) and the historian Alexander Xenopol, who has written on the philosophy of history. Other writers on philosophy are the sociologist Demetrius Gusti, John Petrovici, whose studies have mostly been published in the magazine *Cultura Română*, Constantine Antoniade, the Roumanian interpreter of Carlyle, Marinus Stefănescu, and Radu Djuvara. There is also an aphoristic literature, represented by Iorga's "Gânduri shi Sfaturi" which is perhaps his most careful work, and the "Cugetările" of Adina Gr. Olănescu, an original and stimulating book.

As befits a Latin people, oratory has always had a great vogue in Roumania. Early Roumanian parliaments had to grapple with a series of fundamental questions, which would naturally develop eloquent speakers. Of their successors,

Take Jonesco was generally agreed to hold the palm; his speeches with reference to Roumania's entry into the war beside the Allies are considered among the greatest of our generation. Others who distinguished themselves on that and other occasions were Nicholas Filipescu, former head of the Conservatives, Dr. I. Cantacuzene, Emanuel Antonescu and Titulesco. The debates on agrarian reforms, universal suffrage and other important pre-war problems had developed the oratorical powers and reputation of the Liberal leader John J. C. Bratiano, Nicholas Iorga, the historian, A. C. Cuza, the anti-Semite, and Constantine Banu, as well as others who have now disappeared from the scene. Perhaps the chief of these was the Conservative Peter Carp, who spoke always with eloquence and authority; his colleague, Alexander Marghiloman, was famous for the clearness of style and elegance of his diction. Since the war, many new figures from the provinces have appeared on the parliamentary platform, especially Transylvanians who had won a reputation in and outside of Hungary for the vigor and classic style of their public addresses; among them may be mentioned Vaida Voevod, Julius Maniu, Father Lucaci, Octavian Goga.

The Roumanian law-courts have always been schools of oratory. Law and politics are as closely allied in Roumania as with us; in fact, Roumania could do well with fewer lawyers and more engineers and business men. A large number of the most promising legal students finished their training in Paris, since Roumanian law is much the same as French. This residence in Paris contributed greatly to their polish. Of this last generation, Take Jonesco, Nicholas Titulesco, C. Arion, Constantine Cernescu and N. Mitescu have been perhaps the most eloquent; they maintain the tradition of which Eugene Statescu, Titus Maioresco and Delavrancea were among the distinguished representatives in the past.

University and Academy lectures are also the occasion of much genuine eloquence, and are thronged by the public. In fact, I was unable even to pass the threshold of the Academy when desirous of hearing Constantinescu on his discoveries in the transmission of power, or Iorga on Bessarabian history. The pre-war lectures on philosophy of Titus Maioresco and of Dumitrescu Iashi were always crowded, as are to-day's of Iorga on history, P. Negulescu's on philosophy, and the law lectures of Titulesco and Istrate Micescu.

One cannot close without reference to the Roumanians who have written in some foreign tongue. Perhaps the best-known writer on things Roumanian was the late Queen Elizabeth, "Carmen Sylva." She did a most valuable work of popularizing Roumanian literature for the English, French and German publics. Hélène Văcăresco, though really a French poetess, has contributed much by her translations to knowledge abroad of Roumanian ballads and other poetry. The Princess Henriette Sava-Goïu ("Adrio Val"), intimate friend of Queen Marie, did valuable work as a translator. The Countess de Noailles was also a Roumanian, of the Bibesco family; and Princess Marthe Bibesco won a prize from the French Academy with her "Les Huit Paradis"; Americans remember her "Memoirs," published in the *Saturday Evening Post*. G. Bengescu is an authority on Voltaire, and editor of the standard critical bibliography of his works. As was said not long ago by Louis Barthou, of the French Academy: "There is no other Allied country where the French language is spoken as it is in Roumania, with so much ease, grace and force. Some weeks ago," he continued, "M. Bratiano, at a banquet where I had the honor of presiding, gave us the delightful surprise of a talk in which he spoke French such that we, hearing him, felt we could take lessons from him in the language which after all we ought to speak well ourselves." And that was no empty persiflage!

Queen Marie writes mainly in English, her native tongue. She has brought out several volumes of fairy tales and stories—"The Lily of Life," "The Dreamer of Dreams," "Ilderim" (which has recently been staged), and her brilliant apostrophe to Roumania, "My Country." During the war she wrote a series of sketches and articles, full of deep feeling, for the "Figaro," "Revue de Paris," etc. Her style is strongly tinged by the poetical influences of Roumania and of her Roumanian environment.

CHAPTER XXVI

INTELLECTUAL LIFE OF THE NEW ROUMANIA

It has been my good fortune, in the course of six trips through Roumania, and particularly in lecturing there in 1927 on our American political, intellectual and university life, to come to know a different Roumania from that which greets the ordinary tourist or business man. Not merely the large centers, like Bucharest, Jassy and Cluj, but provincial cities like Craiova and Sibiu (Hermannstadt), support and encourage literary, theatrical and musical activities which compare favorably with those of our own cities. I have spoken on the platform more than two thousand times, in various countries; and I have never had more appreciative audiences than those which crowded the halls of Kishineff, e. g., or Czernowitz, or more enjoyed the discussions which followed; nor have I ever been better reported. One who was brought up in a newspaper office judges a people in part by its newspapers; and here Roumania stands well, though politics still bulks too largely in journalism there; as in France, some newspapers would not exist without the financial support of a political group. But the great dailies, like the "Dimineatza" and the "Universul," with their large income from advertisements and sales, are not dependent on political aid, and are no more partisan than, e. g., the New York "Herald-Tribune" or the London "Daily Telegraph." The "Universul," which used to be the organ of Take Jonesco, is strongly nationalistic, anti-Hungarian and anti-Jewish; its Director, Stelian Popescu, former Attorney-

General, is affiliated with the Liberals. The "Dimineatza" and "Adevĕrul," morning and evening editions published by one company, are of democratic leanings, and have in general supported the Peasant-Nationalist combination, whose official organs are the "Dreptatea," and the "Patria" of Cluj. The official Liberal organ is the "Viitorul," and the French daily which has appeared for half a century, the "Indépendance Roumaine," is of Liberal antecedents. There is an admirable financial daily, the "Argus," whose director, Gafencu, has been a high official in the Foreign Office; this publishes editions also in French and German. Of the other Bucharest dailies, several are of high literary excellence, notably Prof. Iorga's "Neamul Românesc," Gr. Filipescu's "Epoca," the "Cuvântul" and "Curentul," and the "Lupta" with E. Fagure. There is a German daily in Bucharest, several in Transylvania, and a large number of Hungarian dailies and weeklies, which compare well for journalistic enterprise and literary excellence with those of Buda-Pesth. There are also good Hungarian theatrical companies, with well-attended seasons in the Transylvanian cities; Russian companies tour Bessarabia; there is an excellent Yiddish company in Bucharest. Roumanians are fond of the theater, and radio has not dealt the stage as serious a blow as in England and America. But for a generation, in the nineteenth century, the Roumanian stage was thoroughly French; Roumania had produced a great writer for the stage, Caragiale, but his comedies were neglected for those of Molière and Scribe. The Roumanian theater-going public saw, and still sees, French novelties earlier than many a French provincial audience. But in 1906, a famous revolt took place; a group of young Roumanians, with Prof. Iorga and other literary leaders at their head, rebelled against this French dominance, and insisted that the National Theater should present Roumanian plays; and to-day, metropolis and provincial centers offer the classics and the latest productions of Roumanian playwrights. Caragiale's mordant and amusing satires; Alecsandri's "Despot Voda" and "Fântâna Blandusiei"; B. P. Hăsdeu's "Rasvan shi Vidra"; Delavrancea's trilogy—a general favorite—of "Apus de Soare," "Viforul," and "Luceafărul"; G. Diamandi's Chemarea Codrului"; and Al. Davila's "Vlaïcu Voda," are continually produced. There are admirable actors and actresses; indeed, Roumania has furnished the Paris stage with some of its most famous players. I need recall only "Max," ornament of the Comédie Française in the days of Sarah Bernhardt, and such well-known Roumanian actresses of the present day as Marie Ventura, Elvire Popescu and Alice Cocéa.

Roumanian music, like Roumanian literature, takes its origin from the peasantry, in the haunting melodies of the folk-song, with its gay challenge to the dance, or its touching reminiscence of the distant forests or of past happiness; and (like Roumanian writers) composers and artists have gone to Western Europe, and particularly to Paris, for training. Of the present generation, two are especially well-known —Stan Golestan (musical critic of the "Figaro") and Georges Enesco. Golestan was charmed in childhood by the "doïne," those infinitely varied songs of the Roumanian peasantry which express the "dor"—the "yearning" for greater happiness, exactly the "saüdade" of the Portuguese folk-songs which Keyserling has just called the supreme expression of the Portuguese spirit. With his memory full of these songs and their gypsy variants, young Golestan went to Paris and became one of the first pupils of Vincent d'Indy and the Schola Cantorum; one sees also the influence of Auguste Sérieux, Albert Roussel and Paul Dukas. Golestan has written a "Symphonie Roumaine," "Rapsodie Roumaine," "Rapsodie concertante" for orchestra and violin, "Sonata" for piano and violin, "Quatuor à cordes," "Thème, variations et danse," and numerous doïne and popular songs. Enesco is perhaps better known as a superb virtuoso on the piano and violin, and as a conductor, than as a composer; but he rivals his older friend Golestan in his creative ability, to which we owe several sonatas, a "Poème Roumain," several rhapsodies, suites and symphonies, and the lyric drama "Œdipe Roi," to the text of Edmond Fleg. Others of this vital and active group of young Roumanian musicians are Constantine Nottara, Marcel Mihalovici, Georges Enacovici, Nonna Otescu, Alfred Alessandresco, M. G. Andrico and many others. Berlin also attracts young Roumanians, especially pianists, like Dorel Handman. One of their number, Prof. Constantine Brailoïu of the Conservatory, has carried through one of the most remarkable investigations of our times. For three years, under the auspices of the Society of Composers of Bucharest, he has directed the gathering of Roumanian folk-songs. Thousands of phonographic records, supplemented by motion pictures in the case of dances, are now at the disposal of the student; the songs were also annotated by a competent philologist, and a card was devoted to every singer, giving his (or her) name, age, occupation, antecedents, education, travels, etc. Each song has also its series of cards, sometimes a hundred or over, showing where and by whom it was sung; and an ingenious system of notation makes clear the permanent underlying elements in the song, and the variants, regional or personal. Similar thorough work has been done with Roumanian games, and the Năsturel Prize of the Roumanian Academy was awarded in 1931 to G. T. Niculescu Varone for his monumental work describing games previously unrecorded, with an alphabetic and bibliographic index of all Roumanian popular games.

Roumanian intellectual life is centered in the universities, to a greater degree than with us, and culminates in the Roumanian Academy—a venerable institution, whose different sections form channels for the expression of every form of scientific, historical and literary investigation; the high esteem in which it is held is shown by King Carol's speech opening its annual meeting of 1931. Its admirable library, free to the public, is much used; and it is to such a degree a popular institution that the proceedings of its sections are fully reported in the daily papers. Mention of libraries recalls the unique Bratiano Library, to which Mme. Elise Bratiano has devoted an affectionate care which makes it perhaps the best collection for the specialist in the history of southeastern Europe, as it is certainly the most luxuriously convenient for the student that I have ever used; based on the remarkably complete library which Ionel Bratiano had accumulated, it is housed in an addition to his own home, and sufficiently endowed for new purchases and administration.

Roumanian youth flocks to the universities, which are incredibly overcrowded; that of Bucharest boasts some twenty thousand students, and that of Jassy has more than Munich; and practically every Roumanian scholar and scientific man lectures or teaches in the universities or the affiliated institutions. They are also the recognized medium for foreign lecturers, of whom many visit Roumania each year, especially from Paris. Indeed, the French influence is almost as strong in the universities as in the literature; but German scientific thought and investigation is closely followed; Prof. Werner Sombart of the University of Berlin lectured in 1931; and as I discovered from my own courses there, the young Roumanian students and their instructors have great curiosity about the United States, and regret that our remoteness and high prices keep them from knowing our institutions better. Admirable original work is being done by Roumanian specialists, particularly in medicine and in bacteriology, in which Prof. Cantacuzene's authority is universally recognized. The Geological Museum, monument of Prof. Mrazec's labors, and the Natural History Museum, to which Haeckel's collaborator, Prof. Antipa, has devoted a lifetime of devotion, are institutions of the first rank; and Prof. Tzigara-Samurcash's Ethnographical Museum is a revelation of the artistic endowment of the Roumanian peasant. The Roumanian Academy and the universities and technical institutions issue valuable publications, among which should be mentioned the "Annales scientifiques" of the University of Jassy, the bulletins of Prof. D. D. Gusti's Institute of Social Sciences in Bucharest, those of Prof. Racovitza's Institute of Speology of Cluj, the "Buletinele Shtiintzifice" of the Universities of Jassy and Cluj, and the Proceedings (in German) of the Natural History Society of Sibiu. Under great difficulties there appear a host of scientific and technical reviews, of which the "Gazeta Matematică" carries great weight, Roumania having produced admirable mathematicians and physicists; one of the latter, Constantinescu, has achieved world-wide renown through his discoveries, especially in hydraulics; another, Niculae Dinculescu, is well known for his work on the polarization of light. Another periodical now over 20 years old is "Natura." The Jassy Society of Doctors and Naturalists has been publishing its Proceedings for almost a hundred years. Archæology is worthily represented by superb publications, quite comparable with our own, of

which the latest are the Bulletins of the Roumanian Classical
School in Rome. Another vigorous and highly regarded review is Prof. Rădulescu-Motru's "Revista de Filozofie,"
now in its sixteenth volume.

In a previous chapter I have carried the story of Roumanian literature up to 1920. In the following decade, there
has been a surprising development of the novel—the most
surprising feature being that the Roumanian novelist is
reasonably well paid, although he can count on no such overseas public as his colleague in England, France, Spain or
Portugal. Four men stand out conspicuously among the
novelists of to-day—Liviu Rebreanu, Ionel Teodoreanu,
Cezar Petrescu and Camil Petrescu. Rebreanu created a
profound sensation with his novel "Ion," the story of a
young peasant, his land-hunger and his love, quite comparable with the master-pieces of Reymont and Hamsun.
More profoundly affecting was his war novel, "Pădurea
Spânzuratzilor" (The Grove of the Gallows). Here he
handled the poignant theme of the Austro-Hungarian officer
who had to fight against his brothers in the Allied Armies;
the hero is a Transylvanian Roumanian who finally decided to join the Roumanian Army, is captured and hanged.

Ionel Teodoreanu, a profoundly acute observer, sketched
in "La Medeleni" the history of an old Moldavian family,
and in his "Bal Mascat" (Masked Ball), the nervous life of
society in present-day Bucharest. Cezar Petrescu, a newspaper man turned novelist, won instant renown with his war
novel "Intunecare" (The Darkening), a keen study of the
social upturn caused by the war. He followed this up with
"Calea Victoriei," a picture of the new Bucharest, under
the title of its Fifth Avenue. In "Comoara Regelui Dromichet" (The Jewel of King Dromichet), he satirizes modern
artificial life, as penetrated by an ingenuous villager. Camil

Petrescu, the poet and dramatist, has also just published a successful war novel, "Ultima Noapte de Dragoste, Întaia Noapte de Războiu" (Last Night of Love, First Night of War), in which he brings out the senseless stupidity of the contest. This received the 1931 Brătescu-Voineshti Prize of the Society of Roumanian Authors, and the first edition was sold out in a fortnight. G. I. Mihăescu, short story-writer, has gained prominence by his novel "Bratzul Andromedei," (Andromeda's Arm), a brilliant psychological study. And one must not forget Sadoveanu's "File Sânge-rate" (Blood-stained Leaves), one of the first war stories published in Roumania. The Orthodox Church is repre-sented by Rev. Grigore Pishculescu (Gala Galaction), who writes delightful essays and short stories.

In recent poetry, Pillat has continued his lyric strains, and in conjunction with "Perpessicius," has brought out a useful Anthology of recent Roumanian verse. Al. Philippide achieved fame in 1921 with his "Aur Sterp" (Barren Gold), and increased it in 1930 with his "Stânci Fulgerate" (Cliffs Lightning-struck). Lucian Blaga has produced several dra-matic sensations, beginning with "Pietre pentru Templul Meu" (Stones for My Temple); "Zamolxes" and "Mesh-terul Manole" are others of importance. Minulescu keeps publishing charming verse and stories, and successful com-edies. Ion Barbu and Demostene Botez are admirable poets. Nichifor Craïnic continues to write excellent verse, and wields much influence through his newspaper column and his periodical "Gândirea," which is opposed to the ra-tionalistic tendencies of "Viatza Românească." He was just awarded the national poetry prize of 100,000 lei. Of the younger dramatists, Al. Kiritzescu is most in the public eye, with his "Marcel & Marcel," "Cuib de Viespi" (Wasp's Nest) and "Florentina." Otilia Cazimir, a woman poet, who won a Roumanian Academy prize with her volume "Fluturi de Noapte" (Night Butterflies), has just published another collection, "Cântec de Comoară" (Jewel Song). Roumanian painting and sculpture have been more affected by modernistic tendencies than their poetry; so far, there has appeared no Roumanian Gertrude Stein.

In history, Alexandru Marcu has distinguished himself by his "Conspirators and Conspiracies in the Period of Roumanian Political Renascence, 1848–1877," to which the Academy awarded a prize in 1931. Excellent work is being done in the history of Roumanian art and architecture, especially by the architect G. Balsh. Prof. Paul Henry of the French University Mission to Roumania has just published an admirable work on "Les Églises de la Moldavie du Nord," also crowned by the Academy.

Ibrăileanu, the literary critic, has increased his reputation not merely by authoritative studies in Roumanian literature, but also by his masterly essays on Tolstoy and especially Proust. Eugen Lovinescu is publishing a history of Roumanian literature in several volumes; and a new monumental dictionary of the language is coming out, under the editorship of Prof. I. A. Candrea, the "Dictzionar Enciclopedic Ilustrat al Limbei Române." This is based on studies of 850 books and manuscripts, in the course of which over 600,000 citations were made and are being utilized, for about 45,000 words; it includes also a dictionary of geography and history, composed by Prof. Gh. Adamescu. Interest in the language and literature compares favorably at this moment in Roumania, with that in any other country. Besides the prizes which I have mentioned above, in 1929 the distinguished jurist C. Hamangiu (Minister of Justice in the Iorga Cabinet of 1931), gave the Roumanian Academy the funds for an annual prize of 200,000 lei, to be awarded in successive years to the best novel, dramatic or poetical work, literary critique, painting or sculpture, musical composition, and legal work.

Roumanian literary men and artists do not forget that their nation is closely bound with the Balkans; indeed, several of the most distinguished of their number have come from Macedonia. In the Inter-Balkan Conference of October, 1930, a committee was appointed, headed by a Turkish scholar, Hambudah Subhi, to lay the intellectual foundations for the Balkan Union dreamed of by Venizelos and Take Jonesco. This committee is arranging for the interchange of teachers and students in the Balkan universities, the establishment in the Balkan countries of summer schools like that which Prof. Iorga has developed at Vălenii de Munte, and other means of closer acquaintance. Roumania has a great advantage in her friendly relations with all the Balkan countries, and Roumanian writers and university leaders take a keen interest in this movement.

But Paris still remains the Mecca for ambitious young Roumanians; and several of the best Roumanian writers still use French in their books. Panaït Istrati, a former Danube roustabout, has made a success in French comparable to that of Conrad in English, and keeps drawing on his Roumanian reminiscences. Princess Marthe Bibesco, daughter of Ion Lahovary and granddaughter of Vodă Bibesco, wrote her interesting memoirs in English in "The Saturday Evening Post"; but she continues to publish her books and plays in French, though some, like her charming "Isvor, le Pays des Saules," are also available in English and in Roumanian. Her cousin Prince Antoine Bibesco (husband of Elizabeth Asquith) won success on the French, English and German stage with his clever comedies "Laquelle?" and "L'Héritier."

Roumanian writers from Transylvania make use of German, also, and one, Oscar Walter Cisek, won honorable mention for the Kleist Prize in 1929 with his novel "Die Tatarin." In English, Konrad Bercovici has had a career like that of Istrati. He too came from the lower Danube region, and draws from the rich stock of peasant and gypsy tales for his short stories; it is a pity that he has recently succumbed to the lure of sensationalism. We have available in English also a considerable body of translations from the Roumanian, including at last Eminesco's poems, in the version of Miss Pankhurst and I. O. Stefanovici; these are also being translated into Polish by the poet Zagadlowicz.

Not to be outdone by Boston, Roumania has also an Index Expurgatorius, revived recently, to the general amusement, by the Orthodox Church; but its chief result has been to advertise the books concerned, Tudor Arghezi's "Icoane de Lemn" (Wooden Eikons) and D. V. Barnoschi's "Neamul Cotofănesc," which are somewhat like Sinclair Lewis's "Elmer Gantry."

This brief sketch will suffice to show the intensity of the intellectual life of present-day Roumania—the best possible augury for her future.

CHAPTER XXVII

ROUMANIAN POLITICS SINCE THE WAR

THE Roumanians are a "politically-minded" people, and no one can understand Roumania without some knowledge of Roumanian politics. It has been my good fortune to know personally most of the leading figures, both of the generation of Marghiloman, John J. C. Bratiano and Take Jonesco, and of that of to-day; and repeated visits to Roumania, and constant reading of the Bucharest newspapers, enable me to present this subject with at least much sympathy.

The war ended sooner in Eastern Europe—in fact, the collapse of the Bulgarian front in September 1918 was the real end of the struggle—and with the disappearance of the occupying Germans, the Marghiloman Ministry resigned, on Oct. 23. It had defended Roumanian interests against the exploiting invaders—Dr. Antipa, Minister of Agriculture, gives details in his story of the occupation published by the Carnegie Peace Fund—and it had presided over the reincorporation of Bessarabia, first of the lost provinces to return; but it had to bear the stigma of having at least collaborated with the Germans, and gave way to a military cabinet, presided over by Gen. Coanda, with Gen. Văitoianu (Liberal) Minister of the Interior and of Justice, and Gen. E. Grigorescu, Minister of War. This served as a bridge to the Liberal Ministry of John J. C. (Ionel) Bratiano, inaugurated Nov. 29, 1918; this was the cabinet which defended Roumanian interests with such persistency at the

Paris Peace Conference. Transylvania was represented in it by Dr. Vaida Voevod, Stephen C. Pop, and Vasile Goldish. It governed without a Parliament, by decree, and angered the Allies greatly by Bratiano's refusal to sign the treaties with Austria and Bulgaria, as too humiliating.

There was a general demand for a parliamentary election; Gen. Văitoianu was made Premier in Sept., 1919, and the elections were held soon afterward. In spite of the Premier's Liberal affiliations, the Liberals won only 120 seats of the 321; the Transylvanian Nationalists, headed by the men who had fought for Roumanian rights under the Hungarians, and the Peasant Party, under Mihalache, a teacher who showed marked aptitude for politics, had the majority, and proceeded to form a Ministry headed by Dr. Vaida Voevod. Gen. (now Field-Marshal) Averesco, head of the People's Party, an organization closely affiliated with the Liberals, at first collaborated with this Ministry; but in March 1920 he overthrew it, and formed his first cabinet, with Argetoianu as Minister of Finance. In June, he strengthened it by adding Take Jonesco as Foreign Minister, and Titulesco as head of the Treasury. This cabinet carried through important fiscal reforms, and laid the foundations of the present tax system, but it had a minority backing in Parliament, and Gen. Averesco held elections in May, 1920. With the help of the Liberals, he carried 292 constituencies, and governed till December 1921, when John J. C. Bratiano, the consummate political leader who headed the Liberal Party, decided that the time was ripe for his return; and after a stopgap Take Jonesco Ministry, lasting only a month, Bratiano stepped in again, and governed Roumania for four years.

"Ionel" (Jack) Bratiano was a man of the first rank. His early ambition was to distinguish himself in the building up of the country his father had consolidated, and he began his career as a civil engineer; but politics soon attracted him, and his mastery over men brought him immediate success. Perhaps it was his engineering training which made him impatient of the inefficiency of the politicians, and the defects of a democracy based on an illiterate electorate. At any rate, he believed in governing with a firm hand, and was always practically a dictator. The Liberal Party, headed by the Bratianos and their immediate associates, was what Mr. Bryan or Mr. Roosevelt would have characterized as a party of predatory wealth. They controlled the National Bank of Roumania, the Roumanian Bank (Banca Românească), and other great financial and commercial enterprises, and were as discriminating in the granting or withholding of credits as any good Republican banker in Pennsylvania in the Pinchot campaign. Bratiano himself, and his brother Vintila, had seen the confusion caused by Roumania's dependence upon Germany and Austria in 1914, and had made up their minds that Roumania should henceforward stand upon her own feet financially. There was a widespread demand for the use of foreign capital in the development of the country—a demand specially voiced by the Transylvanians, and with which Prince Carol had sympathy; this fact counted probably as seriously against him as his wild oats, in the machinations which led to his exile. But the Bratianos held firm for development with Roumanian capital alone.

Bratiano held his elections in March 1922, in the good old-fashioned way, winning 309 of the 387 seats. Dissatisfaction with the tyrannical methods of the elections was so deep in Transylvania, where they were compared with those held under the Magyars, that the Transylvanian Nationalists kept away from the coronation ceremonies of King

Ferdinand and Queen Marie in their midst, at Alba-Julia, as a protest. Nor was this feeling improved by legislation giving the party which secured as high as 40% of the votes, 50% of the seats in Parliament, and depriving of representation any party which did not secure 2% of the total vote. Legislation is difficult in a body split into many different parties; but this savored too much of the steam-roller.

The chief problem confronting Parliament was the succession to the throne. Under pressure applied by the Bratianos, Crown Prince Carol was forced to abdicate leaving his young son Michael successor; and since Ferdinand was well along in years, it was desirable to have a Regency Council provided for, which should be securely Liberal in sympathies. This was voted on Jan. 4, 1926. Soon afterward, Bratiano decided to withdraw from power for a time, and resigned, recommending the King to call Gen. Averesco and the People's Party to the helm; their affiliations were close with the Liberals, and they agreed not to touch the legislation by which the subsoil and its treasures had been declared government property, to the great alarm of the foreign oil and mining companies operating in Roumania; they were also sound, from Bratiano's point of view, on the question of keeping foreign capital out of Roumania.

Gen. Averesco held elections on May 25, 1926, taking advantage of all the means in his power, and winning 292 out of 387 seats. Gafencu, editor of the leading Roumanian financial and commercial paper, the "Argus," and later a minister in the Maniu administration, tells an amusing story of this election. He was campaigning for the opposition in Bihor, Transylvania, and set out the day before in his car from Oradia-Mare for Beiush. Travel is very carefully supervised on such occasions, and he had provided himself with a general pass from the Prefect—who had however telephoned the first post of gendarmes to stop Gafencu and put his car out of commission. So he was promptly halted and his tires slashed; but to his surprise, when the gendarmes discovered that he was a Nationalist candidate, they made him an honored guest, and told him there was no need of any campaigning; that "our candidates" were sure to win. "Our candidates?" asked Gafencu. "Yes, the Roumanian Nationalist candidates." "Well, then, why do you stop me, and let Hungarians pass who are voting with the People's Party and flying the Hungarian flag and singing the Hungarian anthem?" "Orders are orders; but it's all useless. There are more of us." And so events proved. Even with all the force of the administration behind them, the combined People's—Liberal—Hungarian vote was only 34% in Bihor, 39% in Arad, 43% at Sălaj, 54% in Satul Mare, and 45% in Temesh-Torontal (Banat). In the next election, a year later, held by the Liberals, the Hungarians were in opposition, and polled only 12.84% in Bihor, 14% in Arad, 18.90% in Satul Mare, and 27.94% in Temesh-Torontal. But in the perfectly free elections held under Maniu, Dec. 12, 1928, whose impartiality was officially praised in Parliament by the head of the Hungarian Party, all these cities showed the truth of the gendarmes' statement to Gafencu. In Bihor, the combined Peasant-Nationalist vote was 65%, the Hungarians 19%; in Arad, 75% and 12%; in Sălaj, 64% and 27%; in Satul Mare, 66% and 24%.

Gen. Averesco soon showed too much independence to suit Bratiano, and in June 1927 Averesco fell and Bratiano again held elections along the same lines, securing this time 318 of the 387 seats. Titulesco again left his diplomatic post to serve as Foreign Minister, July 6; a fortnight later, King Ferdinand died, to be followed by Ionel Bratiano on Nov. 24. The Regency Council for little King Michael was therefore constituted, consisting of Prince Nicholas (Carol's younger brother), the Patriarch of the Orthodox Church, Dr. Miron Cristea, and the Chief Justice of the Supreme Court, G. Buzdugan.

On Ionel Bratiano's death, his brother Vintilă succeeded him as Premier and as head of the Liberal Party. Vintilă Bratiano (who died in December 1930) had all his brother's firmness, but lacked his ability to handle men, and persisted in managing everything personally in smallest detail. A favorite anecdote about him told of a distinguished financier going to Ionel Bratiano and begging him to use his influence with Vintilă, whereupon Ionel threw up his hands and confessed that since boyhood he had never succeeded in making Vintilă budge an inch when he had made up his mind. Vintilă saw however that the political situation was dangerous, with the Peasant-Nationalist majority of the voters chafing under these three elections which had kept a minority in power by extra-legal means, and proposed to Iuliu Maniu, head of the Nationalist-Peasant coalition, that they hold new elections with a joint ticket, and divide the cabinet half and half, the Liberals however to keep 55% of the seats in Parliament. Maniu, knowing that a large majority of the electorate was behind him, declined to enter into this combination, and read an energetic protest in Parliament on Dec. 7, 1927, against the dictatorial way in which the country was governed by the Liberals. As this had no result, the opposition decided upon a demonstration; on the 18th of March, 1928, over 100,000 peasants gathered in Bucharest and went on record for new, free elections; and on the first of May, several hundred thousand gathered at Alba-Julia and passed resolutions to the same effect. Both meetings went off with perfect order, and gave admirable testimony to the peacefulness and common sense of the Roumanian peasant. It was voted that the party should withdraw from Parliament, but hold a meeting of its members in Bucharest the day Parliament opened; and on July 26 this gathering did take place, passing bitter criticisms of the Liberals, and contesting their right to speak in the name of the nation.

By this time, Roumanian finances showed the effect of the boycott of foreign capital; New York, London and Paris had scant sympathy with a régime which had ostentatiously declined their aid except on conditions which seemed unjustified, and had been alarmed by the mining legislation, which had smacked of confiscation. The leu had reached the point where a stabilization loan would hold it; and money was sadly needed for other purposes. Foreign banking interests declined to help Bratiano out, and he resigned on Nov. 3, 1928. An effort was made to form a non-partisan cabinet, under Titulesco; but that proved impracticable, and on Nov. 10, Maniu formed the first purely Peasant-Nationalist ministry, with Mironescu in the Foreign Office, Vaida Voevod Minister of the Interior, Michael (Mihai) Popovici in the Treasury, Mihalache Minister of Agriculture, Iunian Minister of Justice, and Madgearu, of Industry and Commerce. Elections were held on Dec. 18, 1928 without government interference; 349 Peasant-Nationalists were chosen, 13 Liberals, 5 People's Party (with whom the venerable Prof. Iorga had combined his forces), 5 Peasant's Party of Dr. Lupu—an able and fearless stormy petrel of Roumanian politics—and 15 Hungarian Nationalists; in the majority were 11 Germans, 4 Zionists (the Jewish vote was divided between Zionists and Social Democrats, thus cutting down their proportion), 2 Bulgarians, 2 Ukrainians and 9 Social Democrats.

The first task of this government was to take the financial and legislative steps necessary for renewed connection with the banking centers. Discrimination against foreign capital was removed; provisions in the mining laws which came perilously near confiscation, were altered; independent corporations were formed for the administration of government assets, like the railways, monopolies, etc.; and the laws governing the creation of stock companies were put on a basis more liberal to foreigners. This Parliament also tackled the problem of decentralization, and decided on a program of regional autonomy, both of provinces, counties and communes. The Opposition found this too radical, and left their seats, on July 14, 1929, to return only at the request of King Carol on Nov. 15, 1930.

The death of Chief Justice Buzdugan, and appointment in his place on the Regency Commission of C. Sărătzeanu, a lawyer connected with a member of the Maniu Ministry, called attention afresh to the disadvantage of such an executive organ in a country where momentous decisions might have to be made at a moment's notice. The people were sick and tired of politics, disappointed that the Peasant-Nationalists had not succeeded in conjuring away the financial, commercial and agricultural crisis, ready for a firm hand. Carol had always been popular among the people, thanks to his complete democracy; the army was devoted to him, except for a few political generals; the Transylvanians had always found him especially sympathetic with them; and Roumanian public opinion in general was perfectly willing to accept his guidance, in the hope that his ambition and solid abilities might lead the country out of the doldrums, when the professional politicians seemed powerless. There was a general expectation that he would return when the time was ripe; and in the spring of 1930, conditions became wholly favorable. Prince Nicholas headed the little group of faithful army officers and political personalities in Bucharest which engineered the return from Paris, originally planned for June 4; there was a hitch, and the rumor got out in Paris, so that one alert American correspondent wired his agency that Carol would be back in Bucharest within the week; but the news was kept out of Roumania, except for a small group of state officials and military officers. Plans had been elaborately made, and the first part of the program went off smoothly; Prince Carol, who posed as the chauffeur of the Roumanian Military Attaché, himself ran the car from his chateau at Coësmes, near Nancy, to Munich on June 5th. Early the next morning—this time as the Military Attaché, with important papers—he started in a French Farman biplane (which had made a famous flight to Lake Tchad and Madagascar) for Cluj, the French pilot having no idea of his identity. Col. Precup sent Capt. Cristescu out with a fast plane to meet him; the aviator, on passing Oradia, noticed a big white plane making a forced landing some distance out of the city; he circled down and found it was the prince. The oil supply had sprung a leak; Capt. Cristescu helped them out, and gave them a 15 minutes' start, as their machine was much slower. But when he reached Somesh Sat, the aviation field where the prince was expected, he had not arrived; so Capt. Cristescu set out again, and this time came upon quite an amusing scene. The Farman had run short of gasoline, and had had to come down on a peasant's mowing in Vadul Crishului, near Bihor. The indignant peasant had demanded 1500 lei ($9) damages; and as the prince and the pilot had only French money, he refused to take it. A large share of the natives of the hamlet soon assembled, and the prince was busy answering questions about the cost of an aëroplane ride, the noise of the engine, etc., when a local notary stepped up, who recognized the prince, and matters were at once adjusted. But not till 7:10 P. M. did they all reach Somesh Sat. The arrival had been scheduled for the early afternoon, and the prince was to have been accompanied from Cluj to the Bucharest landing field by a fleet of planes; but in view of the lateness of the hour, only two planes left, the prince in one, piloted by Capt. Oprish, and Col. Precup in the other.

Those who knew expected the plane in Bucharest by 7 P. M.; and telephone inquiries puzzled the officials there all through the early evening, as well as the crowds which came out, larger than those which normally expect the mail plane. That arrived on time at 9:30 o'clock, and the landing lights were switched off; but the crowd remained. A few minutes later, another plane was heard; it signaled for lights, the flares were set, and at 9:40 P. M., June 6, 1930, Carol was back in Bucharest.

The news spread like wild-fire over the city; but every effort was made to keep it from international circulation. However, two clever correspondents succeeded in getting it out, one indirectly by a telegram to a Swedish friend, the other by a direct personal conventional cable to New York, so that his paper had a clean day's "scoop" on one of the chief news items of our time. Bucharest was immediately descended on by dozens of correspondents, and the following fortnight was of intense interest.

Meanwhile Carol lost no time. He went to Queen Marie's palace at Cotroceni—she was absent in Germany—and telephoned Premier Maniu, who came at once to the palace, and then left for consultation with his cabinet over the constitutional features involved. It had at first been thought that the simplest method would be for Sărătzeanu to resign from the Regency Council in favor of Prince Carol, who should then govern in the name of his son, little King Michael; but a brief discussion made it obvious that that would be a clumsy and unsatisfactory subterfuge and that what the country really wanted was to have Carol as King, fully responsible for the direction of its affairs.

While the cabinet debated, Carol continued his interviews, with Prince Nicholas at his side. At 3 A. M. Saturday came Gen. Averesco and the Transylvanian poet-politician, Octavian Goga, leaders of the People's Party and partisans of Carol's return; Gen. Averesco gave out touching and valuable reminiscences later of his conversations with King Ferdinand and Ionel Bratiano on the subject of Carol's exile. At 5, Gen. Prezan, Chief of Staff, who it was hoped might form a non-partisan ministry in case of need, had an interview; at 6:30, Dr. Lupu, the sturdy independent, whose judgment is highly regarded. Dr. Lupu had had close affiliations with the Liberals in the past, and there was great curiosity about their probable attitude. It was realized that Vintilă Bratiano would doubtless continue the policy of his brother Ionel, of hostility toward the naming of Carol as King; but hopes were held of the younger generation, of whom the most conspicuous was the former Foreign Minister Duca; and Dr. Lupu had two long interviews with him on Saturday. Help came however from an unexpected quarter in the Liberal Party; Ionel's son George Bratiano, Professor of History in the University of Jassy, declared immediately in favor of recognizing Carol as King of Roumania; and when it became evident that under Vintilă Bratiano, the party was to follow an attitude of "watchful waiting," George Bratiano declared himself, and not his uncle Vintilă, legal head of the Liberal Party, and formed his own organization, which boasts an imposing array

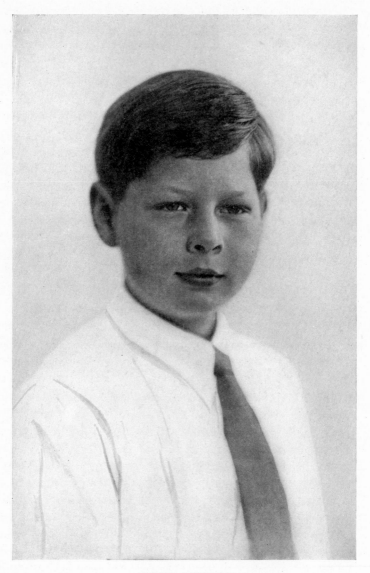

PRINCE MICHAEL

of names, better known however in the intellectual and scholarly world than in that of commerce and finance. The Liberal leader Constantine Argetoianu likewise welcomed King Carol in the name of his group.

Saturday, June 7, 1930, was a day of feverish consultations in Bucharest. The cabinet debate, at which were present also Iunian, Manoïlescu and Michael Popovici, broke up at 4 A. M., to reassemble at 9. The Parliament was to have met, but no formal session was held; excited deputies and senators gathered in groups and discussed the situation. At 11:30, Dr. Lupu came in straight from Cotroceni, and reported that the prince, who was feeling the strain of the journey and the night's consultations, had asked him to say for him that he felt no animus against any one and was anxious to collaborate with all for the good of Roumania. Prof. Iorga, the prince's former tutor, who had always been zealous in his defense, welcomed him back in an editorial in his paper, the "Neamul Românesc."

The cabinet came to no conclusion Saturday morning, and Premier Maniu again visited the prince at Cotroceni, returning at 2 with a request from Carol that the cabinet come to a decision at once on the question of regency vs. kingship. The debate continued; it is understood that Maniu, Vaida and Madgearu felt that it was unseemly that the same ministry which had sworn allegiance to King Michael, should now proclaim Carol King; and that the others disagreed with them. At 5:30 P. M., it was finally decided that Premier Maniu should meet Princes Carol and Nicholas and the Patriarch, and make two proposals: if Carol was willing to become a Regent, the entire Ministry was at his disposal, and the ceremony would take place at 11 Sunday morning, by the decision of a National Assembly. If however Carol wished to be King, Maniu would resign, a new ministry under Iunian, Mihalache or Mironescu would be formed, and this ministry would preside over the Assembly.

The latter course was chosen, and the city was immediately electrified with the news. Sunday morning, the streets were jammed, especially the Calea Victoriei, Bucharest's chief artery, and those about the Parliament. I was held tight for over an hour on the Calea Victoriei, though anxious to get to the Parliament, and had to content myself with a vivid realization of the enthusiasm of the crowd, as Carol drove by in a state barouche beside his brother Nicholas, on his way to the Assembly. There, the two houses had annulled the act of Jan. 4, 1926, an edict of the Crown Council, by which Carol had renounced his succession to the throne. Lawyers had pointed out that the act was never legal, for you cannot renounce what is not yours; but the safer course was followed. Then the heads of the various parties delivered their speeches of allegiance to the new king; the leaders of the various national minorities—Hungarians, Germans, Bulgarians, Ukrainians, Mohammedans and especially the Jews—were particularly cordial. Most notable was the moving address of Prof. Iorga, who told of his interview with King Ferdinand on that winter day of 1926, and the tears with which the King had told him that he had finally been persuaded to sign the edict. Then, about 3:30 in the afternoon, Carol came in and delivered a brief and admirable speech of acceptance. Their enthusiasm told him, he said, that it was the machinations of a few which had driven him into exile of over four years; he was assured that his own affection for his native land, was reciprocated. Standing before representatives of all Roumanians, from the Dniester to the Theiss, from Hotin to the Black Sea, from Boian to Vatra Dornii, from Sătmar to Săcele, he could not fail to be conscious of the 800,000 dead, whose lives had been the price of Roumanian union; he would devote his own to the preservation of those boundaries they had won. He begged them all to collaborate with him to establish the new kingdom on a firm foundation; only so could the difficulties of the situation be met. He would cherish friendly relations with their neighbors. They all knew how rich Roumania is in material resources; he hoped she would take her rightful place in the learned and scientific world. He could not close without reference to his greatest joy in returning—that he was with his beloved son, and could make certain that he should be educated with the warmest love of country. He thanked his brother, and the others of the Regency; and he made the warmest appeal to them all to unite in promoting the good of Roumania. "Roumanians from the four corners of the land, be one in your thoughts, be one in your feelings; on to the work!"

The new King followed his own advice. Up before daylight, he worked till into the evenings; and the bureaucracy soon discovered that a new, firm hand was on the reins. One of the Paris correspondents had put the full address of his paper at the top of each sheet of his dispatch, and given a substantial fee to the operator; but his paper wired that only two sheets came through, and the rest was missent. This came to the King's ears, and he promptly summoned the head of the government telegraph service and warned him that another such mistake would have serious consequences. Some days later, he asked the Mayor to come to the palace, and on his arrival, told him he wanted his company in a drive around the city which he had not seen for so many years; to the Mayor's astonishment, Carol drove his runabout directly to the City Markets, and there walked from stall to stall talking with the dealers about conditions—not a secret service agent about, but a huge and delighted crowd accompanying him. This he has followed up at irregular intervals by unexpected visits to city and government institutions, to occasional consternation of officials, but with enthusiastic general approval.

I had the good fortune to see much of the King that week, and was especially impressed with the answers to questions proposed by the foreign correspondents at a joint interview in the palace on June 11th. The questions were handed in in writing, and were answered frankly and fully by the King, with obvious sincerity, and in language which bore evidence to his thoughtfulness and culture; it is well known that he has kept up his wide reading throughout his exile; and no other prince in Europe has the advantage of knowing life from the standpoint of one who has seen almost every man's hand against him. He won general admiration for his sure and tactful handling of the various problems which immediately confronted him, and for the boundless energy with which he attacked them; his wide experience of life was immediately fruitful to Roumania.

King Carol was confronted with a very difficult situation. Roumania had not had one good year since the war; for most other countries, 1919–20 and 1928 had seen prosperity; but the record in Roumania had been only of bad years, and worse. The currency had been stabilized, it is true; but the prices of all farm produce were dropping rapidly, the farmers were deeper in debt every month, and the country was burdened with an expensive administration, which the politicians were loth to surrender. Premier Mironescu resigned as soon as the King had been inaugurated, and Carol set about forming a ministry in which all parties should be represented, under the direction of Gen. Prezan. This proved impracticable, owing largely to the attitude of the Liberals under Vintilă Bratiano; and on June 13, the King commissioned Maniu to form another Peasant-Nationalistic cabinet, which could work in harmony with the majority of Parliament. This had Mironescu as Minister of Foreign Affairs; Vaida Voevod, Interior; Iunian, Justice; Mihai Popovici, Finance; Pan Halippa (Bessarabian), Labor; Manoïlescu (a very able man, who had been arrested and tried by Bratiano for acting as intermediary between Carol and his partisans), Communications; Madgearu, Commerce and Industry; Costăchescu, Education; Mihalache, Agriculture; and Gen. Condeescu, War. This cabinet went to work to grapple with the situation, and laid the foundations for the "Budget of Sacrifice" and for the loan negotiations carried out under its successor. But it suffered from the tremendous fall in farm prices—a thing which always hurts the party in power—and was severely criticized for its failure to punish adequately some anti-Jewish outbreaks, due primarily to the bitter feeling of peasant debtors against their chattel mortgageors. Premier Maniu, who had led an active political life for 35 years, and his right-hand man, Dr. Vaida Voevod, retired; and in October 1930 a new Peasant-Nationalist Ministry was formed under Mironescu, who retained most of his former associates, with some shifts; Transylvania, who had just lost her oldest campaigners, was represented by Hatziegan, the new Minister of Labor—Halippa remained as Minister without portfolio—and Voicu Nitzescu, Minister of Justice, while Dr. V. V. Tilea, a scholarly young Transylvanian of long experience in London, became one of the Under-Secretaries. This Ministry carried through the new budget, with its slashing reductions of personnel and salaries, and the loan which was concluded in Paris in March, 1931; then it resigned, in order to give the King the opportunity he desired, of forming a government including all political factions.

King Carol, and Roumanian public opinion, turned in this crisis to Roumania's ablest diplomat, Titulesco. He has the great advantage of universal respect and esteem, and a lack of enmities, due partly to his long freedom from the hurly-burly of continuous activity in home politics, partly to his tact and personal charm. Recalled to Bucharest, he promptly consulted the party chieftains, and set about the difficult task of forming a cabinet which should include representatives of all the leading parties and yet work with a Parliament overwhelmingly Peasant-Nationalist. Success at first seemed likely to crown his efforts; but the heads of smaller political groups stood out; and he finally found himself forced to name a cabinet of specialists; prominent in his list were Prof. Iorga, the historian, Rector of the University of Bucharest, as Minister of Education; Gen. Condeescu, War; Gen. Mihail Ionescu, head of the State Railways (C. F. R.), Communications; Dr. I. Cantacuzene, Public Health; and Prince D. Ghica, Minister to Italy, Foreign Affairs. But it is understood that pressure was applied for the appointment as Minister of Finance of C. Argetoianu, a man of great force and varied political career, and too firm a believer in strong centralized government to suit the majority in Parliament. Before this prospect, Titulesco withdrew; and the King turned to his former tutor, Roumania's most distinguished scholar, Prof. Iorga, who had just accepted the post of Education in Titulesco's list, and kept it (with the Premiership) in his new Cabinet, announced on April 18, 1931. This included Manoïlescu, one of the ablest men in Roumania, as Minister of Industry and Commerce; Supreme Court Justice C. Hamangiu as Attorney-General; Gen. Shtefănescu-Amza, War; Dr. Vâlcovici, head of the Temeshvar Polytechnic, Public Works and Communications; Gh. Ionescu-Siseshti, Agriculture; Dr. Cantacuzene,

Public Health; Prince Ghica, Foreign Affairs, and C. Arge-toianu, Finance. In mid-July, 1931, Manoïlescu resigned to become Governor of the National Bank; Rector Vasilescu Carpen of the Bucharest Polytechnic was appointed Minister of Commerce in his stead; Hatziegan, Minister for Transylvania, also resigned, and was replaced by Valer Pop; Jean Pangal took charge of the Press and Information Department. King Carol attends Cabinet meetings, after the American fashion. King Ferdinand had kept in touch with his Ministries through the Minister of the King, always an experienced diplomat (Mishu, and then Hiott); but with the Regency, this post was abolished.

The Iorga Ministry dissolved Parliament and appealed to the country; the Liberal Party, now for years out of office, was the core of the new combination, and forms the leading group in the new Parliament elected (with apparently a certain amount of government interference, as of old) in early June, 1931. Of the nearly 390 members of Parliament, the government coalition, with about 50% of the recorded votes, received 287 seats (the Roumanian system is designed to provide a large working majority to the party which leads at the polls); next came the Nationalist-Peasant Party, with 16%, and 30 seats; next, to general surprise, the branch of the Liberal Party headed by George Bratiano, with 12 seats; Gen. Averesco and his People's Party had 10; Dr. Lupu, 7; Dr. A. C. Cuza and his Anti-Semites, 8; the Anti-Usury and Freemen's League, 6; Social Democrats, 7; Magyar Party, 11; Jewish Party, 4 (the Jews in general voted under other party heads); and the Worker's Bloc (Communists), 5. The latter were eliminated in the course of the Parliamentary vote on disputed elections. Parliament got to work in mid-June, with a program of intense economy (Prof. Iorga himself has sacrificed several lycées, gymnasien, trade, professional and other schools, most of which had been established for local political reasons, like many Normal Schools with us) and encouragement of agriculture and industry. Minister Argetoianu's message on the financial situation was not pleasant reading, but indicates an earnest effort to strike at the root of the trouble.

Women do not yet have the general suffrage in Roumania, but there is an active woman's suffrage movement, headed for years by Princess Alexandrina Cantacuzene; and in 1930 and 1931 a group of women under Mme. Calypso Botez did active work for the Nationalist-Peasant Party. In March 1930 a woman mayor (primar) was elected in the village of Voineshti, county of Vaslui—Mme. Luiza Zavloski, wife of a local school-teacher. Although women may not vote for members of Parliament, some actually have; in 1927, women members of the Faculty of the University of Jassy voted for the Senator who stands for the University, and the same was true in the Senatorial election of 1931 for the University of Bucharest; an attempt was made to invalidate the latter election on this ground, but unsuccessfully.

It is worth remembering that Roumania and Czecho-Slovakia are the only countries in that part of the world which have enjoyed parliamentary government, unsullied by assassination, ever since the war. Their neighbors, Hungary, Jugo-Slavia, Poland and Turkey, are dictatorships; Russia is in the hands of a small group of dictators; Bulgaria and Greece have suffered crisis after crisis, with melancholy events accompanying them. Although perhaps hardest hit by the world crisis, the Roumanian peasant and city-dweller have kept their heads. It would be idle to pretend that they are satisfied with their government; dissatisfaction with the administration exists even in the United States and Great Britain. The Roumanians are a long-suffering and tolerant people; they have shown an admirable willingness to take King Carol on trial. Just as in Spain, there is a strong Republican under-current among the young people; and a long continuance of hard times, or a conspicuous failure of Parliament and King to meet squarely the tremendous problems facing Roumania, may possibly lead, as in Spain, to a dictatorship and a subsequent republic. The Roumanian people seem more inclined to a constitutional monarchy, nor is Roumania's King involved with powerful ecclesiastical and aristocratic interests; the Roumanian monarchy and monarch are closer to their people even than the British. Perhaps all European monarchies are doomed; but if Roumania's King can succeed in guiding his country out of the present financial gloom, he is likely to have nearly as long a reign as his great-uncle, Carol the First.

CHAPTER XXVIII

THE later Middle Ages saw a constant increase in the size and number of landed estates in Roumania as in other parts of Central and Eastern Europe. During the Renaissance, the process was accentuated, and the peasant not merely lost ground economically, but the few rights he still retained were encroached upon. Michael the Brave presented whole villages and all their inhabitants to bishops and generals; and in the 17th century, the peasant becomes a chattel. He could still be taxed; but in the 18th century his master gained control even of his cattle and other belongings; and so many fled the country that the problem had to be faced. When Constantine Mavrocordato began his administration of Wallachia in 1741, he found 140,000 families paying taxes. In 1755, a census reported only 35,000. He made the first reforms in 1746 and later, as we have seen; but they remained largely a dead-letter through the opposition of the boyars. The first genuine improvement dates from the beginning of the 19th century, when under Alexander Moruzi (1805) in Moldavia and Contantine Ypsilanti (1806) in Wallachia, the relations between land-owner and peasant were regulated. In Moldavia the peasants were divided into classes according to the number of oxen they owned; each land-owner had to rent out to a peasant a given area of land according to his class, and the peasant paid a tenth of the produce.

Had conditions been favorable, these reforms might have

created a prosperous peasant class; but the extortions of the Phanariote rulers, internal disorders, Ypsilanti's revolt and the rebellion of Tudor Vladimirescu, followed by the ravages of Russian, Austrian and Turkish armies and an epidemic of the plague, upset all regular government. A million peasants are said to have fled the country during this unsettled period. Nor was General Kissileff's administration or the Organic Regulation calculated to improve the peasants' status, since it was the allegiance of the great boyars which the Russians desired. The peasant was no longer a serf, to be sure; but the area which he might expect for tillage was reduced from Moruzi's allowance. The highest class of peasant (with at least four oxen and a cow) received only 3¾ acres of plow-land and meadow, and 6¼ of pasture! The peasant had to give his landlord 14 days a year of work with oxen and plow, and up to 72 days (in the smaller Moldavian villages) of individual labor. A special grievance was that they had to leave their harvest lying till the landlord had selected his share, and it often spoiled. In 1848, uprisings among the peasants led to the provision that the land-owner should have only ten days in which to make his selection, and that local courts should be created with jurisdiction over disputes between master and peasant. These measures however proved entirely inadequate.

Prince Cuza's agrarian reform of 1864 was the first great step forward of our day. Serfdom had just been abolished in Russia. The country was seething with discontent. Cuza's great minister Kogălniceanu worked out a plan, and submitted it to the Chamber. It was rejected by the boyar majority; Cuza's *coup d'état* carried it, and a plebiscite justified him by 713,000 votes against 57,000.

What distinguished Cuza's reform was that it actually took some of the boyar's land away and gave it to the peasant for his own. The peasant was to pay for it in 15 annual installments. Up to ⅔ of a boyar's land (not counting forest) could be expropriated. If that did not suffice, government land could be drawn upon; this had just been increased by the confiscation of about 9000 sq. mi. of convent lands. The government was to give the boyar 10% bonds, and the peasant compensate the government. But this scheme also had serious disadvantages. Fifteen years, with the heavy interest charges involved, was too short a period; over 30% of the peasant's income had to go to these installments and taxes, according to John Ghica's "Convorbiri Economice." The prices paid were also too high, considering that four piasters (16c) made an ordinary day's wage; the average payment had to be 500 lei ($100) or over, up to 563 lei. The parcels of land were too small—about 12 acres on the average—to support the ordinary family, and became still more inadequate when divided up between the children. So they rented more land from the boyar, and paid in kind or in day's work, as before. Agriculture was on a low level, and model farms are still scarce; wide-spread agricultural education is perhaps the greatest need of the new Roumanian state, which has been encouraging manufacturing and city life at the expense of the farmer.

Cuza's reforms, fundamental and creditable as they were, did not reach far enough. The census of 1901 showed 4061 estates of over 250 acres, and 933,328 less than that area; $21/_{22}$ of all the farms were under 25 acres. Over half of these were between 2½ and 10 acres. Premier Carp had, to be sure, improved matters in the '90s by opening up government land, in 12½, 25 and 62½ acre parcels, to peasants who needed larger farms, on a 36-year payment basis, with an initial loan from the Rural Bank of 600 lei, later raised to 700. The interest rate, which had been 10%, was lowered to 5, and in 1895 to 3.

With a well-educated peasantry, and diversified agriculture, these measures might have sufficed. But the handicap of ignorance, lack of capital and exclusive cereal culture was too great. Economists have often pointed out that the new class created by the agrarian legislation was neither fish, flesh nor fowl, or, rather, partook of all three. His farm being so tiny, the average peasant was both a land-owner, a renter (of the additional land necessary) and an agricultural laborer. A crisis, like the hard years 1906–07, brought matters to a head, and the desperate peasants rose in what almost amounted to revolution. The army's loyalty was sorely tried, for they had to fire on their own fathers and brothers; but the uprising was suppressed, and the government set about a more thorough-going reform. The large estates were still more pared down, and state land was set at the peasants' disposal much more generously. A minimum wage was established. A period of great financial prosperity set in, and the peasant benefited.

Nevertheless, the situation was far from healthy. At the beginning of the war, the total arable land of the Kingdom—about fifteen million acres—was almost exactly divided between small peasant holdings, and great estates; medium-sized farms, the ideal of this legislation, covered only about a million acres. The war hastened tardy ambitions for justice to the peasants, and in 1917, at the direct instigation of King Ferdinand, new agrarian legislation was passed. This was supplemented by agrarian laws in each province. The Carnegie Endowment for International Peace having just published a masterly survey of this whole subject, Dr. David Mitrany's "The Land and the Peasant in Rumania," I need give here only a brief summary. In Bessarabia, the province most closely affected by the Russian Revolution, the inflexible maximum which might be retained was fixed at 100 hectares (247 acres); all above that was expropriated. In the Old Kingdom, large estates were allowed to keep up to 500 hectares of arable land, plus vineyards, orchards, woods and waste land. In Transylvania and the Banat, expropriation proceeded more leisurely; here also large estates could retain up to 500 hectares, depending on their size. The Bucovina, a region of smaller farms, set the limit at 250 hectares. In general, foreigners and absentee landlords were expropriated in full. Since the first laws did not provide enough land for the claimants, the Garoflid Law of 1921 was passed, which incidentally endeavored not to break up the most modern farming enterprises. As a result of these various laws, about 6,000,000 hectares were expropriated and divided among about 1,400,000 peasants.

As would be inferred, the area of the resultant holdings is too small for profitable working; and many economists have assumed that Roumania's eclipse as a wheat-exporting country is due to this feature of the reform. Dr. Mitrany's admirable studies show that other factors have been potent. There has been a series of dry years, to complicate the industrial depression; whereas the average rainfall for 1814–1914 was about 24 in., for 1919–1923 it was only 22½; in 1924, only 21½; 1927 was very dry; and in 1928, no rain fell from late May till the winter snows.

There was also extensive government interference. To ensure cheap bread for the cities, the government set a low fixed price for wheat. This led the farmers to increase their cultivation of Indian corn (already gaining on wheat), and especially of barley and oats, which have gained 1,750,000 acres since the war. Then the government tried an export tax on wheat, which of course had a similar effect; the tax was not abolished until 1931. Now there is an export bounty, and a stamp-tax on bread. There is no doubt that the reform has improved the peasant's material status, and he eats much more wheat bread than before the war. In the recent world-wide agricultural crisis, wheat prices have suffered more than the rest; and Roumania feels keenly the effects of cut-throat competition from near-by Russia. All in all, it seems certain that Roumania will never regain her former importance in wheat exporting. The area sowed to wheat has dropped a million acres since the war, and this will not quickly be recovered, especially as Roumania will soon become a manufacturing country, and absorb more and more of her own surplus.

The reform caused, curiously enough, little change in the farming procedure of the average peasant. In the past, with his teams and labor, he had cultivated the land of the large proprietors. Now a portion of this land became his own; but he handles it on the same lines as before. The reform has, to be sure, moderately enriched him; but the succession of bad years, his lack of capital, the scarcity of money, and the exorbitant interest (generally 3% a month) which he has to pay, have led to an appalling poverty in many of the country districts, especially in Bessarabia. The success of the recent negotiations for a loan to create a Farm Credit institution, is encouraging; but if bad years and low prices persist, conditions such as we have had to cope with recently in Arkansas, will not be lacking in Roumania. It speaks well for the patience of the Roumanian peasant that he has borne these hardships with so little complaint.

The great land-owners often suffered seriously, also. The

original plans for expropriation contemplated equitable compensation; but the rapid depreciation of the currency defeated this, though the compensation was raised; and at the end, land which was worth, say $100 an acre, was taken for about $3 an acre—and that paid in State bonds, which are quoted at about 50%. No wonder the former Hungarian land-owners felt that the measure was one of confiscation; and it was small comfort to them that Roumanian and former Russian land-owners were in similar case.

England and France insisted on payment in gold in full for the Bessarabian estates owned by subjects of theirs, and Roumania had to pay this, as a price for the Bessarabian Treaty (see my "Bessarabia," pages 227-8). A somewhat similar effort on the part of Hungarians expropriated in Transylvania and the Banat led to the celebrated "Hungarian Optant" controversy before the League of Nations, in which success crowned the Roumanian defense, thanks to the brilliant pleas of Titulesco, Roumania's leading diplomat. Former Hungarian land-owners who had not returned to Roumania by March 3, 1921, were deprived of all their property-rights, and all their land was expropriated. The Hungarians claim that they were denied visas for their return; and since that was undoubtedly correct in some cases, the Roumanian government has agreed to a proposal to compensate them from the Hungarian reparations. Since the Hungarian optants were mainly great land-owning gentry, the Hungarian Social-Democrats maintain that this settlement is a reactionary concession of their government to the land-holding aristocracy which still holds the reins in Hungary.

The land reform is thus shown to be of doubtful economic expediency; but it was an inevitable act of social justice, and must be considered from that viewpoint. It has changed a people largely of farm laborers into a nation of land-holders, and in spite of the crisis, it has revolutionized the peasant's attitude toward life.

CHAPTER XXIX

THE MINORITIES PROBLEM

THE annexation of former Austro-Hungarian and Russian territory brought millions of foreigners into Roumania, many of them bitterly opposed to the new state. The difficulties inherent in all reconstruction (well known to us from our Civil War experience) were enhanced by differences of race, language and religion. A Greek Orthodox state, believing in free non-sectarian education, found itself called upon to regulate the worship of Protestants, Roman Catholics and Jews, to provide free public schools for Hebrews, Germans, Hungarians and Slavs, and to decide the fate of church schools which had been subsidized by the Hungarian state —a procedure unconstitutional in Roumania, and as repugnant to the Roumanian spirit as to the American. Roumania is almost unique in Europe in providing free public school education for all classes, from the kindergarten to the university. Hungary had encouraged parochial and sectarian schools with grants from public funds, and many of them owned large tracts of land.

It was clear that the Hungarian system must yield to the Roumanian, the principle of parochial schools supported out of the taxpayers' money being foreign to Roumania. But these Hungarian and German schools, particularly such admirable institutions as the German gymnasien in Bistritza, Sibiu (Hermannstadt), etc., and the Hungarian Calvinist, Jewish, Roman Catholic and Unitarian institutions in Cluj, Temeshvar, etc., were invaluable, and the Roumanian government, in its anxiety not to lose their services, maintained them with subsidies partly covering their expenses, and confirmed their faculties in their privileges, merely setting a date some years on, by which time they must show that they could use the language of the state. But the Roumanians met in many cases with hostility and disaffection. In the course of several journeys in Transylvania to study this problem, I was astonished at their tolerance. Visiting a Hungarian primary school in Bistritza, I found the children still using primers of pre-war days, extolling the Hapsburgs; and in a certain Calvinist school, the children had just finished singing the Hungarian national anthem! The Roumanian Commissioner of Education for Transylvania in 1918–20 gave me a graphic picture of his troubles. He had urged the Rector of the Hungarian University of Kolozsvár (Cluj) to finish the school year and grant his degrees, which would be recognized by the Roumanian state—and this in spite of the strong feeling the Roumanians had against this institution, which they considered a Hungarian propaganda center. But when he found the Rector was insisting on an oath of allegiance to the Hungarian Republic from his students, now Roumanian citizens, he protested; and when the Rector persisted, he had to close the university before the graduation exercises. I gave a course of lectures in this university, now Roumanian, in 1927, and was interested to hear both German and Hungarian talked by the students, in precincts where the Hungarians severely penalized the use of any language except Hungarian or Latin. In that connection, another personal experience may be of interest. Bishop Nagy of the Calvinist Church in Cluj told me in 1919 that the new Roumanian administration was forcing them to use Roumanian by posting all official notices in Roumanian alone; and I saw this stated in American papers. But I myself had already kept a record of all government announcements I saw posted in Cluj, some sixty in number; only one—and that a post office bulletin—was in Roumanian alone; the rest were bilingual (Roumanian and Hungarian), and about a score in German also.

The Roumanian government gladly took over into its church, school, judicial, administrative and railways systems, thousands of former Hungarian functionaries who spoke little or no Roumanian; the oath of allegiance was all that was required, and even this was omitted for years in many cases, the most striking being that of a well-known bishop. The Roumanians felt however that they might reasonably ask that within a few years these professors, ministers, judges, railway employees, etc., should learn the language of the state—a procedure we followed in Porto Rico and the Philippines, with much less excuse, for after all Roumanian is the language of the majority of the Transylvanians. But they kept extending the time limit. Dr. Gaster told me that in 1925 he was unable to find a single employee in the great railway station of Arad, who spoke good Roumanian; and in June 1930 I found employees there who spoke only Hungarian. Indeed, when, in February 1931, over twelve years after the incorporation of Transylvania, Gen. Ionescu, the new Director of the State Railways, issued an order that all employees must use the state language in working hours, a Hungarian member of the Roumanian Parliament protested against this "intolerance," and hinted that unless the order was modified, he might complain to the League of Nations. The order, however, with the usual mildness, was interpreted to refer only to official use of the language, and the Hungarian member withdrew his threat.

The chief grievance however on the part of the Hungarians was a more serious matter. The Roumanian government provided their children with free public schools in Hungarian, it is true—there are to-day in Transylvania more free public schools in Hungarian than under the Magyars; and it insists on only a few hours weekly in the language of the country (the courses in Roumanian literature, history and geography)—a striking contrast with the Apponyi régime, under which almost all the instruction for young Germans, Serbs, and Roumanians had to be in Magyar. But in these free public schools their children learn Transylvanian history from the Roumanian standpoint—and they themselves are still in large part unreconstructed, still reverence the Hapsburgs and the bygone aristocratic system, regard the Roumanians as barbarous interlopers, and Transylvania an integral part of Hungary, to which she will later return. So they want their own church schools, with their own Hungarian teachers of secular and church history. Nor do the Roumanians interfere; indeed, they still grant subventions to the church schools in Transylvania, and far more generously, proportionately, to the Calvinist and Unitarian institutions than to the Greek Orthodox, who are continually complaining in Parliament of the government's discriminating against them and in favor of Catholic and Protestant schools. But the government lets it be clearly understood that these private sectarian schools must soon meet all their own expenses and not expect aid from public funds, and that they must also meet government standards, especially as regards knowledge of Roumanian among faculty and pupils.

This policy provoked loud outcries from the former enemy subjects, with claims of persecution; appeals were made to the League of Nations, and British-American religious commissions (no member of which ever could talk the language of the country) have several times traversed Transylvania under anti-Roumanian escort, and have turned in reports

which, with every effort to be fair, nevertheless give a misleading picture. One must try to put one's self in the place
of the Roumanians, dealing with former enemies who are
only too often ready to join hands with Hungarian Irre-
dentists. They even caught a Bishop red-handed in trea-
sonable correspondence; but they merely admonished him,
and left him in his episcopal dignity.

This mildness on the part of the Roumanians, so different from Magyar chauvinism, led to the discovery by the
Hungarian Transylvanians that they could disseminate anti-
Roumanian propaganda in Britain and America undisturbed, and we were deluged with it, especially in the religious journals. Indeed, we had the unedifying spectacle of a
Christian denomination urging the American people to force
Roumania to support this sect's schools in Roumania out of
the tax-payers' money—a policy it fights, as regards Roman Catholic parochial schools, in its home city in the
Union! I ran across an admirable example of this propaganda in the weekly published by this same denomination. It
epitomized a sermon preached (in English!) to the visiting
British-Americans by a Hungarian pastor in Transylvania.
His main points were: 1) before the war, his church had
been wealthy, with money in the bank; now, under the
Roumanians, it was penniless; 2) before the war their beautiful church chimes had been admired all over that part of
Hungary; now, their spire was mute; 3) before the war,
they had had broad landed estates; but the Roumanian government had confiscated their land. These statements are all
true, or nearly so, and seem to have succeeded in hoodwinking the visiting clergymen; but on analysis they dissolve
completely. The church funds had been put into Austro-
Hungarian Victory War Loan bonds—a perfectly safe as
well as patriotic investment, since principal and interest

were guaranteed by the Austro-Hungarian Empire, and the principal would be paid out of the indemnity to be exacted from the French, British and Americans. It is only fair to say that this was a forced loan; but that is where the church funds went, all over Hungary—to prosecute the war against the Allies.

The church bells were also a war sacrifice. They were given to the Hungarian War Department to be melted down into cannon. Like many another American, I passed months under shot and shell fired in part from guns made out of church bells. In the deep harmony of the battlefield, we could not distinguish Unitarian from Calvinist, Roman Catholic from Greek Uniate; nor do we bear resentment against the patriotic gesture which sacrificed these chimes; but in the interest of historic truth, I must protest against the deduction encouraged by this pastor.

It was in some respects unfortunate that the land reform involved the estates of the minority schools and churches, as well as those of the Roumanian majority. But here again the deduction from the pastor's statement is misleading. The Roumanian churches and church officials in Transylvania also had to witness the expropriation of their properties beyond the legal maximum—properties trifling in comparison with those of the far wealthier Germans and Hungarians, but all the more treasured by them. No one can deny that in this huge transfer of real estate there have been irregularities and cases of individual injustice; I fear they would have occurred even in the United States if our politicians had supervised the dividing up of the land among their constituents; but that there was any organized discrimination against the minorities, I can deny from my own observations on the spot. In fact, what especially astonished me, in looking over the lists of those who had been assigned allotments in various Transylvanian villages, was the frequency of German and Hungarian names; nor shall I soon forget my surprise on discovering that the first beneficiaries were widows of war veterans, whose husbands, Hungarian subjects, had fought against Roumania in the war! I wondered if our own government, in the distribution of public land after the Civil War, had discriminated in favor of the widows of Confederate veterans. This lack of prejudice in the Roumanians is all the more remarkable when one considers their former oppression at the hands of the Hungarians. In fact, any thorough study of this problem in Roumania, complicated as it is by resentments so deeply rooted in human nature, must result in renewed admiration of the easy-going tolerance of the Roumanian people. All their history bears witness to this, and it has been one of the chief factors in their slow development from a group of shepherds and peasants in the Carpathians, to the leading people in Southeastern Europe. We boast that for a hundred years we have had no armed conflict with our Canadian neighbors. For over a thousand years, in this cock-pit of Europe, the Roumanians have had no battle with their warlike neighbors, the Serbs. Roumania has never known an Inquisition, a pogrom or an expulsion of the Jews, a St. John's Eve, or an auto da fé. For centuries she has received the Jews, Armenians, Greeks, Lipovans, Bulgarians, Gagaoutzi and other sects and nationalities oppressed by the Russian and Turkish Empires. The friction to-day is far less than in various other countries perplexed by their minorities, and Time, the great healer, may be trusted to heal these wounds.

One other complaint remains to be discussed—that of the Baptists. Claims that the Baptists were systematically molested, if not actually persecuted, were wide-spread in England and America; and on my Roumanian lecture tour in

1927 I devoted much time to this question, interviewing scores of high officials, as well as Baptists; I had a long talk on the subject with Ionel Bratiano only a few weeks before his death, and discussed it with Archbishops, Bishops and government officials. I speedily found that the real animus against the Baptists was due to the fact that they proselyte actively from the State Church, like the Methodists in Italy. This was keenly resented. One Orthodox Greek Bishop said to me: "If you Americans desire to spend money in Christian missionary effort, why don't you send your emissaries to non-Christian countries? We were Christians here, actively defending our faith against the infidel, long before America was discovered." On the other hand, the Baptist preachers found a fertile field in parishes which were neglected; and one Orthodox bishop admitted to me that he sometimes felt that their competition had been of value, quickening his priests to a more spiritual ministry and a livelier interest in their parishioners. A cavalry general with whom I talked, told me that his orderly was a Baptist, an earnest, conscientious, God-fearing young man, and that he wished them joy in their campaign.

The government, as Bratiano informed me, was inclined to keep hands off, but various government officials felt sympathy with the prelates of their church. The Baptist custom of "circuit-riding"—serving several parishes—gave offense; complaints were turned in of anti-Roumanian propaganda by Baptist pastors of Hungarian sympathies; and their lack of higher education was emphasized. The Roumanian government insists on a minimum educational qualification for the ministers of the state church, and investigated this matter; I possess a copy of their report, which discloses that less than a dozen of the over 900 Baptist clergymen in Roumania had had a college training, and that the vast majority had only a grammar school certificate. The admirable Baptist Seminary in Bucharest is making an earnest effort to overcome this handicap, with quite insufficient funds, derived mainly from American Southern Baptists. The government has given them the same status and privileges with the Calvinists and Unitarians, and we may now hope for that same tolerance of various churches' efforts in Christian labor, which we enjoy in the United States.

There has also been much complaint in the past of discrimination against the Jews. Up to the World War, the Jews in Roumania were mainly foreign subjects, and it was made very difficult for them to obtain Roumanian citizenship. Now they are citizens, and carry on active electoral campaigns; but there is somewhat the same social discrimination against them in Bucharest as in New York, though there are Jewish professors in the Roumanian universities and higher schools, just as at Harvard and Columbia. Throughout the country, anti-Semitic feeling was kept up during the war by the prominence of Roumanian Jews as assistants to the German administrators, and by the fortunes which were made by numerous Jews at that time and in the post-war period. Roumania, unlike Hungary, Austria, and various American colleges, does not endeavor to keep Jews out of the universities; and they have flocked there in such numbers, thanks to their universal ambition for higher education, that anti-Semitic agitators like Prof. A. C. Cuza of the University of Jassy have been able to create much anti-Jewish feeling among the students, leading occasionally to regrettable outbreaks much like those of 1931 in Vienna and Berlin. It was however pointed out by the great bacteriologist, Prof. Cantacuzene, that this feeling is mainly due to frightful overcrowding of the universities; his own laboratory in the University of Bucharest, which was planned for about 75, had to accommodate 450! In the same way, the anti-Jewish feeling among the peasants is primarily economic, and is due to resentment at the high interest (30–40%) charged by the Jewish money-lenders on chattel mortgages in the towns and villages. Great hopes were entertained of the Peasant-Nationalist Ministry, and as a matter of fact the situation did improve materially; but outbreaks in 1929 were not punished with sufficient promptness and severity to satisfy enlightened public opinion. The great Bucharest dailies "Adevĕrul" and "Dimineatza," which are owned by Jewish capital, criticized the Interior Department for its laxness, and called for action against the nationalistic organizations, the Iron Guard (Garda de Fier) and the Archangel Michael (Arhanghelul Mihail), which somewhat resemble our own Ku Klux Klan in their aims, as Dr. Lupu noted in his speech of June 30, 1931. Finally, in late December, 1930, a youthful member of one of these societies shot the director of the "Adevĕrul," fortunately without injuring him seriously; and the government took up the matter in earnest. It is understood that King Carol feels strongly on this subject and the recent satisfaction of the Roumanian Jews in the United States, as expressed to the Roumanian Minister at their meetings, seems based on a secure foundation.

No better proof of the general appreciation of Roumanian tolerance can be found than that furnished by the League of Nations. The League has made the most thorough investigations of the charges brought; the head of their Minorities Department, Mr. Erik Colban, made a tour through Transylvania, and expressed to me afterwards his feeling that the government was handling a difficult situation with tact and fairness. A great impression was made on the officials of the League by the detailed refutation by the Roumanian government of the equally detailed and surprisingly unfounded charges of the Hungarian religious and school propagandists in Transylvania; I have never read a more convincing document, and was able to verify a number of its statements myself. Indeed, who could fail to be impressed by the Transylvanian school figures which follow:

DENOMINATIONAL SCHOOLS

	Under Hungarians, 1918	Under Roumanians, 1925
Primary		
Roman Catholic Hungarian	377	372
Roman Catholic German	0	53
Calvinist Hungarian	362	684
Unitarian Hungarian	27	44
Lutheran Hungarian	4	14
Lutheran German	258	268
	1028	1435
High Schools		
Roman Catholic Hungarian	25	51
Roman Catholic German	0	1
Calvinist Hungarian	3	9
Unitarian Hungarian	1	2
Lutheran Hungarian	0	2
Lutheran German	5	8
	34	73
Lycées		
Roman Catholic Hungarian	13	17
Calvinist Hungarian	9	11
Unitarian Hungarian	2	3
Lutheran German	9	11
	33	42
Commercial Schools		
Roman Catholic Hungarian	1	4
Calvinist Hungarian	0	4
Lutheran German	0	3
	1	11

This growth of denominational schools was partly due to the desire of former enemy parents mentioned above, to keep Catholic and Protestant children from learning church and secular history from the Roumanian viewpoint; partly also to a fear that the Roumanian state would not be able to provide enough trained teachers for the public schools. This fear proved to be unfounded; and as the financial strain on the denominations is severe in these hard times, and the public schools are satisfactory, we may expect to see the number of these sectarian schools decline. Meanwhile, the government has provided amply for the needs of the minorities, as is shown by the following tables:

Primary Schools

		Under the Hungarians	Under the Roumanians
One school for	1,229	Roumanians	803 Roumanians
"	504	Hungarians	778 Hungarians
"	890	Germans (Saxons of Transylvania)	880 Saxons
"	10,847	Germans (Suabians of the Banat)	2,184 Suabians

High Schools

One school for	732,525	Roumanians	65,909 Roumanians
"	11,979	Hungarians	15,163 Hungarians
"	46,000	German Saxons	28,750 Saxons
No school for		German Suabians	Now one for 38,504 Suabians

Lycées

One school for	586,024	Roumanians	72,500 Roumanians
"	25,110	Hungarians	32,500 Hungarians
"	25,633	German Saxons	20,900 Saxons
No school for		German Suabians	Now one for 154,200 Suabians

The universities and higher technical schools take in students of all the minority nationalities and religions without the faintest discrimination. At the University of Jassy, for instance, I held conference with Bulgarian, Russian and other minority students, several of them from Bessarabia, which also has a variegated picture of minority schools; I would refer to my "Bessarabia" for a description of the dedication ceremonies of a school in a purely Russian town, with speeches in Russian and Roumanian—one of the most inspiriting occasions I ever attended.

Most encouraging has been the growth of better feeling between Hungarians and Roumanians in business, politics, literature and art. In the Cluj Chamber of Commerce, members use whichever language they please and it is at once translated into the other, as with Spanish and English in the New Mexico Legislature. I publish photographs of minority newspapers, which criticize the government with great freedom, as anyone will see who reads Hungarian. I hope these photographs will help to throw light on Zsombor de Szász's statement about the Hungarian and Saxon Minorities, that "their language is suppressed." Having seen Hungarian and German books and newspapers everywhere in Western Roumania, having attended their plays, movies, concerts, etc., having heard Hungarian and German in schools, churches, government buildings, in fact, all about me, I have read such books as Mr. Szász's, Mr. Cabot's, etc., with unbounded astonishment, equalled by that of various Transylvanians with whom I discussed them. They should read the incendiary Irredentist election handbills of the Magyar Party in the 1931 campaign. Still, they are no further from the truth than much of our own literature on conditions under Prohibition, which so greatly puzzle foreigners.

One of Prof. Iorga's first acts as Prime Minister was to appoint Rudolph Brandsch, a prominent German publicist, as Under-Secretary for the Minorities; justified complaints will obviously receive intelligent and prompt attention. He announced also the founding of a chair for the Hungarian language and literature in the University of Bucharest. In 1930, Minister Manoïlescu headed a delegation of Roumanian business men to Buda-Pesth, and started negotia-

MINORITY NEWSPAPERS

POLITICAL CARTOON IN SOCIALIST PAPER: GEN. AVERESCO SAYS TO
EX-PREMIER BRATIANO: "I AM THE BIGGER," AND THE
LATTER REPLIES, "NO, I AM."

tions leading in 1931 to the creation of a Hungarian Chamber of Commerce in Bucharest, and a Roumanian Chamber in Buda-Pesth.

In fine, my own repeated trips through Transylvania and Bessarabia, with the experience derived from giving lectures and conferences in over a score of institutions, from Kishineff to Temeshvar, have led me to agree with Lord Hugh Cecil, Chairman of a special Committee of the Council of the League of Nations, in his letter of March 18, 1926: "In a very difficult matter the Roumanian Government have shown a genuine and admirable desire to meet the claims of justice and humanity."

CHAPTER XXX

RECONSTRUCTION

THIRTEEN years have passed since the Germans left Roumania a thoroughly exhausted and exploited country. Bucharest in 1919 gave me the impression of a still beleaguered fortress. Everything material had to be restored, replaced, obtained, at high prices; the new country had a rapidly depreciating currency and precarious credit; yet it succeeded in clinging to its currency unit, the leu, in spite of having to absorb billions of Austro-Hungarian crowns and Russian rubles; and the leu was approximately stabilized in 1927 (and actually in Feb., 1929), at about 168 to the dollar, 817 to the pound sterling, when in 1926 it had fallen to over 200 to the dollar. As Mr. Titulesco rightly notes, the industrial countries of Western Europe and America have had two years of great prosperity in that period, 1919–20, and 1928, each followed by a collapse; Roumania, an agricultural country, each time affected by drought, failed to share in this prosperity, and suffered the consequences of each crisis, the second of which still grips her; and in the world-wide price fall of agricultural produce, lumber and oil, her chief assets, her position next door to Russia, the chief disturbing factor, has put her at a singular disadvantage. Her moneyed classes had their wealth chiefly in land, and the expropriation of their land at a pitifully low rate has largely destroyed their capital, even though it has led to the solution of a vital social problem. She has had to grapple with the assimilation of four millions of foreigners, most of them former enemy subjects and many bitterly hostile to the new state; and she struggles against the same sort of efforts of corrupt politicians and corrupting concessionaires and capitalists with which our own experience has familiarized us. No wonder that in my several visits to Roumania from 1919 on, generally at two-year intervals, I have found my Roumanian friends discouraged. But I have been able to cheer them; for each time I was astonished at the progress made. If one compares the Bucharest—or indeed, any Roumanian city—of 1919 with the same city to-day, one must be lost in admiration at the advance visible on every side. Conditions are still very trying, but so they are in every adjoining country, and in some which never had to undergo Roumania's Calvary. The country which suffered the severest losses of the World War, is to-day living under a constitutional régime which finds every party and every nationality represented in her Parliament, and a young, experienced and ambitious monarch bending every nerve to promote his country's interests, in close personal contact with the leaders of every constitutional party and every shade of opinion. The schools and universities are thronged with eager young people; the peasants, backbone of the nation, though heavily burdened with debt, are now the owners of their land; and that land, with its enormous agricultural and mineral wealth, lies ready for intensive exploitation, now that foreign capital has at last made up its mind to share in the development. Roumania, given peace and two or three years of good growing weather, will be one of the first countries to recover from the crisis of 1930–31. The qualities which have carried the Roumanian race, through centuries of neglect and oppression, to final triumphant union, will urge them on to helpful leadership.

Of all the problems which confronted the new nation in 1919, the financial was perhaps the most pressing. In half her territory, Austro-Hungarian and Russian banks, co-operatives and other financial organizations had been in control. These had to be assimilated or reorganized in connection with Roumanian institutions, which were, and still are, in sore need of capital. Bank-note circulation at present is only about $7.50 per capita, whereas in pre-war Roumania it was $14. How is the National Bank to obtain the $150,000,000 necessary as a basis for the additional currency required by minimum commercial demands? Banking circles favor loans secured by government assets—the forests, fishing monopoly, the sugar, tobacco, and alcohol monopolies, etc. The National Bank is in excellent condition, and maintains the conservative traditions which won it respect before the war, when Roumanian finances and credit were in the healthiest condition. By law it must keep on hand gold and foreign exchange covering 35% of its issue of bank-notes, and this reserve averages considerably higher; in June 1931 it was 43%. Its capital is 600,000,000 lei; reserves about 350,000,000; sinking fund about 400,-000,000. The bank's legal rate of interest was (in 1931) 8% on rediscount and 9% on commercial loans; it has out over seven billions of lei. It has advanced the state about three and a half. In conjunction with the leading private banks, it established in 1927 a Clearing House; and in 1928, a certified-check service. There is an Industrial Credit Society, with a legal maximum rate of 12%; a Rural Crédit Foncier, and a Society of Agricultural Credit, which are land mortgage banks. During June 1931, the League of Nations sent the French banker Henri Regard to Bucharest to organize the new Farm Mortgage Credit (Creditul Ipotecar

Agricol), in connection with the International Agricultural Credit organization in Geneva.

The new Agricultural Bank (Banca de Agricultură), incorporated in the summer of 1931, has a capital of about $12,000,000, and hoped to have out soon some 35 or 40 million dollars in farm loans. But capital is still greatly needed and should bring in large returns, for the farmers in general are in the hands of petty money-lenders, usually the Jewish village saloon-keepers, who demand exorbitant interest, generally 3% a month; the law against usury of 1931 is designed to prevent any rate over 18%. It astonished an American, who felt lucky if he could get 2% on his checking balance, to discover as late as 1930 that the Roumanian banks still were paying as high as 8%, such is the need of money. The League of Nations calculates that Roumanian farms are mortgaged for about $24.40 a hectare, as compared with $10.97 in Bulgaria, $33.74 in Hungary and $59 in Jugo-Slavia.

In 1929 there was established a Central Coöperative Bank, whose capital of a billion lei was provided, half by the State, and half by the nearly 5000 "popular banks," which have over a million depositors.

Roumania has a number of powerful private banks; the Roumanian Bank (Banca Românească), which has in the past been closely affiliated, like the National Bank, with the Liberal Party, has a paid-in capital of 153,000,000 lei, reserve of 75,000,000 and a yearly balance of 3,867,000,000. The Banca Marmorosch, Blank & Co., whose headquarters in Bucharest is one of the best examples of recent Roumanian architecture (by George Cantacuzene), is still larger; on its paid-in capital of 125,000,000 with a reserve of 138,000,000, it does a business of over 4,500,000,000 lei.

The Roumanian Commercial Bank, the Roumanian Bank of Credit, the Banque Chrissoveloni, and the Banca Generală (which applied in June 1931 for a moratorium due to a run of depositors) all show large balances; and there are several smaller institutions which follow standard banking practice. They are highly profitable; in 1930, their net profits (in per cent on paid-in capital) were: the Banca Românească, over 48%; Banca Generală and Banca Marmorosch, Blank & Co., 45%; Roumanian Bank of Credit, 28%; Roumanian Commercial Bank, 24%; Banca Chrissoveloni, 13%; dividends run as high as 17, 18 and even 25%. One of the chief uses to which the new loan is devoted, is to make available to agriculture and industry some part of the capital so sorely needed. Bank runs in August 1931 led to the forming of a super-bank, the Guarantee Banking Syndicate, with capital of a billion lei.

The general policy of Roumania since the war has been to industrialize the country; manufacturing has been encouraged by protective tariffs and other government action, with the result that to-day there are in Roumania some 4000 establishments, using about half a million horse-power; this does not count electric power works. In order of number, these are flour-mills and other food manufactories; saw-mills, furniture factories, etc.; textile mills: steel and other machine works, the largest in the Banat; chemical establishments; building material enterprises; leather goods factories; paper mills, publishing houses, etc.; potteries; glass works; and electro-technical establishments. The average dividend in recent years has been about 9%.

Interesting testimony to the progress made by Transylvania and the Banat since the union, is offered by a Bulletin of the Cluj Chamber of Commerce in 1927, compiled by Dr. Mozes Farkash, a Hungarian Transylvanian. He points out that in the period 1916–1927, production in their iron and steel industry had increased ⅓; in leather goods and chemicals, ½, while in textiles it had doubled. The new factories have the latest machinery, and the abundance of natural gas is a great advantage.

Roumania offers many inducements to the manufacturer, chief among them abundance of excellent labor and of cheap power. It is calculated that about 4,500,000 horse-power (on the basis of minimum autumn flow) can be made available. Natural gas has long been used in Transylvanian establishments; recent discoveries, particularly on Standard Oil property not far north of Bucharest, will revolutionize conditions in that city. We have already seen how bountifully Nature has endowed Roumania with oil and coal.

But Roumania is still far from meeting her own needs in manufactures, although even locomotives are turned out in Roumanian shops. Her exports will continue to be prevailingly oil, lumber, grain, cattle and other natural products. When the National Peasant Party came into power, they inaugurated a policy of freer trade, with a view to encouraging imports as well as exports; and Roumania is one of the few countries which have followed the recommendations of the League of Nations (in 1927) and lowered their tariff barriers. In 1929, a new tariff reduced, e. g., the duty on plows over 40%, scythes 25%, threshing machines 50%, etc. But the tremendous fall of farm prices in 1930 neutralized the good effects of this reduction. Roumania is still the second or third maize-exporting country in the world; in 1928, she exported 47,314 carloads (of ten tons) of Indian corn; in 1929, 37,449; in 1930, 118,080. 37% of her area is given up to its cultivation (⅓ more than wheat). Unfortunately, the Roumanian farmer has still much to learn about corn-growing, his average production of

990 kg. per hectare falling much under that of Jugo-Slavia (1350), Hungary (1680) and Czecho-Slovakia (1790). Nevertheless the excellent season of 1929–30 raised hopes—dashed by the fall of prices (50% in the case of wheat) which brought the national income from agriculture, (in 1929, 96½ billions of lei,) down to 58¼ in 1930; nor did the actual farmers benefit much by the improvement of prices in April 1931.

The agricultural states of Central and Eastern Europe were all anxious for freer trade and lower tariff barriers, and were all hard hit by the collapse. Briand's Pan-Europe proposals, and the later German-Austrian Zollverein plan, had a powerful effect; and Roumania and Jugo-Slavia, fellow-sufferers in agricultural distress, held a conference at Sinaia in the summer of 1930 to decide on some form of common action. It was there determined to act jointly in efforts to dispose of agricultural surplus to manufacturing countries, and to try to induce Czecho-Slovakia, their ally in the Petite Entente, to enter into an agreement with them to take a certain proportion of their exports, in return for the sale to them of a similar share of their imports of manufactures. A committee was even appointed to examine the possibility of a Customs Union between Roumania and Jugo-Slavia; with their 32,000,000 inhabitants, this would make a respectable unit in European commerce. Germany and Austria invited Roumania and Jugo-Slavia to join their proposed Customs Union, and it is understood that only courtesy to French objection deferred favorable discussion, or even acceptance of the proposal.

Still more remarkable was the Conference in Bucharest before that of Sinaia, between Roumania, Jugo-Slavia and their former enemy Hungary, for joint agricultural action. 1930 had seen a Balkan Conference, in which Roumania also was represented, and which would have delighted Take Jonesco's heart. In November 1930 another economic conference was held in Paris, at which Minister Manoïlescu spoke in the name of all South-eastern Europe, asking that European states in need of farm products, extend preferential treatment to European producing states. These evidences of a new European friendliness were followed in February 1931 by the Economic Conference of Central and Eastern European States in Bucharest, which resulted in the appointment of a permanent Committee to study closer economic relations. Bulgaria, Hungary, Lettonia, Poland, Jugo-Slavia, Czecho-Slovakia and Roumania took part in the Conference, which in a way was preliminary to the International Grain Conference held in Rome late in March 1931. It is worth observing that this step towards Pan-Europa is at the expense of the great grain-exporting countries outside Europe—Canada, the Argentine, Australia, etc. —and meets also with Russian hostility.

Roumania has not only to consider her farmers' indebtedness; the State itself, like all neighboring countries, has only been able to progress since the war by borrowing. Pre-war Roumania had balanced budgets and excellent credit; and Greater Roumania, though in large part racked and devastated almost to beggary, succeeded in balancing her budget for several years. But then deficits occurred. Foreign capital had not been encouraged by the Liberal Party, and had taken fright at the Mining Act of 1924, which nationalized the subsoil, and appeared likely to deprive foreign oil and mining companies of their property, like somewhat similar Mexican legislation. Many Roumanians claim that the great oil companies now closed markets for Roumanian oil, and instigated a financial boycott; in any case, the State found it difficult to obtain money, especially as legislation of 1922 kept the State from offering any part of its revenues as security for a loan.

This situation was met by the new Mining Act of March 28, 1929, which confirmed in their rights till 1974 companies which were exploiting their property on July 4, 1924, and thus put an end to a period of uncertainty which had slowed down operations, and impaired Roumanian credit. Other legislation that same year created the Autonomous Office of the State Monopolies of Roumania. This gave corporate existence to the various state properties and monopolies, making it possible to pledge their revenues as security for loans, or lease their exploitation to outsiders. These properties and monopolies are of great value; they comprise the state's mineral wealth (metals, oil, gas, salt, coal, etc.) and the royalties from them; the railroads; the P.T.T. (post, telegraph and telephones, the latter of which were taken over in 1930 by the International T. and T. Corporation of N.Y., which also operates the telephones in Spain and Portugal); the port facilities; Roumanian Maritime Service (which has just let contracts for six new steamers of about 6500 tons each; it runs express steamers to the Ægean and Eastern Mediterranean); the River Navigation Co., which has a fleet of steamers, tugs and barges on the Danube and other streams; the hot springs and other watering-places, in which Roumania is very rich; the State monopolies—tobacco, matches, salt, playing-cards, etc.; the vast forests; the fisheries; metal works belonging to the State; and the State domains. These (outside of the mineral wealth) are calculated to be worth nearly a billion dollars. In 1913, these paid over 5% on their value; in 1927, only 1½%. It must be borne in mind that besides the considerations mentioned above, Roumanian currency had been

under a tremendous strain; in 1919–20, the total value of
the currency in circulation was $165,000,000; the deprecia-
tion of the leu brought this down in 1921, to $155,000,000;
in 1922, to 105; in 1923, to 85; 1924–7, about 90—as compared with $135,000,000 in 1915 for pre-war Roumania,
with only 40% of its size and resources.

The stabilization of the leu in 1929, and the new legislation just described, at last made it possible for Roumania
to obtain loans of reasonable size. The first, in 1930, designed primarily to support the leu, was of $72,000,000,
supplemented by one of $30,000,000 from the Swedish
Match Trust (in return for a 30-year concession of the
match monopoly). $35,000,000 were set aside for the most
pressing needs of the State railways.

The railways of pre-war Roumania were well-built and
admirably run. In 1915 they totaled 3702km. (about 2350
miles), with 932 locomotives, 1790 passenger coaches, and
23,600 freight cars; there was a large surplus; in 1912, the
net revenue was $10,000,000 (on a gross of $22,000,000);
in 1915, $4,000,000 (on the same gross). The lines in the
new territories added about 7600km. to the system; but the
war had wrought devastation. On leaving Roumania, the
Germans destroyed the chief bridges, and much equipment;
they took along the best of the rolling stock. When the
Roumanians undertook railway reconstruction, they had to
rebuild 155 bridges, including the great Danube bridge at
Cernavoda. There were only 265 usable locomotives, and
7800 freight cars. The repair shops were largely dismantled.
Millions of ties needed replacing; the Germans had carried
off even rails, leaving the double track line to Constantza
with only a single track. The Bessarabian railways had to
be made standard gauge. Locomotives and cars were
bought and rented; to-day equipment is nearing normal,

with 2200 locomotives (of 70 different models!), 3300 coaches and 55,000 freight-cars. New lines are being built; the routes in former Austro-Hungarian and Russian territory must be centered on Bucharest, and also connect different sections of Roumania. In April 1931 one of the new links was opened in Bessarabia, much shortening the time from Kishineff south and southwest.

In July 1931 Gen. M. Ionescu, Director of the State Railways, opened the first section of the line from Brashov (Kronstadt) to Buzău, which pierces the Carpathians with several tunnels, one over 2½ miles long, and connects Transylvania directly with the Danube ports. The new line Bucharest—Piteshti—Curtea de Argesh—Râmnicul—Vâlcea—Sibiu, now under construction, will cut several hours off the time between Bucharest, Arad and Western Europe; and the new bridge across the Danube near Panciova, for which the Roumanian and Jugo-Slav governments have recently drawn up plans, will shorten the route between Roumania and the West by 12 hours. International freight service has been greatly improved recently; freight to and from Paris now takes from a week to ten days, according to the route; the shipper has his choice of nine, via points as remote as Breslau and Modane. Express service (grande vitesse) is provided by the through passenger trains. These make good time considering the mountainous country through which they run; the "Trajan Express," from Bucharest via Craiova to Temeshvar, covers the 356 miles in about 11 hours—much the same speed as on our Western mountain roads.

There is excellent air service, connecting Bucharest with Sofia, Salonica, Constantinople, Czernowitz, Warsaw, Vienna, etc.; it is now possible to go from Paris to Bucharest in one day.

The second loan, of $52,000,000, was signed in Paris March 11, 1931; it was issued at 86.5, and bears 7½% interest. This was devoted largely to agricultural credit needs, but also to the railways. The latter have suffered not merely from the crisis, but also—as in all other countries—from motor competition. This is being met by improvement of the service, which is especially striking in international connections, both freight and passenger; there are through sleepers from Bucharest to Buda-Pesth, Vienna, Warsaw, Prague, Venice, Paris, etc. The service is good, passenger train delays being no greater than with us.

Some of this loan was also ear-marked for highway development. Roumania is still only on the threshold of the automobile age; in a country well toward the size of California, and with four times its population, there were in 1929 only 26,500 automobiles, 5000 autobusses and 4500 motor-trucks; in 1930, 32,000 automobiles. But the need of better highways has long been felt, and in August 1929 the state highways were formed into the "Autonomous State Road Office," which is to spend the sums allotted out of the loan of 1931 and subsequent ones.

Pre-war Roumania, and the Austro-Hungarian accessions, had excellent paved roads, but not enough of them. The new office has classified the highways as State, district, regional and communal; of the state roads, corresponding to our Lincoln Highway, Roumania proper has (1931) about 1500 miles reckoned as good, and 1150, fair; the former Austro-Hungarian provinces, 1200 and 1400 respectively. The Russians had left the prairie province of Bessarabia in the same condition as the Dakota of my boyhood; even to-day, if you don't like the road in Bessarabia, you try the adjoining prairie; and a heavy rain ties up all road transport. Bessarabia has the area of Vermont and New Hampshire together; in a hundred years of occupation, the Russians had constructed only about 40 miles of paved road! Even to-day, the Office finds only those 40 miles of good paved highway in Bessarabia, 12 of fair, and 7 of poor; there are over 4000 miles of roads in Bessarabia the Office declines to catalogue other than "unclassified"! Since Roumania imports predominantly American cars—about 80% of the automobiles one sees are American—and our automobile exports have been checked by tariff reprisals in Italy, France, Germany, Spain, and many other countries, American financial interests have every reason to help Roumania put these highways into shape for the enormous automobile development which will follow the passing of the crisis in grain, oil and lumber prices.

The State has also recently classified its various public debts, and consolidated most of them. The total amounts to 6,670,210,495 lei (as of Jan. 1, 1931). The Consolidated debt (in lei) is thus classified:

PAYABLE IN FOREIGN CURRENCIES

Pre-war debts	698,304,029
War and post-war debts	3,508,161,608
7% Stabilization loan (1929)	1,351,831,561
Interest on 8% I. T. T. loan (1930)	73,000,000
Roumanian share in European Danube Commission loan	18,145,125
	5,649,442,323

PAYABLE IN GOLD

Pre-war consolidated debt	64,943,072
Post-war consolidated debt	734,837,204
Floating debt:	

Treasury bonds	44,297,044
Debt Administration, commissions, miscellaneous, etc.	140,190,852
Funds for extraordinary diplomatic and administrative needs	36,500,000
	6,670,210,495

Like most other countries in 1931, Roumania faces a budget deficit. Over half of the revenue comes from indirect taxation; in the 1931 budget, the sums are estimated at:

	Lei
Customs duties	4,775,000,000
Tax on alcoholic liquors	1,250,000,000
Other consumption taxes	2,882,000,000
Business tax	2,000,000,000
Amusements tax	100,000,000
Stamp taxes	4,150,000,000

as contrasted with 9,310,000,000 from direct taxation. These do not include all taxes on consumption; that on tobacco, for instance, is counted in the revenue from the Autonomous Government Corporations, which was fixed at 5,577,-917,747 lei.

In these hard times, budget estimates based on consumption have proved to be illusory everywhere. When the price of a carload (10 metric tons) of wheat, fell from 94,000 lei in June 1928 to 32,000 in October 1930; of corn, from 96,600 lei in September 1928, to 27,500; of barley, from 71,000 in May 1928 to 18,500; and when gasoline and kerosene fell over 50% during 1930 alone—an enormous fall in revenue must result. The budget for 1930 had already foreseen a deficit; the customs receipts (import and export taxes) had fallen over a billion lei short of the estimates; the taxes on beer, wine and spirits brought in less than ⅔

(743,000,000 lei) of the receipts. So Mihai Popovici, the Transylvanian Finance Minister whose fate it has been to shape Roumanian budgets in three hard years, cut down, e. g., customs estimates from six billion to less than four, and slashed department estimates by what was called the "curve of sacrifice," every State employee (beginning with the King) accepting a cut in salary of from 10% up. He also incurred further unpopularity by discharging thousands of State employees whose services did not seem absolutely necessary. The government undertook also a campaign to reduce prices, somewhat along the lines of that instituted by Mussolini.

Roumania is largely dependent on foreign trade; with her grain, oil, lumber, live stock and other farm products, she buys manufactures and pays her debts. The keen competition and over-production of recent years hit Roumanian exports; and in April 1930 the government established a National Export Institute, to study the situation and suggest remedies. This body at once attacked two problems: that of raising wheat export standards, as foreign buyers complained of inadequate grading of the wheat; and the proper sorting of eggs. In the latter, an immediate improvement resulted; and for the former, a huge grain elevator extension program at Constantza, has been adopted, and the first new units are under construction. In recent years, Roumanian exports have varied from about 28 to 38 billion lei, and imports from 24 to 38. A striking feature has been the increase of trade with France:

	(In millions of francs)		
	1928	1929	1930
Exports to France	184	233	374
Imports from France	164	150	171

Exports to Germany also increased from 211 million marks in 1929 to 237 in 1930; the new commercial treaty will improve relations, especially the privileges given Roumanian barley, which is preferred by German brewers.

In spite of the depression, Roumania had a favorable trade balance of 6¼ billion lei ($37,500,000) in 1930, as contrasted with an excess of imports over exports in 1929 of nearly a billion lei.

In international relations, Roumania's policy has been one of close harmony with France. The "Little Entente" of Jugo-Slavia, Czecho-Slovakia and Roumania—an agreement for common action in case of aggression—is now ten years old, and was reaffirmed in May, 1931. Originally formed as a safeguard against any Austro-Hungarian revival, it has largely lost its earlier associations, and is becoming predominantly economic; it would not be surprising to see it lead to a customs union. A French military commission has been working with the chiefs of all three armies, in an effort to mold a homogeneous instrument which would be a respectable safeguard of peace, since it would represent a population nearly equal to that of Italy or France.

I point out elsewhere the great improvement in relations with Hungary. The treaty with Poland has been recently renewed, and Roumania forms a link between the "Little Entente" and Poland. This treaty is designed as a safeguard against Soviet Russia, which both countries regard as a neighbor of uncertain tendencies. The Russians have never acknowledged the rightfulness of Bessarabia's union with Roumania (see my "Bessarabia" for a fuller discussion of the controversy), nor do they consider their appropriation of the Roumanian treasure sent there during the war for safe-keeping, any compensation. There have been several attempts, nevertheless, to negotiate a treaty with Russia, but as yet they have all failed.

Recent Roumanian relations with Germany and with Italy have been somewhat chequered. There were serious financial difficulties with Germany, remaining from the war, and these have only just been regulated. The long-continued efforts for a liberal commercial agreement have met with only partial success; and the proposal of an Austro-German Customs Union complicated this situation. Not till the summer of 1931 was a trade agreement with Germany finally negotiated, under which Germany facilitates the import of Roumanian products (especially barley) and Roumania gives the most favored nation rates to German manufactures. Roumania is not much affected by the Hoover moratorium.

Italy and Roumania have always been friendly; but Mussolini's sudden wooing of Hungary has given Roumania pause, as the Italian policy was obviously to face Jugo-Slavia and France with a Bulgarian-Hungarian-Italian combination. Roumanian statesmen, knowing from long experience the dangers of any aggressive alignment in the Balkans, and profoundly desirous of peace, have done their best to keep on the previous friendly terms with both Italy and Jugo-Slavia. Roumania has in Italy a Roumanian Chamber of Commerce (in Milan), a Roumanian House (in Venice) and the Roumanian Archæological School in Rome, and excursions of students and business men from one country to the other, take place every year.

An effort has recently been made to foster closer relations with Spain, and a contract for Roumanian oil was made with the Spanish Government shortly before King Alfonso's downfall; a new direct steamship line was then inaugurated. It is a pity that neither Great Britain nor the United States pay much attention to Roumania, where they nevertheless have important financial investments at stake. A gallant fight to arouse interest is being made by the Society of Friends of Roumania in the United States, with headquarters at 36 W. 44th Street, New York, under the general direction of Mr. Wm. Nelson Cromwell, a well-known New York lawyer. They publish an excellent well-illustrated quarterly, "Roumania," and maintain a permanent secretary. In Roumania similar work is done by the Friends of the United States. Intellectual relations however are much closer with France, and French professors, generals and statesmen keep visiting Roumanian centers. Let us hope that London and New York will support similar pilgrimages, to Roumanian advantage, and our own.

All in all, few countries can view the present world depression with more equanimity than Roumania. The census of Dec. 29, 1930, gives her 18,025,237 inhabitants. We must agree with the judgments recently expressed by Charles Dewey, American financial expert in Poland: "In general, economic conditions in Roumania seem to rest on a firm foundation. It can hardly be expected that great prosperity can be reached in brief time; but with all her natural resources, with hard work and well-judged plans, one can feel sure that positive results will be obtained in a comparatively short term of years;" and by Prof. Parker Willis of Columbia University and the New York *Journal of Commerce*: "Roumania is a country of enormous natural wealth. Her deposits of oil, natural gas, minerals and metals assure her a brilliant future as an industrial country and few will be able to rival her. With her fertile soil and hard-working population . . . she will be able to pass through crises even severer than this of 1930. . . . I am firmly convinced that the day will come when the great problem in Roumania will be, not how to secure foreign capital, but how to regulate its entry into the country."

I catalogue here merely a few of the most interesting, valuable or widely known books dealing with Roumania and
the Roumanians. I include a few in Roumanian, since any one
familiar with Italian, Portuguese, or Spanish will have little
difficulty with the language.

Ackerley, Fred G. A Rumanian Manual for Self-tuition.
London, K. Paul, Trench, Trübner & Co., 1917. 1446 pp.
A good introduction to the language.

Adamescu, Gheorghe. Istoria literaturii Romậne. Bucharest,
Alcalay, 1910. (reprinted with brief postscript 1920).
559 pp., numerous illustrations. A standard Roumanian
literary history, frequently revised.

L'agriculture en Roumanie. Album statistique. Bucharest,
Ministère de l'Agriculture et des Domaines, 1929. Valuable collection of maps and statistics.

Analele Academiei Romậne. Seria I (1867–1878). Seria II
(1879–1923). Seria III (1923, în continuare). I.)
Memoriile sectziunii istorice. II.) Memoriile sectziunii
literare. III.) Memoriile sectziunii shtiintzifice. IV.)
Desbateri. The chief channel of learned publication in
Roumania; works of importance often have a French
summary.

Antipa, Gr. Dunărea shi Problemele ei Shtiintzifice, Economice shi Politice. Cartea Românească, 1921. 192 pp. The
Danube question treated by a scientist of German training and international reputation.

Antipa, Gr. L'Occupation ennemie de la Roumanie et ses con-
séquences économiques et sociales. (*in* Histoire Écono-

mique et Sociale de la Guerre Mondiale, Série Rou-
maine.) Publications de la Dotation Carnegie, etc. Yale
University Press, New Haven (n. d.; 1929?) 185 pp.
Valuable description of exploitation of Roumania by
Central Powers.

Antipa, Gr. Pescăria shi pescuitul în România. Bucharest,
1916. Dr. Antipa, head of the Bucharest Natural History
Museum, is Roumania's leading ichthyologist.

Arhiva pentru Shtiintza shi Reforma Socială. A stimulating
review, edited by Prof. D. Gusti, Professor of Sociology
in the University of Bucharest.

Axelrad, Philip. Dictzionar Complet Român-Englez . . .
Complete Roumanian-English Dictionary. New York,
Biblioteca Română (c. 1918). A reasonably satisfactory
dictionary, with brief summary of grammar.

Axelrad, Philip. The Elements of Roumanian; a Complete
Roumanian Grammar, with Exercises. New York, Biblioteca Română, 1919. 108 pp.

Bănescu, N. Historical Survey of the Rumanian People. Bucharest, Cultura Natzională, 1926. 60 pp.; illust. Read-
able brief sketch of Roumanian history.

Bartók, Béla. Volksmusik der Rumänen von Maramures.
München, Drei Masken-Verlag, 1923. 224 pp.

Bengescu, George. Les Golesco. Une famille des Boyards let-
trés roumains au xixe siècle. 284 pp.

Bercovici, Konrad. Ghitza and Other Romances. New York,
Boni & Liveright, 1921. 227 pp. Graphic and fascinating
stories of Roumania.

Bercovici, Konrad. That Royal Lover. New York, Brewer &
Warren, 1931. Unfounded gossip about prominent Rou-

manians. "The narrative lacks the convincing quality essential in a work which professes to be history." (Springfield *Republican*.)

Berkowitz, Joseph. La question des Israélites en Roumanie. Paris, Jouve, 1923. 798 pp.

Bernatzik, Hugo Adolf. Ein Vogelparadies an der Donau. Bilder aus Rumänien. Tierwelt-Volksleben. Berlin, Wasmuth, 1929. 96 pp.; numerous plates, many of peasant types.

Beza, Marcu. Paganism in Roumanian Folklore. London, Dent, 1928. 161 pp.; illustrations and bibliography. Many of the old pagan customs have survived among the people, and are here described.

Beza, M. Papers on the Rumanian People and Literature. London, McBride, Nast & Co., 1920. Excellent essays on the Church and people, Englishmen in Roumania, English influence on Roumanian literature, and folk poetry.

Beza M. Rays of Memory. Translated by Mrs. Lucy Byng. London, J. M. Dent; New York, Dutton, 1929. 144 pp. Interesting recollections, beginning with childhood in Macedonia.

Beza, M. Rumanian Proverbs Selected and Translated by M. Beza. London, 1921. 63 pp. Roumanian and English on opposite pages.

Bibliographie roumaine. Bulletin mensuel de la librairie de Roumanie en général et de la librarie roumaine de l'étranger. Bucharest, 1879 on.

Boldur, Alex. La Bessarabie et les relations russo-roumaines. Paris, 1927. Scholarly study of the Russian treatment of Bessarabia.

Boutière, Jean. La Vie et l'Œuvre de Ion Creanga. Paris, Gamber, 1930. 254 pp.; 25 illustrations. The leading Roumanian story-teller, as seen by a French critic.

Brailsford, Henry Noel. Macedonia. London, Methuen & Co., 1906. 340 pp.; 31 photographs and 2 maps. Intensely interesting; has a chapter on the Macedonian Roumanians. Out of print.

Bratiano, Elise J. Les hommes d'Etat pendant la Guerre: Lettre ouverte à M. William Martin. Bucharest, Scrisul Românesc, 1929. 16 pp. Admirable presentation of John J. C. Bratiano's rôle in the war, by his widow.

Brote, Eugen. Die rumänische Frage in Siebenbürgen und Ungarn. Vienna, 1895. 432 pp.; map.

Bucuresti. Bucharest, Cartea Românească, 1929. Excellent collection of 30 photogravures of Bucharest parks and buildings. Bibliography.

Bucuta, Emanoil. Românii dintre Vidin shi Timoc. Bucharest, 1923. 132 pp. Study of the Roumanians in Serbia.

Buletinul Cărtzii Româneshti, Bucharest, Cartea Românească. Monthly list of new books, published since 1927.

Bulletin de l'Institut pour l'étude de l'Europe sud-orientale. Bucharest, 1914–24; since 1924, Revue Historique du sud-est européen. Paris, Gamber. This quarterly, edited by the historian Iorga, is valuable also for its bibliography.

Bulletin statistique de la Roumanie, publié par la Direction Générale de la Statistique du Ministère de l'Industrie et du Commerce. Bucharest, 1909 on. The governmental statistical publication. Contains not merely statistics but also essays on various economic and other topics.

Byng, Mrs. Lucy Margaret (Greenly) Schomberg. Roumanian Stories; Preface by Queen Marie. London and New

York, John Lane, 1921. 287 pp. A well-chosen collection, in translation.

Cabot, John Moore. The Racial Conflict in Transylvania. Boston, The Beacon Press, 1926. 206 pp. The revision of an Oxford thesis, written by an American Unitarian with pro-Hungarian bias.

Cazacu, Dr. P. Moldova dintre Prut shi Nistru. Jassy, Viatza Romînească, 1925. 345 pp. By far the most detailed and judicious account of Bessarabia under the Russians, and of the transition period, by a chief actor; admirably written.

Ciobanu, Shtefan. Basarabia, Monografie. Kishineff, 1926. A valuable collection of essays on Bessarabia.

Clark, Charles Upson. Bessarabia. New York, Dodd, Mead & Co., 1927. 333 pp.; illust., map and bibliography. Pronounced by the "American Hebrew" "a reliable and well-documented work, presenting much new material of a valuable nature . . . singularly free from the fatal taint of subjectivity."

Clark, C. U. Greater Roumania. New York, Dodd, Mead & Co., 1922. 477 pp., illust., maps and bibliography. A description of Roumania in the early post-war period, with full account of American Red Cross, Food Commission and other work, and interviews with King Ferdinand, Queen Marie, John Bratiano, Take Jonesco, etc.; out of print. See preface.

Credit Position of Roumania. Bulletin 17 of Institute of International Finance. New York, New York University, July 31, 1928. Convenient recapitulation of financial and economic possibilities, and of public debts.

Deák, Francis. The Hungarian-Rumanian Land Dispute. New York, Columbia University Press, 1928. 272 pp.

Presentation from the Hungarian viewpoint, of the controversy up to 1928.

Densusianu, Ovide. Histoire de la langue roumaine. Paris, 1901–14. 2 v.; republished Bucharest, 1929. A standard work.

Densushianu, Ovid. Literatura română modernă. Bucharest, 1920–21. Vol. I–II; re-issued later.

Dictzionarul geografic al României. Publicat de Societatea Regală Română de Geografie. Bucharest, 1898. 5 vol. Standard pre-war work of reference.

Dobrogea. Cincizeci de Ani de Vieatză Românească. Bucharest, Cultura Natzională, 1928. (= Analele Dobrogei, IX, vol. I). 793 pp.; 213 illust.; 2 plates of ancient coins. Collection of valuable essays, commemorating the 50th anniversary of the annexation of the Dobrudja; beautifully printed.

Dobrogeanu-Gherea, C. Studii critice. Bucharest, 1923–28. vol. 1–5. Valuable critical studies.

Dragomir, Sylvius. The Ethnical Minorities in Transylvania. Geneva, Sonor, 1927. 129 pp.; map. Detailed answer to Szász.

Drutzu, Serban *and* Popovici, A. Românii în America. Bucharest, Cartea Românească, 1926. Our American Roumanians have their newspapers, societies, cultural organizations, etc., as described here.

East, W. G. Union of Moldavia and Wallachia. London, 1929. Valuable historical study.

Economic Survey of Roumania. Reprinted from "The Economist." London, n. d. (1929). 51 pp. Short articles by Madgearu, Mihai Popovici, S. Radulescu, Aristide Blank, and other authorities.

Eminesco. Poems by Eminesco; translated by Sylvia Pankhurst and I. O. Stefanovici. London, Kegan, Paul &
Trench, 1930.

Ephemeris Dacoromana. Annuario della Scuola Romena di
Roma. Roma, Libreria di Scienze e Lettere. The publication of the Roumanian School in Rome. Vol. IV contains a biography of Parvân, the leading Roumanian
archæologist, who died in 1927.

Evans, Ifor Leslie. The Agrarian Revolution in Roumania.
Cambridge, The University Press, 1924. 197 pp.; maps.
Valuable study, in briefer compass than Mitrany's, but
still timely.

Les Forces économiques de la Roumanie en 1930. Bureau
d'Études de la Banque Marmorosch-Blank & Cie. Bucharest, Cultura Natzională, 1931. Excellent summary
of Roumanian resources, trade, commerce, etc., prepared
by a leading bank; maps and illustrations.

Galitzi, Christine Avghi. A Study of Assimilation among the
Roumanians in the United States. New York, Columbia
University Press (etc., etc.), 1929. 282 pp. A description
of Americanization of our Roumanians.

Gaster, Dr. Moses. Children's Stories from Roumanian Legends and Fairy Tales. London, Raphael Tuck, 1923.
Illust. by C. E. Brock. Scholar and artist here combine
to explain Roumania and Roumanians to our children.

Gaster, M. Crestomatzie română, texte tipărite shi manu-
scrise, sec. XVI–XIX, dialecte, literatură populară.
Leipzig, 1891. 2 vol. The standard collection, showing
the development of the language from the earliest documents on.

Gavanescul, Gen. C. Rasboiul nostru pentru Intregirea Nea-
mului (Our War for the Union of the People) (August,

1916–April, 1918.) Jassy, Serviciul Geografic al Armatei, 1918. Numerous maps. A semi-official account of the war, which received the Nasturel Prize of the Roumanian Academy.

Gerard, Emily. The Land Beyond the Forest. Facts, Figures and Fancies from Transylvania. With Map and Illustrations. London, Blackwood, 1888. 2 vol. 340 and 370 pp. The keen and fascinating observations of the English wife of an Austrian officer. She devotes several interesting chapters to the Roumanian peasantry, the Roumanian literature of Transylvania, etc. Out of print.

La Grande Roumanie. Album édité à l'occasion des fêtes de l'Union. Paris, l'Illustration, 1929. Beautiful illustrated collection of articles, e. g., one by Henri Focillon on l'Art roumain.

Great Britain. Admiralty. A Handbook of Roumania. London, H. M. Stationery Office, 1920. An excellent picture of Roumania, in its geographical and allied aspects before the war.

Great Britain. Foreign Office. Historical Section. Roumania. London, 1920. 144 pp.; tabs. Good brief sketch of Roumanian history.

Grothe, Hugo. Zur Landeskunde von Rumänien, Kulturgeschichtliches und Wirtschaftliches. Frankfurt a. M., Keller, 1906. 23 Abbildungen (davon 3 im Text), 4 Karten und ein Mehrfarbendruck. 126 pp. A thorough study of the physical geography, agriculture and commerce of Roumania, with good chapters on the history, language, agrarian legislation, peasant arts and national characteristics. Footnotes give valuable lists of books on the subjects treated.

Hamilton-Zay, Lucy. My Note Book on Rumania. Bucharest, Cartea Românească, n. d. (1922?). Preface by Louis E.

Van Norman. 62 pp.; numerous illustrations. Interesting comments on Roumanians and their life, by an English-woman who has lived long among them.

Hoppé, Emil Otto. In Gypsy Camp and Royal Palace; Wanderings in Rumania. With a Preface by the Queen of Rumania; with Decorations by Bold and 32 Illustrations by the Author. London, Methuen & Co. (1924). 240 pp.; illust.; plates.

Hughes, Annie. Roumanian Conversation Grammar and Key. Heidelberg, J. Groos, 1920. 330 pp. (Key 56 pp.).

Iorga, Nicolae. Art et littérature des Roumains. Paris, Gamber, 1929. 98 pp. + 72 pl. Cursory sketch on broad lines, noting cultural influences.

Iorga, N. The Byzantine Empire. Translated from the French by Allen H. Powles. London, 1907. 236 pp.

Iorga, N. Drumuri shi orashe prin România. Bucharest, Ed. II. 236 pp. Delightful excursions through Roumania with its leading historian.

Iorga, N. Geschichte der Rumänen und ihrer Kultur. Hermanstadt, Krafft & Drotleff, 1929. 375 pp. Übertr. v. H. Rösler-Albrich. For use in German schools, in Roumania and outside.

Iorga, N. Histoire des Roumains de Transylvanie et de Hongrie. Bucharest, Göbl, 1916. 2 vol. The standard recent Roumanian handbook on this theme.

Iorga, N. A History of Roumania: Land, People, Civilization. Translated from the 2d. enlarged edition by Joseph McCabe. London, T. F. Unwin, 1925. 284 pp.; fold. map. A translation of Iorga's standard history.

Iorga, N. Istoria României. Bucharest, Suru, 1920, and reissued since. 475 pp. The favorite Roumanian school history, interesting and well illustrated.

Iorga, N. Istoria Românilor prin calatori. Bucharest, 1920–22. 3 vol. Learned study of early travelers' accounts of Roumania.

Iorga, N. Sate shi mânăstiri din România. Bucharest, 1905. 1 vol. Interesting pictures of the villages and their convents.

Kennard, Dorothy Katherine (Barclay) Lady. A Roumanian Diary, 1915, 1916, 1917. New York, Dodd, Mead & Co., 1918. 201 pp.; front.; plates. Interesting war diary, now out of print.

Kiritzesco, Constantin. La Roumanie dans la guerre mondiale (1916–1919). Bucharest, Cartea Românească, 1927. 97 pp.; maps and illust. Brief outline of the course of the war.

Kirke, Dorothea. Domestic Life in Rumania . . . with 8 Illustrations. London, Lane, 1916. 290 pp.; front.; plates. Interesting description of the home life of the people.

Labbé, Paul. La vivante Roumanie. Ouvrage illustré de 55 gravures, et d'une carte en noir. Préface de M. Gaston Doumergue. Paris, Hachette, 1915. 207 pp.; 32 plates. This lively account of a trip through Roumania includes full descriptions of Roumanian agriculture, salt mines, oil fields, fisheries, etc. The cuts are very interesting.

Libros, M. La situation économique et financière de la Roumanie en 1930. Bucharest, Dacia, 1931. Authoritative study, by a leading financial editor.

Lindenberg, P. König Karl von Rumänien. Ein Lebensbild dargestellt unter Mitarbeit des Königs. Berlin, Hafen-Verlag, 1923. Interesting for its light on international relations.

Lupu, Dr. N. Roumania and the War (Columbia University Quarterly, XX (1918), pp. 312–329). An appeal for sympathy, from one of Roumania's frankest public men.

Madgearu, Dr. Virgil. Roumania's New Economic Policy. London, P. S. King & Son, 1930. 63 pp. Summary of recent statistics and economic legislation.

Maiorescu, Titu. Critice. Bucharest, 1928. 3 vol. A reprint of Maioresco's critiques, perhaps the most authoritative in that field.

Marian, S. Nunta la Români. Bucharest, Ed. Academia Română, 1929. Study of wedding customs, by a leading folk-lorist.

Marian, S. Sărbătorile la Români. Bucharest, 1898–1899. 1901. 3 vol. The folk festivals in Roumania.

Marie, Queen of Roumania. The Country that I Love. London, Duckworth, 1925. 175 pp.; illust. Queen Marie's fond tribute to her adopted country.

Martineau, Alice Vaughan-Williams (Mrs. Philip). Roumania and Her Rulers. With Preface by the Infanta Beatrice. London, S. Paul & Co., 1927. 210 pp.; front.; plates; ports. An intimate account of Roumanian royalty and aristocracy.

de Martonne, Emmanuel. La Valachie; Essai de Monographie Géographique. Avec 5 cartes, 12 planches hors texte et 48 figures dans le texte. Paris, Colin, 1902. 387 pp. A scholarly and interesting work, with excellent bibliography, by a trained geologist and geographer.

Mawer, E. B., translator. Rumanian Fairy Tales and Legends. Four Illustrations. London, Lewis, 1881. 124 pp.

Mehedintzi, S. Le pays et le peuple roumain. Bucharest, 1927. Excellent sketch, by a leading historian.

Metesh, Sht. Ce a scris N. Iorga, viatza shi activitatea sa. Bucharest, 1921. A bibliography of Iorga's astoundingly fruitful activity, up to 1921.

Miller, William. The Balkans; Roumania, Bulgaria, Servia and Montenegro. With New Chapter containing their History from 1896–1922. (Story of the Nations). New York, G. P. Putnam's, Sons, 1923. 3rd edition. 538 pp. Still valuable and authoritative.

Mitrany, David. The Land and the Peasant in Rumania (*in* Economic and Social History of the World War). New Haven, Yale University Press, 1930, 627 pp. A most valuable account of the peasant and land reform. See my review in "American Historical Review," XXXVI, 644.

Mrazec, Ludovic. L'industrie du pétrole en Roumanie. Gotha, 1917. Scientific description of the oil fields.

Murgoci, G. M. *and* Burca, I. P. România. Serie noua. Bucharest, Socec, 1919 (and later). 233 pp. illust., maps. A widely used school text-book on Roumania.

Negulesco, Gogu. Rumania's Sacrifice; her Past, Present, and Future. Translated by Mrs. C. de S. Wainwright. New York, The Century Co., 1918. 265 pp.; illust. with photographs and maps. A book of interest and value, but marred by inadequate proof-reading; no dependence can be put on proper names.

Noyes, James Oscar. Roumania; the Border Land of the Christian and the Turk. New York, Rudd & Carleton, 1858. 520 pp.; 23 plates. Interesting account of the Roumanian Principalities just as they became independent.

Olszewski, Georges. Bucharest (Bucureshti). Notes historiques et estampes. 1929. Charming colored reproductions of old prints.

Oprescu, George. Peasant Art in Roumania. London, The Studio, 1929. 182 pp.; illust.; plates, map, bibliography. The best introduction to the subject; a beautiful and scholarly work, with numerous photographs from the author's collections.

Oprescu, George. Tzara noastră. Bucharest, Cultura Natzională, 1922. Brief and lavishly illustrated account of peasant art, in Roumanian.

Ozanne, J. W. Three Years in Roumania. London, Chapman & Hall, 1878. 227 pp. Out of print.

Pantazzi, Mrs. Ethel Greening. Roumania in Light and Shadow. London, T. F. Unwin, 1921. 279 pp.; front., illust., map, pl. Interesting description by an Englishwoman long resident in Roumania. Out of print.

Pantazzi, Ethel Greening *and* Theodorini, Julieta. Strolls in Old Corners of Bucharest. Bucharest, 1926.

Papahagi, Tache. Images d'ethnographie roumaine. Bucharest, Societatea Cultural-Natzională Apostol Margarit, vol. I, 1928; vol. II, 1930, pp. 173, 230; 749 photographs; text in Roumanian and French. Admirable introduction to Roumanian peasant types and life.

Parkinson, Maude Rea. Twenty Years in Roumania. London, G. Allen & Unwin, 1921. 255 pp. Interesting comments of an Irishwoman who lived twenty years in Bucharest.

Pârvan, Vasile. Dacia; an Outline of the Early Civilizations of the Carpatho-Danubian Countries. Cambridge, University Press, 1928. 216 pp., pl. The fundamental account of the early history of what is now Roumania.

Pârvan, V. Getica. Bucharest, 1926. A most erudite study of the primitive inhabitants of Roumania; in Roumanian, but with a summary in French. See my review in "American Historical Review," XXXII, 841.

Patterson, Rev. R. Stewart. Romanian Songs and Ballads. Preface by Mrs. Take Jonesco. London, J. Long, 1917. 128 pp. Excellent translations by an English clergyman long resident in Bucharest; out of print.

Philippide, Al. Originele Românilor. Iashi, 1927–29. 2 vol. An interesting study, by one of the best modern writers.

Pillat, Ion *shi* Perpessicius. Antologia poetzilor de azi. Bucharest, 1925–1928. vol. I–II. Admirable selection of modern Roumanian verse.

Pillat, Ion *and* Popescu, Stefan. Florica, n. d. Poems inspired by the Bratiano country home; magnificently printed and illustrated quarto volume, obtainable from the Biblioteca I. I. C. Bratiano, Bucharest.

Pittard, Eugène. La Roumanie: Valachie-Moldavie-Dobroudja. 50 illustrations, dont 35 hors texte d'après des photographies prises par l'auteur. Paris, Bossard, 1917. 320 pp. Fascinating book, written by a trained anthropologist; the photographs are most unusual.

Pizanty, Mihail. Petroleum in Roumania. London, 1931. Authoritative statement by the editor of the "Monitorul Petrolului."

Popovici, Andrei, Ph.D. The Political Status of Bessarabia. Washington, Ransdell, Inc., for Georgetown University, 1931. 290 pp., 5 maps, illust. The latest study of Bessarabia's international situation.

Popoviciu, Dr. Gh. Diferentze shi asemănări în structura biologică de rasă a popoarelor României. Cluj, "Ardeal," 1924. 11 pp. A serological study of the different races in Roumania.

Protection des Minorités en Roumanie. League of Nations, Geneva, 1925. 163 pp. Detailed reply of the Roumanian

Government to the charges brought by the Reformed, Unitarian and Catholic Churches of Transylvania.

Puscariu, Sextil I. Etymologisches Wörterbuch der rumän- ischen Sprache. Heidelberg, C. Winter, 1905. 235 pp. Ex- cellent for derivations.

Pushcariu, Sextil I. Istoria literaturii române. Sibiu, Editzia mare, 1930. Excellent sketch of the literature.

Rommenhöller, Carol Gustave. La grande Roumanie, sa structure économique, sociale, financière, politique et particulièrement ses richesses. La Haye, M. Nijhoff, 1926. 634 pp.; tables. Excellent description of the coun- try; also available in German (see following).

Rommenhöller, Carol Gustave. Gross-Rumänien. Berlin, Puttkammer & Mühlbrecht, 1926. 735 pp.

Rommenhöller, C. G. Die Reichtümer Rumäniens und ihre Ausbeutung. Als Manuskript gedruckt. Berlin, 1929. 158 pp. Sketch of Roumania, largely for German busi- ness men.

Roumania: a Quarterly Review. Published by the Society of Friends of Roumania, 36 W. 44th St., New York. An ex- cellent means of keeping abreast of progress in Rou- mania.

Roumania, Ten Years After. Boston, The Beacon Press, c.1928. 143 pp. Report of the Commission, sent in the summer of 1927 to investigate the condition of the racial and religious minorities embraced within Greater Rou- mania, by the American Committee on the Rights of Religious Minorities. For a discussion of the work of these commissions, which the Roumanians think failed to appreciate their difficulties, see Chapter XXIX.

Roumania Today. New York, Industries Publishing Co., n. d. (1928), 35 pp. Brief sketch of Roumania, largely economic.

La Roumanie agricole. Bucharest, 1929. 455 pp. Valuable and well illustrated description of Roumanian agriculture.

La Roumanie: Conférences faites à l'Union Française par MM. Lacour-Gayet, de l'Académie de Sciences Morales; de Martonne, Professeur à la Sorbonne; Jean Richepin, de l'Académie Française; Charles Diehl, de l'Académie des Inscriptions et Belles-Lettres; R.-G. Lévy, de l'Académie des Sciences Morales; Mircea Djuvara, Conseiller juriste à la Conférence de la Paix . . . Introduction de Paul Gaultier. Paris, Union Française, n. d. (1919). 282 pp. An excellent introduction; the chapters on the history, the land, the art, the economic situation, etc., are all by specialists.

La Roumanie en Images. Paris, L'Hoir, 1919. Vol. I. (only one out). Magnificent collection of photographic reproductions of Roumanian landscapes, costumes, peasant types, historic monuments, modern architecture, etc.

Rumania. Illustrated Supplement of the "Manchester Guardian," Nov. 28, 1929. Valuable collection of articles on Roumania.

Rumänien. Sondernummer, Völkermagazin. Berlin, Mai, 1929. 144 pp. Interesting summary, especially valuable for its illustrations, among which are many of distinguished Roumanians.

Savadjian, Léon. The Campaign against the Treaty of Trianon. Paris, Revue des Balkans, 71 rue de Rennes, 1929. 28 pp. Arguments against Lord Rothermere's pro-Hungarian campaign.

Seton-Watson, R. W. Corruption and Reform in Hungary. London, Constable & Co., 1911. 197 pp. Indispensable to any judgment on Hungarian problems.

Seton-Watson, R. W. The Rise of Nationality in the Balkans. 4 maps. New York, Dutton, 1919. 308 pp. Excellent general introduction.

Seton-Watson, R. W. Roumania and the Great War. London, Constable & Co., 1915. 102 pp.; bibliography, ethnographical map and index. Written to explain Roumania's neutrality to British readers, it is still by far the best short introduction in English to the story of Roumanian historical development; I recommend the bibliography to supplement this brief list.

Shaineanu, Lazar. Dictionar universal al limbei Române. 5th ed. Craiova, 1925. 875 pp. An excellent general dictionary, of the type of the small Larousse.

Society of Friends of Roumania. Bulletin dedicated to Her Majesty Queen Marie of Roumania. October 18, 1926. New York, Society of Friends of Roumania, 1926. 108 pp.; illust., plates, ports.

Spaull, Hebe. Peeps at Roumania. With 12 full-page illustrations; 4 in color. London, A. & C. Black, 1930. A brief popular account; one of the Black color books.

Stahel-de Capitani, H. Rumänien . . . mit 94 Abbildungen, einer wirtschaftlichen Karte und einer Eisenbahnkarte. Zürich, Tschopp, 1925. 143 pp.; 94 illust., ports., maps, bibliography. Good brief description.

Stanley, Henry. Rouman Anthology, or Selections from Rouman Poetry, Ancient and Modern . . . with an Appendix, containing translations of some of the poems, etc. London, Stephen Austin, 1856. 226 pp. The first English study of Roumanian poetry.

Steed, Henry Wickham. The Hapsburg Monarchy. 4th ed. with new preface. London, Constable & Co., 1919. 304 pp. Of great learning and influence, especially at the Peace Conference.

Stefanesco, I. D. L'évolution de la peinture religieuse en Bucovine et en Moldavie, Paris, 1928.

Sturdza, Alexandru A. C. La femme en Roumanie, sa condition juridique et sociale dans le passé et le présent. Paris, V. Giard & E. Brière, 1911. 158 pp.

Sturdza, Alex. A. C. La Terre et la Race Roumaines. Paris, Laveur, 1904. 724 pp.; 10 maps, 186 illust. A scholarly, encyclopædic and profusely illustrated book.

de Szász, Zsombor. The Minorities in Roumanian Transylvania. London, Richards Press, 1927. 414 pp. Highly exaggerated statement of situation of Hungarian and German minorities. See Chapter XXIX.

Tafrali, O. Le monastère de Sucevitza. Jassy, 1929. 103 pp. Valuable study of one of the most interesting convents and its art.

Tentoonstelling van Roemeensche Kunst. Gemeente Museum voor Moderne Kunst te's-Gravenhage. 3 Tot 25 Mei, 1930. With 30 plates of paintings and sculpture by Roumanian artists exhibited at the Hague.

Teutsch, Fr. Die Siebenbürger Sachsen. Hermannstadt, (Sibiu), 1929. 367 pp. The history of the Transylvanian Germans, by one of their leaders.

Tichner, Henrietta M. Roumania and her Religious Minorities. London, A. M. Philpot, 1925. 100 pp. A reply, by an American Jewess, to "The Religious Minorities in Transylvania," the report of the Anglo-American Commission of 1924 to the minority churches of Transylvania.

Tiktin, Hariton. Rumänisch-deutsches Wörterbuch. Bukarest, Staatsdruckerie, 1903–25. 3 vol. Added t.-p. in Rumanian. Issued in 30 parts, paged continuously. A very scholarly dictionary.

Tiktin, Hariton. Rumänisch Elementarbuch. Heidelberg, C. Winter, 1905. 228 pp. Excellent grammar.

Titulescu, N. La réforme agraire en Roumanie et les optants hongrois de Transylvanie. Paris, 1924. 188 pp. An authoritative statement of the Roumanian case.

Transilvania, Banatul, Crishana, Maramureshul, 1918–1928. Bucharest, Cultura Natzională, 1929. 3 large volumes. 1582 pp.; numerous maps and illust. Valuable articles, especially on history, culture, religious sects, etc.

Uhlig, C. Die Bessarabische Frage. Eine geopolitische Betrachtung. Breslau, 1926. Discussion of the Bessarabian problem, with anti-Roumanian tendencies.

U. S. Dept. of Commerce. Rumania: an Economic Handbook. Washington, Govt. Print. Off., 1924. 167 pp. Of great value.

Van Teslaar, Dr. James Samuel. When I was a Boy in Roumania. Boston, Lothrop, Lee & Shepard, Co., 1917. 179 pp.; illust. Embodies Dr. Van Teslaar's recollections of his boyhood in Roumania.

Vicol, Dr. Roumanie balnéaire et climatique. Bucharest, 1926. Roumania's mineral springs and health resorts.

Wace, Alan John Bayard and M. S. Thompson. The Nomads of the Balkans: an Account of Life and Customs among the Vlachs of Northern Pindus. With 42 illustrations and 2 maps. London, Methuen, 1914. 332 pp. An authoritative account of the Macedonian Aromanians, based on many months of life among them, with a bibliography, grammar and glossary of the Macedonian dialect of Roumanian. Out of print.

Whitman, Sidney. Reminiscences of the King of Roumania. With portrait. New York, Harpers, 1899. 367 pp. An abstract of King Charles' memoirs, throwing much light on international as well as Roumanian affairs.

Winlow, Clara Vostrovsky. Our little Roumanian Cousin. Boston, The Page Co., 1917. 113 pp.; front., plates. For children.

Xenopol, Alexandru Dimitrie. Istoria Românilor. Bucharest, 1924–1930. Valuable history, available also in French translation (Histoire des Roumains, préface par A. Rambaud, Paris, 1896).

ADDENDA

Humphreys, R. J. E. Economic Conditions in Roumania (dated May, 1931). London, H. M. Stationer's Office, 1931. 92 pp. A thorough study of the situation, by the Commercial Secretary of the British Legation in Bucharest; published for the Department of Overseas Trade.

Le Recensement Général de la Population de 1930. La Population Actuelle de la Roumanie . . . Direction du Recensement Général de la Population, Bucureshti, 1931. 45 pp.; illustrations. The preliminary figures of the 1930 census.

Tibal, André. La Roumanie. Préface par Auguste Gauvain. Paris, Editions Rieder, 1930. Pp. 154. A compact and accurate introduction to modern Roumania.

Riker, T. W. The Making of Roumania . . . 1856–1866. Oxford University Press, 1931. Pp. viii, 592; map. A scholarly study of the subject, in its international aspects. See my review in "Roumania."

THE NEW CENSUS

According to the preliminary figures of the 1930 census, Roumania now counts 18,022,962 inhabitants; only 1,959,-000 live in municipalities. The chief cities are: Bucharest, with 632,000; Kishineff (Chishinău), 116,000; Czernowitz (Cernăutzi), 111,000; Jassy (Iashi), 102,000; Galatz, 102,-000; Cluj, 99,000; Temeshvar (Timishoara), 91,000; Oradea Mare (Grosswardein), 82,000; Ploeshti, 77,000; Arad, 77,000; Braila, 68,000; Brashov (Kronstadt), 58,000; Constantza, 57,000; Craiova, 57,000; Satul Mare, 51,000; and Sibiu (Hermannstadt), 49,000.

INDEX